The Contested Diplomacy of the European External Action Service

The creation of the European External Action Service (EEAS), the EU's new diplomatic body, was accompanied by high expectations for improving the way Europe would deal with foreign policy. However, observers of its first years of operation have come to the opposite conclusion.

This book explains why the EEAS, despite being hailed as a milestone in integration in Europe's foreign policy, has fallen short of the mark. It does so by enlisting American institutionalist approaches to European questions of institutional creation, bureaucratic organisations and change. The book examines the peculiar shape the EEAS's organisation has taken, what political factors determined that shape and design and how it has operated. Finally, it looks at the autonomous operation of the EEAS from a bureaucratic theory perspective, concluding that this is the best way to understand its course. Including data gathered from elite interviews of politicians and senior officials involved in the institutional process, an assessment of official documentary evidence and a survey of EEAS officials at the organisation's beginning, it sheds new light on a controversial tool in the EU's foreign policy.

This text will be of key interest to scholars and students of European Union foreign policy, public administration, and more broadly to European Union and European politics, as well as to practitioners within those fields.

Jost-Henrik Morgenstern-Pomorski is a Lecturer in Political Science with a special focus on European and American politics at Maastricht University, the Netherlands. He was awarded a Marie Curie Early Stage Researcher position at Loughborough University, UK, and was a visiting PhD student at the University of Cambridge, UK.

Routledge/UACES Contemporary European Studies

Edited by Chad Damro
University of Edinburgh, UK
Elaine Fahey
City University London, UK
and
David Howarth
University of Luxembourg, Luxembourg, on behalf of the University Association for Contemporary European Studies

Editorial Board: Grainne De Búrca, European University Institute and Columbia University; Andreas Føllesdal, Norwegian Centre for Human Rights, University of Oslo; Peter Holmes, University of Sussex; Liesbet Hooghe, University of North Carolina at Chapel Hill, and Vrije Universiteit Amsterdam; David Phinnemore, Queen's University Belfast; Ben Rosamond, University of Warwick; Vivien Ann Schmidt, University of Boston; Jo Shaw, University of Edinburgh; Mike Smith, University of Loughborough and Loukas Tsoukalis, ELIAMEP, University of Athens and European University Institute.

The primary objective of the new Contemporary European Studies series is to provide a research outlet for scholars of European Studies from all disciplines. The series publishes important scholarly works and aims to forge for itself an international reputation.

For more information about this series, please visit: www.routledge.com/Routledge-UACES-Contemporary-European-Studies/book-series/UACES

37 The EU in the Global Investment Regime
Commission Entrepreneurship, Incremental Institutional Change and Business Lethargy
Johann Robert Basedow

38 The Dynamics of EU External Energy Relations
Fighting for Energy
Francesca Batzella

39 Claiming Citizenship Rights in Europe
Emerging Challenges and Political Agents
Edited by Daniele Archibugi and Ali Emre Benli

40 The Contested Diplomacy of the European External Action Service
Inception, Establishment and Consolidation
Jost-Henrik Morgenstern-Pomorski

41 Power Politics, Banking Union and EMU
Adjusting Europe to Germany
Shawn Donnelly

The Contested Diplomacy of the European External Action Service

Inception, Establishment and Consolidation

Jost-Henrik Morgenstern-Pomorski

LONDON AND NEW YORK

First published 2018
by Routledge
2 Park Square, Milton Park, Abingdon, Oxon OX14 4RN

and by Routledge
711 Third Avenue, New York, NY 10017

Routledge is an imprint of the Taylor & Francis Group, an informa business

© 2018 Jost-Henrik Morgenstern-Pomorski

The right of Jost-Henrik Morgenstern-Pomorski to be identified as author
of this work has been asserted by him in accordance with sections 77 and
78 of the Copyright, Designs and Patents Act 1988.

All rights reserved. No part of this book may be reprinted or reproduced or
utilised in any form or by any electronic, mechanical, or other means, now
known or hereafter invented, including photocopying and recording, or in
any information storage or retrieval system, without permission in writing
from the publishers.

Trademark notice: Product or corporate names may be trademarks or
registered trademarks, and are used only for identification and explanation
without intent to infringe.

British Library Cataloguing-in-Publication Data
A catalogue record for this book is available from the British Library

Library of Congress Cataloging-in-Publication Data
A catalog record for this book has been requested

ISBN: 978-1-138-03946-9 (hbk)
ISBN: 978-1-315-17583-6 (ebk)

Typeset in Times New Roman
by Wearset Ltd, Boldon, Tyne and Wear

**In memory of
Dave Allen**

It [European Political Cooperation] is essentially suited to reacting to events: anything more would require a much closer harmonization of EPC and EEC activities. In the long run this would presumably require a much larger secretariat [...]; it would, in fact, require the establishment of both a common foreign policy and a common European diplomatic service.*

David Allen, 1982

* Reprinted from *European Political Cooperation*, David Allen, Reinhardt Rummel and Wolfgang Wessels, Postscriptum 1982 by David Allen, pp. 170–176, Copyright 1982, with permission from Elsevier for Butterworth Scientific.

Contents

List of illustrations	x
Acknowledgements	xi

1 Introduction: constructing the EU diplomatic service   1

*Assessing the EEAS and its added value to Global Europe: in the
eye of the beholder(s)? 2*
Literature on the EEAS: the nature of the beast 5
Bureaucratic change and the long road to the EEAS 8
Research design 10

2 The long road to EU diplomatic capacities   18

*The European Commission's external service – developing and
trading up 19*
The organisation of European Political Cooperation 24
*Member states and the reorganisation of European foreign
policy 28*
Parliamentary activism over two decades 34
Conclusion 38

3 Bureaucratic change in EU foreign policy   45

The emergence and change of bureaucratic institutions 46
The politics of structural choice 55
Bureaucracy and bureaucratic politics 57
The phases of emergence of the EEAS 63
The three stages of institutional development in the EU 68
Conclusion: the three stages of bureaucratic emergence 72

viii   *Contents*

4 The shape of things to come: the inception of the European External Action Service   79

*The European Convention: background, organisation and
   objective 80*
Agents at work? Working Group VII on External Action 87
Plenary struggles and intergovernmental agreements 95
A stable compromise: the fate of the draft Constitutional Treaty 99
Conclusion 100

5 Navigating the 'politics of Eurocratic structure': the establishment of the European External Action Service   106

All about access: member states and the EEAS negotiation 107
Protecting prerogatives: the European Commission 116
*From cheerleader to controller and back again? The European
   Parliament creates leverage 121*
Towards the 2010 decision 127
Conclusion 130

6 Bureaucracy, competition and control: the consolidation of the European External Action Service   135

*The EEAS as an emerging bureau: maximising budgets, shaping the
   service or bureaucratic politics? 136*
*Building on quicksand? The EEAS and its institutional
   environment 145*
The many faces of control: European Commission 146
*The many faces of control: the Council Secretariat, the President of
   the European Council and the member states 152*
The many faces of control: European Parliament 158
Conclusion 160

7 Sailing on a second wind? Trajectories of consolidation for the European External Action Service   169

Developments inside the EEAS 169
*EEAS and the Juncker Commission: Spitzenkandidat meets
   European Council nominee 171*
EEAS and European Council and Council of the EU 174
EEAS and Parliament 175
*Charting the course ahead: the politics of diplomatic structure and
   trajectories of the EEAS 177*

Contents ix

8 Conclusion: towards a European foreign ministry? 184

Inception 185
Establishment 186
Consolidation 187
The EEAS and institutional change in the EU 192

Appendix 1	198
Appendix 2	210
Appendix 3	219
Appendix 4	224
Appendix 5	226

Index	228

Illustrations

Figure

4.1	Convention structure and membership	82

Tables

1.1	Three-phase framework of bureaucratic creation	8
1.2	Core questions and approaches by development phase of EEAS	11
2.1	Selected member states' positions on CFSP integration	30
2.2	Selected member states' views on organisation structures in CFSP	32
2.3	Progressive institutionalisation of European Political Cooperation 1970–1986	35
2.4	Selected European Parliament positions on the organisation of Union external affairs 1978–2001	37
4.1	Categories of reform considered during Convention	90
6.1	EEAS budget 2011–2016	137
6.2	Perception of support by other EU bodies	143
6.3	Control mechanisms for the EEAS by actors	162

Acknowledgements

When beginning the research for this book in 2010, I was frequently asked how I could study something that did not yet exist. It turns out that the EEAS came and grew much faster than the research process. Not only has the EEAS been established, but it is already operating under its second High Representative. As it turns out, I could have started earlier!

I would like to thank all those officials and politicians who volunteered their time to answer my questions and whose contributions are an invaluable part of understanding how the EEAS came about.

I gratefully acknowledge the funding this project has received from the European Commission through a PhD position in the Inter-Institutional Cooperation in the EU (INCOOP) Initial Training Network at Loughborough University.

The two central figures of my time at Loughborough were Dave Allen and Mike Smith, once referred to as the 'twin pillars of Loughborough' at an EUSA conference. Dave was an incredible inspiration from the first day at Loughborough and is unfortunately not with us to see this book published. For this reason, I have dedicated this book to his memory. Mike has helped enormously with his comments and advice, his drive towards structure and meaningful arguments, as well as his keen eye for Germanisms. I owe him great thanks also for his support and advice in the years after the PhD. I would also like to thank Helen Drake for all her support during and after the dissertation and for her role in that wonderful association of researchers that is UACES. Mark Webber, Lee Miles and Rob Dover gave valuable comments in the process, too. It was a genuine pleasure to share an office with fellow INCOOP researcher Nikola Tomic and see the Boston Celtics and Baltimore Orioles with Borja Garcia. As part of the INCOOP network, I had the opportunity to spend time at the University of Cambridge and I would like to thank my host Julie Smith, as well as Christopher Hill, Geoffrey Edwards, and Ariella Huff. At Maastricht, thanks go to Heidi Maurer and Paul Stephenson who just may have to hear a little less about the EEAS in the future.

I would also like to thank Renaud Dehousse, Simon Duke, Andrea Lenschow, Christine Neuhold, Guy Peters, Berthold Rittberger, Ben Tonra, Sophie Vanhoonacker and Richard Whitman for their comments and encouragement at various stages of the research process.

xii *Acknowledgements*

Thanks go also to Chad Damro, Elaine Fahey and David Howarth at the Routledge UACES Contemporary European Studies series for their support, and to Andrew Taylor and Sophie Iddamalgoda for managing the process with swift and friendly professionalism. And, of course, thanks go to two anonymous reviewers for their comments and suggestions incorporated in this book.

My family has been an inexhaustible source of support. I would like to thank my parents, Grete and Rudi. This book could not have reached publication without Karolina's seemingly inexhaustible encouragement and patience, and her insightful comments, for all of which I am very grateful.

Maastricht, 19 October 2017

1 Introduction
Constructing the EU diplomatic service

On the surface, the creation of the European External Action Service is just a footnote to the wider changes introduced by the Lisbon Treaty; the EEAS is mentioned a mere three times in the treaties. Yet, it has captured the imagination of politicians, journalists and academics alike in more ways than many other organisational changes introduced by the latest reform of the European Union's basic legal framework. The EU's main business may still be regulation, but it has started processes that directly touch upon the prerogatives of the state. Recent scholarship has begun to explore the 'integration of core state powers' (Genschel and Jachtenfuchs 2016), and the creation of the EEAS as a supranational diplomatic service is an obvious case in this line of inquiry.

The EU's diplomatic service holds the key to both the EU's contribution in external relations with the wider world as well as contributing to the development of EU foreign policy. It connects previously separate policy fields in European integration: the external relations driven by the European Commission and foreign policy in the hands of the member states. That being said, the EEAS is not an organisation created on an empty political and bureaucratic drawing board. It is a merger of previously existing administrative structures with an infusion of new personnel provided by the member states. When considered as an administrative merger, it has many features of the traditional administrative reorganisation. The literature on the EEAS has focused more on the diplomatic nature of the organisation than its administrative or bureaucratic qualities. While understandable, this misses the potential explanatory power of established institutionalist approaches.

In this book, I propose an alternative view of the EEAS and its creation. The EEAS is best understood as a bureaucracy, created in a process of institutional change by actors attempting to imbue the new administrative structure with diverging political objectives. Combining insights from different strands of institutional theory in different phases of an organisation's creation makes it possible on the one hand to explain the links between these phases and on the other hand to discern the legacies of the past in newly emerging challenges to administrative structure. This bureaucratic-institutionalist framework of institutional creation will be used to give answers to the three core questions identified in the literature: why the EEAS was created, what the EEAS is, and what forces drive

2   Introduction

its operation. After a brief overview of the main questions emanating from the academic debate on the EEAS, this chapter develops a bureaucratic-institutionalist framework that provides for a targeted investigation of the EEAS's evolution as a new actor in the EU's foreign policy system, and answers these core questions coherently.

But why is understanding the EEAS as a bureaucratic actor and the 'nature of the beast' relevant? First, there is of course the academic point of view that 'administrative reorganisations are interesting in their own right. The effectiveness of political systems depends to a substantial extent on the effectiveness of administrative institutions, and the design and control of bureaucratic structures is a central concern of any polity' (March and Olsen 1989: p. 69). In this light, the EEAS is an administrative reorganisation at the core of EU politics. Combined with the insight that these administrative changes are continuously ongoing, or, as Moe expressed it, 'The game of structural politics never ends' (Moe 1989: p. 284), an understanding of the origins of the organisation gives a clearer view of its future. Understanding the nature of the EEAS and its evolution tell us about the EU as a political system. Second, observers argued that in its first years the EEAS had mixed success. Looking at this performance assessment, it is relevant to understand whether and in what these observations are grounded and what this means for the EU's role in the world. Thus, before introducing the book and its main claims, it is necessary to take a first look at how the EEAS was assessed by a variety of audiences: first, the media; second, the think tanks dealing with EU politics and, third, academics studying EU foreign policy in the broadest sense. This will give the opportunity to investigate the many different standards applied to the organisation before the book moves to highlight the organisational roots of many of the findings presented in these assessments.

Assessing the EEAS and its added value to Global Europe: in the eye of the beholder(s)?

Assessing the work of the EEAS was, at least for the early years of the organisation's existence, a favourite pastime of political observers in journalism, European and national think tanks, and the academy. An overview of these assessments and their evolution over time is given below. The main expectations and failure to fulfil them will then be assessed in view of what this reveals about the assessors' views of the EEAS.

From early on in the EEAS's life cycle, criticism was reported by media outlets in various European countries both on a leadership and organisational level. The German magazine *Der Spiegel* reported early in 2010 that (High Representative) 'Ashton has only been in office for 100 days, but she is already running into stiff criticism', a sense more than echoed by the BBC, which detailed the difficult process of setting up the basic organogram of the organisation (BBC 2010). After the setting up of the EEAS, media outlets with a focus on the EU described critical personnel management issues (EUobserver 2011), which were dismissed at the time in a letter by the spokesperson of Ashton as 'unsubstantiated tittle-tattle' (Mann 2011). Others reported 'a paralysis in EU foreign policy' (The Economist blog 2011), only to see similar claims levelled by foreign ministers of some member states a year later: 'bureaucracy and bad management are hampering the effectiveness of the EU's new diplomatic service one year after its launch' (EUobserver 2012). Outlets more critical of European integration in general naturally also reported more gleefully about these and other failings (Telegraph 2009, 2011, 2012).

While this could be subsumed under media reporting that focuses on the negative to have a good headline, it is telling that reports by think tanks echoed many of the concerns raised in press reports about the performance of the service (Howorth 2014). Think tanks were softer in their judgement of the performance of the EEAS in its first years of operation. The Brussels-based Center for European Policy Studies (CEPS) argued for a 'generally positive' assessment of performance, but admitted that ' "Teething problems" should not come as a surprise to anyone, given the complexity of setting up an institution of this kind' (Helwig *et al.* 2013: p. 69). Despite this positive tone, Helwig *et al.* detailed large numbers of functional issues in relations between the EEAS and EU institutions and, more specifically, the overall approach by the Commission towards the EEAS, its limited willingness to share information and a sense of withdrawal of positive ideas on how to use the external relations tools at its disposal (2013: pp. 31–46). Relations with the Commission were made more complicated by the Commission's internal dynamics in external relations, as the authors discuss in greater detail. Managerial issues in the delegations were added on top of this list (Helwig *et al.* 2013: pp. 62–68).

Lehne's paper for the Carnegie Endowment for International Peace (Lehne 2011) assembles a more critical list arguing that the EEAS was not well suited to dealing with the external effects of internal policies, was struggling to gain benefits from internal and external collaboration in the field, and was not yet of significant size for full impact. Hemra *et al.* in a report for the Royal Institute of International Affairs found 'significant shortcomings' (Hemra *et al.* 2011: p. 5) preventing the EEAS from operating like a fully functioning diplomatic service, and identified strategy, leadership, and delivery challenges. Nevertheless, the authors highlighted areas in which the EEAS can develop added value in the future through an entrepreneurial approach to EU foreign policy making and by strongly involving member states. Duke reviewed the commentary and identified two categories of short-term and long-term changes that would be required for the EEAS to fulfil its role and end a period of 'navel gazing' (Duke 2012). Other think tank pieces, building on these early evaluations, actively proposed reforms to the EEAS in the timeframe of the EEAS review (e.g. Blockmans and Hillion 2013; Lehne 2011), at least implying that manifold changes would benefit the EEAS's operative abilities. A detailed look at how the EEAS interacts with national diplomacies (Balfour and Raik 2013) revealed the mixed views held by national governments on what the EEAS could and should do. Balfour and Raik also note how for the EU and member states involved 'the travails of working

4   *Introduction*

together during the past two years have proven to be one of the most serious set-backs to the first steps of the EEAS's existence' (Balfour and Raik 2013: p. 1).

One of the more damning reports emerged not from the world of foreign policy think tanks but from an EU institution in its own right, the European Court of Auditors (ECA). In its 2014 Special Report on 'The Establishment of the European External Action Service', the ECA highlighted that in its view the 'establishment of the EEAS was rushed and inadequately prepared' (ECA 2014: p. 8), which resulted in unrealistic assumptions and decisions that hampered the organisation's functioning (ECA 2014: p. 10). The report is even more critical of the structures that were created, judging them to be 'more complex than the foreign policy structures it replaces' and having a heavy tilt towards senior management positions (ECA 2014: p. 12). The report finds communication with the Commission to be 'partly effective', but notes that the trajectory of coordination was positive (ECA 2014: p. 19). The benefits from the permanent chairing arrangement in the Council of the EU had 'not been fully realised' (ECA 2014: p. 23). The ECA did not necessarily hold the EEAS responsible for all of the listed shortcomings, but also criticised the institutions for their unwillingness to plan ahead and set funds aside strategically, rather than insisting on a 'budget neutral' implementation. The EP took this assessment as a means to note that the EEAS 'is not yet a fully-fledged Union diplomatic service because of resource constraints' and reiterated the need to address imbalances and streamline EEAS's senior management (EP 2014). Even the institutional assessment from an indirect stakeholder at the EU level in 2014 remained rather less than a ringing endorsement.

While academic work on the early years of the EEAS has not as its main objective looked at the performance of the EEAS, a number of articles did contain assessments of the EEAS's performance in the period 2010–14. Beginning with early warnings on how many practical issues would be faced by this new organisation when it was still a 'European foreign ministry' (Hill 2003), the academic debate has focused on the implementation of vague rules. Aside from the by-now familiar claim of bureaucratic turf battles documented in areas where EEAS competences intersect with the Commission and member states (Smith 2013; Tannous 2013; Ramopoulos and Odermatt 2013), the academic assessment has highlighted critical elements in agenda-setting: Vanhoonacker and Pomorska argued that while 'capacity' was being built through the creation of the service, mobilisation of partners remained low (Vanhoonacker and Pomorska 2013: p. 1328). They judged the follow up to strategic priorities as 'unconvincing', even as they stressed the efforts of the new organisation to build credibility (Vanhoonacker and Pomorska 2013: p. 1329). In a similar vein, Edwards highlighted the structural constraints that may be the cause of the EEAS (diplomatic) performance issues (Edwards 2014: p. 129). Like Balfour and Raik in the think tank world (2013), Adler-Nissen conceptualised the relationship between the EEAS and the national foreign ministries as a 'struggle' for 'symbolic power' (2014), a structural set-up not conducive to the type of policy engagement asked of member states foreign services (Hemra *et al.* 2011). Pomorska and

Introduction 5

Vanhoonacker identified 'resistance to the EEAS' by the member states themselves (Pomorska and Vanhoonacker 2015). In a study of the politics of information of the EEAS, Vanhoonacker and Blom found the EEAS to have the upper hand (Vanhoonacker and Blom 2015). Bicchi showed the relevant role played by the network of delegations and the EEAS in this respect (Bicchi 2014), just as Maurer and Raik illustrated the adjustment issues in the core delegations in the US and Russia (Maurer and Raik 2014). In addition to these studies on the performance of the EEAS in its domain, scholars have studied internal aspects of the organisation's functioning, such as the creation of an esprit de corps (Juncos and Pomorska 2013) and training and recruitment (Cross 2011; Duke 2012). From an administrative perspective, Henökl and Trondal find increasing autonomy of the new organisation (Henökl and Trondal 2013, 2015). Riddervold and Trondal (2017) look at the outcome of the 'organisational settlement' vis-à-vis the European Commission for the 'nascent' EEAS, a process similar to the one identified as consolidation in this book (Chapters 6, 7). The results show different potential benefits that have yet to materialise.

The ability of the organisation to reach a positive assessment appeared structurally impaired. Most of these studies expressly addressed the overall performance of the EEAS, with the exception of Ramopoulos and Odermatt (2013). In a narrow sense, they are not performance measurements. Such an overall performance assessment would first need to identify what benchmarks would be applicable. Which benchmarks are applicable to the EEAS is largely defined by what the observer believes the EEAS is or should be: a diplomatic service, a European agency, an external relations section of the European Commission, or something else entirely. It would require a decision on whether the organisation should be accountable to the expectations of those who conceived it, those who put it into law, or those actors now exercising control over the organisation. As this book will show, making such a choice of benchmark may be more difficult than looking at the letter of the law. Nevertheless, the collected evidence points to a dysfunctionality that is built into the organisation and, crucially, its operating environment.

Any assessment of performance is dependent on what the assessor believes the EEAS to be – what expectations and benchmark is developed for the task set of the EEAS. But the task set itself was contested; the people and collectives engaged in its creation have different views on nearly all features of the EEAS: its (legal and institutional) status, its scope of activity, and its staffing. No assessment of any relevance can be made before knowing what the contestation of the EEAS was about and how it was – or was not – resolved over time. The confusion of the assessors reflects the divergent objectives of the many creators, as this book will demonstrate.

Literature on the EEAS: the nature of the beast

Eight years into the EEAS's life as an organisation, the academic literature has started to address a range of fundamental questions surrounding the European

6 *Introduction*

External Action Service. But so far it has done so in a quite dispersed way, largely relying on the presentation of empirical data (Juncos and Pomorska 2015: p. 239). Because of the nature of these contributions, there has been limited headway in conceptualising the service and linking the different phases of its creation.

The literature has grappled with the question *why and how the EEAS was created*. Despite the acknowledgement that EU foreign policy is on a trajectory of institutionalisation (Smith 2004), it still appears a puzzle that new roles were bestowed on a new organisation in the field in 2010. The research on why the EEAS exists has come from a wide range of theoretical perspectives, often resorting to abstract theories of international relations and sociology. Kluth and Pilegaard (2012) offered a neorealist interpretation of the establishment of the EEAS. In essence, they see the EEAS as a Franco-British creation that allows what the authors call these 'major powers' to control EU foreign policy machinery and to 'to rein in the diplomatic efforts of less capable Member States in relation to global security issues' (Kluth and Pilegaard 2012: p. 319). Their contention that the thrust behind the service was essentially British and French sits uneasily with the growing body of evidence on the role of other member states as well as that of the EU institutions in creating the new service (e.g. Raube 2011, 2012). It also ignores the fact that the original decision to create the service was opposed by British representatives and accepted by the French only in a logrolling exercise at the European Convention (see Chapter 3). Another attempt at explaining the organisation's existence from a principal agent perspective highlighted the 'rationales' behind the establishment of the EEAS (Kostanyan 2014). Kostanyan contended that the EEAS was created mainly to increase the efficiency and coherence of EU external action (2014: p. 180). The implicit assumption in this line of argument is that politicians' rhetoric can be equated to their objectives and that member states are solely responsible for the decision, as they are the main foreign policy actors. While member states certainly take centre stage in the creation of the service, the picture is considerably more complex due to the nature of the forum in which the EEAS was conceived.

Another element in the investigation of the EEAS is related to a categorical question: *what is the EEAS?* A study into the nature of the organisation is at the heart of institutional research on the European Union and has been discussed in the literature, largely disconnected from the organisation's creation and creators, and mostly on the basis of a traditional legal-institutionalist analysis (Juncos and Pomorska 2015). The EEAS as a 'sui generis' – or one of a kind – organisation is appealing from a legal-institutionalist perspective (van Vooren 2011), but does little to categorise the EEAS and explain its characteristics and behaviour with reference to a larger group of phenomena (see Bátora 2013 for a discussion). Vanhoonacker and Reslow analysed the service on the basis of the 'rational design of international institutions' approach and with knowledge of its institutional and political heritage inside the Commission and the Council Secretariat (Vanhoonacker and Reslow 2010; Koremenos *et al.* 2004). While they admit that a 'sui generis' argument on the EEAS is possible, they also

Introduction 7

make it clear that 'most of the design elements are not that different from those facing other international institutions' (Vanhoonacker and Reslow 2010: p. 17). Henökl (2014) proposed analysing the EEAS as a case of the emerging 'European diplomatic space'. A more conceptual approach proposed by Bátora relies on sociological theory to discuss the EEAS as 'interstitial organisation', i.e. an organisation that 'spans organizational fields and draw[s] upon and recombine[s] resources from these' (Bátora 2013: p. 599). This is a forward-looking analysis of the EEAS as an organisation with potential for 'organizational learning and innovation' (Bátora 2013: p. 599). This discord in the literature on the nature of the EEAS has been captured succinctly by Adler-Nissen (2015). She highlighted the under-theorised nature of the investigation into what the EEAS is (Adler-Nissen 2015: p. 17) and identified the main trends in the approaches used. The most common approaches were rationalist studies of the EEAS as an agent of the member states (Kostanyan and Orbie 2013; Furness 2013; Murdoch 2012, 2014) and constructivist-organisational approaches to the 'EEAS as a social body' (Adler-Nissen 2015; Cross 2011; Juncos and Pomorska 2013; Henökl 2014).

An additional perspective on the EEAS has come from the study of diplomacy, which was concerned with the particular practices of EU diplomats and whether they differ from the traditional member state diplomats with a rigid career path based on competitive entrance exams and a rotation system of international postings. Adler-Nissen's work on 'Europe's new diplomat' also challenges a neorealist interpretation by seeing the EEAS as a symbolic challenge to member states' diplomacies: 'the EEAS represents a novelty – a quasi-supranational diplomatic corps – leading to uncertainty about the future of national foreign services' (Adler-Nissen 2014: p. 9). Lefebvre and Hillion (2010) picked up the theme of a common European diplomacy, a turn of phrase also used by the European Parliament in its drive for the EU to be a more united international actor (European Parliament 2000). Spence (2012) has looked at the different diplomatic (or not) communities and mind-sets that found themselves inside the EEAS after its creation. An edited volume explores various facets and origins of the EU's new diplomatic system (Smith *et al.* 2016).

These views of the EEAS as organisational innovator, as disruption or challenge of diplomatic practice, however, sit uneasily with the growing body of evidence of underperformance, turf wars and disagreements (Edwards 2014; Juncos and Pomorska 2013; Smith 2013; Tannous 2013) that appear to have characterised the early years of the organisation's life, as discussed above. Consequently, another core question about the EEAS is *how the service operates*. While closely linked to the question of why it was created and how it came about, this is a question that has been addressed independently from the same variety of conceptual perspectives. Vanhoonacker and Pomorska (2013) showed the difficulty the EEAS had in asserting itself as an agenda setter, even if it possessed the prerequisite legal powers. Michael E. Smith (2013) highlighted the bureaucratic politics and potential for confusion and incoherence through the particular nature of the EEAS. Tannous (2013) argued in a very similar vein that

8 *Introduction*

the conflict between parts of the Commission and the EEAS was detrimental to successful external policy. Kostanyan and Orbie (2013) analysed the EEAS's discretion in the Eastern neighbourhood. The only slightly more neutral to positive assessment came in the area of the EU's comprehensive approach to crisis management (Tercovich 2014). But even Tercovich found evidence of a 'competition for competences and resources' (2014: p. 7). These bureaucratic difficulties need to be analysed in view of the political conflicts behind them, as Smith has argued (Smith 2013). This concerns both prior conflicts at the time of creation, as well as later conflicts derived from the nature of the organisation.

One of the challenging elements in this part of the academic debate remains the categorisation of the EEAS, currently seen as determined by its function alone. Looking at the EEAS as a diplomatic organisation in the world of diplomacy may be missing the basic and fundamental characteristics of the organisation that we observe in the real world. The EEAS is not just 'copying the organisational structures, norms, rules and practices [...] of the dominant organisations constituting the diplomatic field' (Bátora and Spence 2015: p. 8), but it is fundamentally driven by the same forces that drive all state organisations. In order to identify what these characteristics of the EEAS are, a consistent, theoretically driven study that links its origins to its operation can provide a structured explanation of the phenomena observed in the early years of the EEAS. Conceptualising the EEAS in this manner, as an integral part of an executive administrative structure at the EU level, widens the available theoretical toolbox. Different elements of institutional theory provide the building blocks to analyse the EEAS first as an object and later as agent of institutional change.

Bureaucratic change and the long road to the EEAS

The history of the administrative structures of the EU in external relations and foreign policy shows a long-term path towards integration on two trajectories, yet the creation of the European External Action Service represents a break with

Table 1.1 Three-phase framework of bureaucratic creation

	Forum	*Actors*	*Decision*	*Driver(s) of change*
Phase I Inception	Convention and IGC	Member states, Convention delegates	Treaty revision (grand bargain)	Political conflict
Phase II Establishment	EU decision-making process	Member states and EU institutions	Legislation	Resource and boundary conflict
Phase III Consolidation	EU policy-making	EU institutions, member states and EEAS	Inter-institutional rules	Self-interested organisation in competitive institutional environment

this dual path. Explaining this bureaucratic change towards a more unified structure through a merger of organisations requires particular attention to the institutional rules of the game that drove the decision-making leading up to and implementing the merger. This book conceptualises the creation of the EEAS in a three-phase framework, in which the individual phases are largely characterised by the rules of the game as depicted below.

The creation of the EEAS starts with its inception as an administrative support body to the political post in EU foreign policy during the European Convention, to be later translated into treaty text by subsequent intergovernmental conferences (IGCs). This inception includes the decision to partially break with the dual structures in EU foreign policy and external relations and create a merged administration out of several administrative sources. The second stage of establishment concerns the implementation of treaty provisions regarding the EEAS, i.e. the legal decision setting up its structure and basic features of operation. The third stage of consolidation is the period that starts with the EEAS's operation as an administrative body that fulfils the mandate and tasks set out in stage two. The third stage covers the tenure of the first High Representative in full, and leads up into the tenure of the second High Representative in 2017.

Inception: forum, actors, decision

The beginning of the EEAS is traced back to the Convention on the Future of Europe, a process of treaty revision that in addition to representatives of the member states included members of the European and national parliaments in order to broaden the political input into a 'grand bargain' change of the EU's treaty base. While the process was still largely driven by member states and their representatives, and in any case required the unanimous agreement of and ratification through the member states, its activist participants shaped many of the agreements reached. The EEAS was in many ways only a footnote in the wheeling and dealing on institutional structure, decision-making rules and substantive policy during the Convention's proceedings, but major administrative change has had more clearly visible impact than changes in decision-making rules. This book charters the relaxing of rules and the variety of views introduced during the Convention that enabled the EEAS to be included in the EU administrative structures.

Establishment: forum, actors, decision

After the partial and contested passing into treaty form of the Convention's treaty proposal, the EEAS had to be created by a specific procedure foreseen in the treaty text. The EEAS did not yet exist as an administrative structure, even though its political leadership, the High Representative, was already in office. At this stage, member states and EU institutions followed a negotiating path similar to regular EU legislation, with an additional element of power for the European Commission President and the High Representative. In fact, it was the High

10   *Introduction*

Representative who was tasked with finding the agreement across the Council of the EU, the European Commission and the European Parliament. The decision-making is thus considerably narrower than the wide-ranging debates of the European Convention. The establishment phase resulted in the Council Decision of 26 July 2010 establishing the organisation and functioning of the European External Action Service (2010/427/EU) and set the stage for a period of consolidation, in which the new organisation found its place in the existing EU administrative and decision-making structures.

Consolidation: forum, actors, decision(s)

Based on the Council decision (Council of the EU 2010), the EEAS now had to consolidate itself as an organisation as well as consolidate its position in relation to the EU administrative and institutional structure. This phase involved internal decision-making in the organisation as well as interactions between the organisation and its environment, including the office of the President of the European Council, the Council of the EU, the European Commission and the European Parliament. Looking at the control exercised by bureaucratic and political bodies allows for an empirical study of the bureaucratic politics of the EEAS. It covers relations with the European Commission and the Council of the EU on working methods, consultation and information processes between the EEAS and the EP and the President of the European Council. In this web of relationships, a consolidated role for the EEAS and its ability to stake out its own area of activity will become visible.

These different phases require approaches that are suited to the environmental conditions of the respective phase. The core questions asked about the creation of the EEAS shift in line with the developmental stage. First, it is imperative to ask why the EEAS was created the way it was. Second, what determined the operational shape of the EEAS? And third, how does the EEAS take up its role in relation to its environment?

Table 1.2 outlines core questions and approaches that will help elucidate the bureaucratic creation of the EEAS. The first phase only involves the creators of the EEAS. From the establishment phase, the EEAS is an actor in its own right. The establishment and consolidation phases share the common conception of the EEAS as an administrative, or bureaucratic, actor with a specific self-interest that it seeks to represent vis-à-vis the rest of the EU structures. Chapter 3 will return to a more in-depth discussion of distinct frameworks applied in the analysis. It will highlight the continuity of bureaucratic-institutionalist thinking about the creation of new bureaucratic actors while distinguishing the difference in mechanisms driven by actors and fora at play in each of the three phases.

Research design

The empirical research presented in this book is based on a 'structured and focused case' in order to allow for potential comparison with other cases (George and Bennett 2005: p. 67). Single cases contribute to the accumulation of

Table 1.2 Core questions and approaches by development phase of EEAS

	Phase I: Inception	*Phase II: Establishment*	*Phase III: Consolidation*
Key questions	Why was the EEAS created as an institutional break with past structures?	How was the EEAS created? What determined its final organisational or administrative shape?	How did the EEAS consolidate itself? How did the EEAS take up its role in the EU administrative and political environment?
Analytical approach	Rational choice historical institutionalism/'enacting coalition'	Rational choice historical institutionalism – 'executing coalition' and 'Politics of Eurocratic structure'	Bureaucracy theories and bureaucratic politics
Driver of change	Political conflict between diverging interests channelled through institutional framework in 'critical juncture'	Resource and boundary conflict	Self-interested organisation in competitive institutional environment
Observations	Short-term change in institutional rules Political disagreements over outcome result in vague compromise	Conflict between political and bureaucratic actors; conflict between bureaucratic actors Negotiated outcome of implemented organisation	Budget maximisation and bureau shaping Attempts at control by established actors; resistance by new organisation Negotiated or enforced cooperation
EU-specific analytical approach	Politics of Treaty reform	Politics of Eurocratic structure	Bureaucratic Politics and Politics of Eurocratic structure

12 *Introduction*

knowledge by either closely adhering to established theoretical frameworks, replication, using a particular case for theory-building, or developing multiple observations from within a case. This book connects several of these approaches to make a contribution to our general understanding of institutional change and behaviour. The research questions presented above are concerned mainly with determining the mechanisms of particular theoretical approaches with a view to refining existing theoretical claims (Rohlfing 2012: p. 4), i.e. they seek to establish the why and how of the creation of the EEAS from an institutionalist-bureaucratic perspective. For this type of investigation of mechanisms and processes, the most suitable method is 'process tracing' (Checkel 2005; George and Bennett 2005). Process tracing is a method that allows in-depth analysis of political decisions and is of particular use when looking at the 'genetic moments' (Capoccia and Kelemen 2007: p. 342) of organisations. It does not necessarily compare variations across cases, but can observe mechanisms of decision-making that are not detectable when analysing outcomes only (George and Bennett 2005). Process tracing is particularly relevant for this study as it covers several connected stages of an organisation's life cycle, making time and temporal order of the events part of the object of inquiry (Buethe 2002; Hall 2012).

The process tracing on the inception and establishment of the EEAS relies on semi-structured elite interviews as well as extensive documentary analysis. The elite interviews were undertaken following guiding questions on the individuals' roles in the preparation of the EEAS, their relationship with other actors, specific negotiation items and related questions. Appendix 5 gives an overview of the interviewees, their institutional affiliation, and their specific fit with the genetic phases of the EEAS. A small-scale survey of officials contributes to the evidence mainly in the fourth chapter on the consolidation of the service to gauge perceptions by EEAS staff. The mix of the evidence base is largely determined by availability of sources (e.g. documentary evidence becomes scarcer as the creation of the EEAS proceeds), and thus varies slightly across the empirical chapters. Many of the interviewees have dealt with the EEAS's creation in several of the three phases and often in different institutional settings. One current Commission staff member had been a member state official supporting the Convention, another had been working in the Council Secretariat before returning to the member state's administration. This enriches the interview data. Appendix 5 presents a detailed overview of the interviewees and their level of seniority as well as which interviewee dealt with the EEAS in which phase. The documentary evidence relies for the most part on official documents of internal proceedings at the EU level, such as proceedings from the European Convention including reports, proposed amendments and verbatim records of debates. They have been published and are available printed and online. They also contain documents from official requests for documents from the European institutions (such as intra-institutional agreements) and member states, which provide a partial but nuanced picture of EU institutions' and member states' preferences. In relation to the third and final stage of institutional consolidation, the methodological set-up changes slightly. Bureaucracy theory has developed clearer

Introduction 13

expectations of behaviour and internal processes. For these reasons, expectations of findings are more precise and a plausibility probe of these predicted findings more appropriate. The chapter on the consolidation of the EEAS (Chapter 6) carries out a 'plausibility probe' (Eckstein 1992) of 'multiple complementary hypotheses' (Rohlfing 2012: 41) to determine whether general bureaucracy claims have an added value in analysing the European External Action Service. On the basis of these different types of evidence, a rounded view can be drawn of the EEAS, and also of its counterparts, at all stages of institutional evolution.

Structure of the book

After identifying the three main questions in the literature regarding the European External Action Service, this chapter has introduced a new bureaucratic-institutionalist framework to explain the organisation's creation. In three distinct analytical phases – inception, establishment and consolidation – specific institutional processes of competition and conflict play out with regard to the EEAS structure that have direct impact on its operation. Chapter 2 describes the EU's foreign policy and external relations system prior to the creation of the EEAS as a baseline. It demonstrates in how far the EEAS marks a break from the past by merging administrative structures with distinct histories and identities driven by staffing and tasks. Chapter 3 takes a bureaucratic view of change in EU foreign policy structures and argues that answering the core questions requires seeing the EEAS as a bureaucratic actor first and foremost. Using three established institutionalist approaches in sequential order captures the processes of bureaucratic creation best. Chapter 4 explains why and how the EEAS came about during the European Convention through the intense political conflict surrounding the organisation. Chapter 5 shows how the establishment of the EEAS by EU legislation was driven by the politics of 'Eurocratic structure'; an inter-institutional conflict over resources and control. In Chapter 6, the consolidation of the EEAS during the tenure of High Representative/Vice-President Catherine Ashton is traced back to internal characteristics of bureaucratic organisations as well as inter-organisational conflict in the EU political system. Chapter 7, the final empirical chapter, continues the investigation into the consolidation of the EEAS during the tenure of Federica Mogherini and the organisation's reorientation towards the European Commission. Based on the knowledge gained from looking at the inception, establishment and consolidation, it develops potential trajectories for the EEAS in its relations with the EU institutional structure. Chapter 8 concludes by showing how a bureaucratic conception of the EEAS answers the three core questions on the EEAS and identifies some surprising findings for scholars of bureaucratic and institutional creation.

References

Adler-Nissen, Rebecca 2014: Symbolic power in European diplomacy: the struggle between national foreign services and the EU's External Action Service. *Review of International Studies*, vol. 40, no. 4, pp. 657–681.

14 Introduction

Adler-Nissen, Rebecca 2015: Theorising the EU's Diplomatic Service: Rational Player or Social Body? In Spence David and Bátora, Jozef (Eds.), *The European External Action Service*. The European Union in International Affairs series. Palgrave Macmillan, London.

Balfour, Rosa and Raik, Kristi 2013: *Equipping the European Union for the 21st century: National diplomacies, the European External Action Service and the making of EU foreign policy*. FIIA Report 36, Occasional Report 1. FIIA: Helsinki.

Bátora, Jozef 2013: The 'Mitrailleuse Effect': The EEAS as an Interstitial Organization and the Dynamics of Innovation in Diplomacy. *Journal of Common Market Studies*, vol. 51, no. 4, pp. 598–613.

Bátora, Jozef and Spence, David 2015: The EEAS as a Catalyst of Diplomatic Innovation. In Spence, David and Bátora, Jozef (Eds.), *The European External Action Service*. The European Union in International Affairs series. Palgrave Macmillan, London, pp. 1–16.

BBC 2010: BBC News Lady Ashton takes flak in EU diplomatic battle. 3 March 2010. Retrievable at http://news.bbc.co.uk/1/hi/world/europe/8546108.stm.

Bicchi, Federica 2014: EU Foreign Policy and the Politics of Information. In Blom, T. and Vanhoonacker, S. (Eds.), *The Politics of Information. The Case of the EU*. Palgrave: Houndmills, Basingstoke.

Blockmans, Steven and Hillion, Christophe (Eds.) 2013: *EEAS 2.0: A legal commentary on Council Decision 2010/427/EU*. Centre for European Policy Studies: Brussels.

Blom, Tannelie and Vanhoonacker, Sophie 2015: The European External Action Service (EEAS), new kid on the block. In Bauer, M. and Trondal, J. (Eds.), *Palgrave Handbook of the European Administrative System*. Palgrave Macmillan: Houndmills, Basingstoke.

Buethe, Tim 2002: Taking Temporality Seriously: Modeling History and the Use of Narrative as Evidence. *American Political Science Review*, vol. 96, no. 3, pp. 481–493.

Capoccia, Giovanni and Kelemen, R. Daniel 2007: The Study of Critical Junctures: Theory, Narrative and Counterfactuals in Historical Institutionalism. *World Politics*, vol. 59, pp. 341–369.

Checkel, Jeffrey 2005: Tracing Causal Mechanisms. *International Studies Review*, vol. 8, no. 2, pp. 362–370.

Cross, Mai'a K. Davis 2011: Building a European Diplomacy: Recruitment & Training to the EEAS. 2011. *European Foreign Affairs Review*, vol. 16, no. 4, pp. 447–464.

Duke, Simon 2012: Now We Are One.... A Rough Start for the EEAS. *EIPAscope*, vol. 1, pp. 25–29.

Eckstein, H. 1992: *Regarding Politics. Essays on Political Theory, Stability and Change*. UC Press: Berkeley.

Edwards, Geoffrey 2014: The Public Face of a Proto-Something...: Diplomacy and the European Union. *Diplomacy & Statecraft*, vol. 25, no. 1, pp. 115–134.

EUobserver 2011: Staff leaving EU diplomatic service amid bad working conditions. 30 September 2011. Retrievable at https://euobserver.com/institutional/113777.

EUobserver 2012: Ministers identify glitches in EU diplomatic service. By Andrew Rettman. 6 January 2011.

Furness, Mark 2013: Who controls the European External Action Service? Agent Autonomy in EU External Policy. *European Foreign Affairs Review*, vol. 18, no. 1, pp. 103–126.

Genschel, Philip and Jachtenfuchs, Markus 2016: More integration, less federation: the European integration of Core State Powers. *Journal of European Public Policy*, vol. 23, no. 1, pp. 42–59.

Introduction 15

George, Alexander L. and Bennett, Andrew 2005: *Case Studies and Theory Development in the Social Sciences*. MIT Press: Cambridge, MA.

Hall, Peter 2012: Tracing the Progress of Process Tracing. *European Political Science*, vol. 12, pp. 20–30.

Helwig, Niklas, Ivan, Paul and Kostanyan, Hrant 2013: *The New EU Foreign Policy Architecture. Reviewing the first two years of the EEAS*. CEPS: Brussels.

Hemra, Steffan; Raines, Thomas; and Whitman, Richard 2011: *A Diplomatic Entrepreneur: Making the Most of the European External Action Service*. Chatham House Report. The Royal Institute of International Affairs, London.

Henökl, Thomas 2014: Conceptualizing the European Diplomatic Space: A Framework for Analysis of the European External Action Service. *Journal of European Integration*, vol. 36, no. 5, pp. 453–471.

Henökl, Thomas and Trondal, Jarle 2013: Bureaucratic structure, geographical location and the autonomy of administrative systems. Evidence from the European External Action Service. ISL Working Paper 2013, no. 7.

Henökl, Thomas and Trondal, Jarle 2015: Unveiling the anatomy of autonomy: dissecting actor-level independence in the European External Action Service. In *Journal of European Public Policy*, vol. 22, no. 10, pp. 1426–1447.

Hill, Christopher 2003: A Foreign Minister without a Foreign Ministry? Or with too many? *CFSP Forum*, vol. 1, no. 1, pp. 1–2.

Howorth, Jolyon 2014: *Security and Defense Policy in the European Union*. Houndmills, Basingstoke: Palgrave Macmillan.

Juncos, Ana E. and Pomorska, Karolina 2013: 'In the face of adversity': explaining the attitudes of EEAS officials vis-à-vis the new service, *Journal of European Public Policy*, vol. 20, no. 9, pp. 1332–1349.

Juncos, Ana E. and Pomorska, Karolina 2015: The European External Action Service. In Jørgensen, Knud Erik, Aarstad, Åsne Kalland, Drieskens, Edith, Laatikainen, Katie, and Tonra, Ben (Eds.): *The SAGE Handbook of European Foreign Policy*, vol. 1, pp. 238–248.

Kluth, Michael and Pilegaard, Jess 2012: The Making of the EU's External Action Service: A Neorealist Interpretation. *European Foreign Affairs Review*, vol. 17, no. 2, pp. 303–322.

Kostanyan, Hrant 2014: The Rationales behind the European External Action Service: The Principal-Agent Model and Power Delegation. *Journal of Contemporary European Research*, vol. 10, no. 2, pp. 166–183.

Kostanyan, Hrant and Orbie, Jan 2013: The EEAS' discretionary power within the Eastern Partnership: in search of the highest possible denominator. *Southeast European and Black Sea Studies*, vol. 13, no. 1, pp. 47–65.

Lefebvre, Maxime and Hillion, Christophe 2010: The European External Action Service: towards a common diplomacy? Swedish Institute for European Policy Studies, European Policy Analysis, vol. 6.

Lehne, Stefan 2011: More Action, Better Service. How to Strengthen the European External Action Service. Carnegie Endowment for International Peace Policy Outlook, 16 December 2011.

Mann, Michael 2011: Unsubstantiated tittle-tattle from anonymous 'sources' (Letter to the editors). EUobserver, 3 October 2011.

Maurer, Heidrun and Raik, Kristi 2014: Pioneers of European Diplomatic System. EU Delegations in Moscow and Washington. Finish Institute of International Affairs FIIA Analysis, no. 1.

16 *Introduction*

Murdoch, Zuzana 2012: Negotiating the European External Action Service (EEAS): Analyzing the External Effects of Internal (Dis)Agreement, *Journal of Common Market Studies*, vol. 50, no. 6, pp. 1011–1027.

Murdoch, Zuzana 2014: Building Foreign Affairs Capacity in the EU: Recruitment of Member State officials to the European External Action Service. *Public Administration*, vol. 92, no. 1, pp. 71–86.

Pomorska, Karolina and Vanhoonacker, Sophie 2015: Resisting the European External Action Service. *European Foreign Affairs Review*, vol. 20, no. 2/1, pp. 21–37.

Ramopoulos, T. and Odermatt, J. 2013: EU Diplomacy: Measuring Success in Light of the Post-Lisbon Institutional Framework. In Boening A., Kremer JF., van Loon A. (Eds.) *Global Power Europe – Vol. 1. Global Power Shift*. Springer: Berlin.

Raube, Kolja 2011: The emerging relations between the European Parliament, the High Representative and the EEAS. Working Paper no. 74, Leuven Centre for Global Governance Studies.

Raube, Kolja 2012: The European External Action Service and the European Parliament. *The Hague Journal of Diplomacy*, vol. 7, no. 1, pp. 65–80.

Riddervold, Marianne and Trondal Jarle 2017: Integrating Nascent Organisations: On the settlement of the European External Action Service. *Journal of European Integration*, vol. 39, no. 1, pp. 33–47.

Rohlfing, Ingo 2012: *Case Studies and Causal Inference: An Integrative Framework*. ECPR Palgrave: Houndmills, Basingstoke.

Smith, Michael E. 2004: *Europe's Foreign and Security Policy. The Institutionalization of Cooperation*. Cambridge University Press: Cambridge.

Smith, Michael E. 2013: The European External Action Service and the security–development nexus: organizing for effectiveness or incoherence? *Journal of European Public Policy*, vol. 20, no. 9, pp. 1299–1315.

Smith, Michael, Keukeleire, Stephan and Vanhoonacker, Sophie 2016: *The Diplomatic System of the European Union. Evolution, change and challenges*. Routledge Advances in European Politics. Routledge: Abingdon, Oxon.

Spence, David 2012: The early days of the European External Action Service: a practitioner's view, *The Hague Journal of Diplomacy*, vol. 7, no. 1, pp. 115–134.

Spiegel 2010: Walking the Thin Line with Catherine Ashton. 8 March 2010. Retrievable at www.spiegel.de/international/europe/european-union-foreign-policy-walking-the-thin-line-with-catherine-ashton-a-682339.html.

Tannous, Isabelle 2013: The Programming of EU's External Assistance and Development Aid and the Fragile Balance of Power between EEAS and DG DEVCO. *European Foreign Affairs Review*, vol. 18, no. 3, pp. 329–354.

Telegraph 2009: EU draws up plans to establish itself as 'world power'. 6 October 2009.

Telegraph 2011: Baroness Ashton's staff: EU foreign corps are 'nightmare'. 30 September 2011.

Telegraph 2012: 17 weeks holiday a year for Ashton's EU bureaucrats. 27 March 2012.

Tercovich, Giulia 2014: Towards a Comprehensive Approach: The EEAS Crisis Response System. *Journal of Contingencies and Crisis Management*, vol. 22, no. 3, pp. 150–157.

The Economist blog (Charlemagne) 2011: Meanwhile on Planet Brussels: Paralysis in European foreign policy. 18 October 2011.

Van Vooren, Bart 2011: A legal-institutional perspective on the European External Action Service. *Common Market Law Review*, vol. 48, pp. 475–502.

Introduction 17

Vanhoonacker, Sophie and Pomorska, Karolina 2013: The European External Action Service and agenda-setting in European foreign policy. *Journal of European Public Policy*, vol. 20, no. 9, pp. 1316–1331.

Vanhoonacker, Sophie and Reslow, Natasja 2010: The European External Action Service: Living Forwards by Understanding Backwards. *European Foreign Affairs Review*, vol. 15, no. 1, pp. 1–18.

Official documents

Council of the European Union

Council of the European Union 2010: Decision of 26 July 2010 establishing the Organisation and Functioning of the European External Action Service 2010/427/EU. Brussels.

European Court of Auditors

European Court of Auditors 2014: Special Report No. 11: The Establishment of the European External Action Service. ECA, Luxembourg.

European Parliament

European Parliament 2000: Report on a common Community diplomacy. (Galeote I Report) A5–2010/2000. Brussels.

European Parliament 2014: Report on discharge in respect of the implementation of the general budget of the European Union for the financial year 2013, Section X – European External Action Service (2014/2086(DEC)). Brussels.

2 The long road to EU diplomatic capacities

Whether the creation of the European External Action Service was in fact a sea change for European diplomacy is a question that cannot be answered without looking at the history of EU external relations and EU foreign policy organisations first. The EEAS was explicitly not newly created in a kind of 'institutional void' (Riker 1998), but merged from distinct organisational sources. The Treaty on European Union (TEU) spells out in article 27 that it 'shall comprise officials from relevant departments of the General Secretariat of the Council and of the Commission as well as staff seconded from national diplomatic services of the Member States'. Understanding the organisational landscape before the creation will provide the background on the basis of which the EEAS was built and thus provide a baseline for evaluating the EEAS as a case of institutional change.

The purpose of this chapter is thus threefold: first, it is to trace the organisational capacity in external relations in the European Commission. Second, it will do the same for the Council Secretariat's administrative organisation for foreign policy. And third, it will analyse the divergent views on these structures present in the member states and the European institutions in the decade before the creation of the EEAS in the 1990s. It begins by tracing the organisational landscape in EU external relations and foreign policy that existed until the creation of the EEAS. The two organisational sources that provided the immediate administrative backbone of the EEAS had evolved to fulfil separate tasks and had developed quite distinct identities. The chapter will first highlight the primary role the European Commission played in developing a network of delegations and the multipolarity of the external relations structure within the Commission headquarters in Brussels. It will then turn its attention to the evolution of the Council Secretariat's structures supporting member states' foreign policy coordination, or European Political Cooperation. Later this cooperation was strengthened and re-fashioned as Common Foreign and Security Policy (CFSP) and acquired a defence policy aspect, the European Security and Defence Policy (ESDP). In a third step, the chapter turns to a deeper analysis of member states' preferences regarding an expanded foreign policy structure during several Treaty reform negotiations of the 1990s and the resulting incremental changes. From the positions discovered in the process, the political landscape and the debate on how the EU ought to organise its foreign policy administration becomes clearer, as do the fault lines of disagreement.

The long road to EU diplomatic capacities   19

The idea of a European diplomatic service, or a European foreign ministry, led by a European foreign minister has been part and parcel of nearly all noted federal visions of European integration put forward during or just after the Second World War, including in the proposals of the Swiss Europa-Union in 1940, of Altiero Spinelli in 1941, and the Pan-Europa Union's 'Draft Constitution for a United States of Europe' in 1942. All contained foreign policy as a competence for a European federation (Lipgens 1986). These ideas have not translated naturally into the institutional reality of the European Union and its predecessors. Even with the creation of the European External Action Service (EEAS), the current institutional structure bears only a very abstract resemblance to the federal ideas of the past. The path to the creation of this latest organisation has been a rather long chain of changes in the practice and later institutional structure of the European Communities and then European Union. This chapter briefly highlights the institutional development in EC external relations and EU foreign policy since the beginning of European integration in the 1950s. A central focus is the proposals and positions in place in the 1990s across EU member states and EU institutions, to develop a sense of how core actors saw the future of EU external relations and foreign policy structures just before the EEAS was created.

While the EEAS is often called the European diplomatic service, it is not the beginning of external representation and foreign policy at the European level. The organisational roots of external relations services in the broadest sense in the EU lie in the European Commission.

The European Commission's external service – developing and trading up

The EU, or at the time the ECSC and later EC, started in its early years to develop a system of representation abroad, which at a much later stage was also reflected in an external relations structure at the headquarters level. This system's growth was anchored on the one hand to the US, with a pioneering role for the Washington delegation, and in the former colonies of the member states, where numbers of missions were largest. The roles of the offices were at first purely informational, or in the case of former colonies focused on technical assistance programming and implementation of the European Development Fund. Staff structure and staff privileges reflected the nature of the representation service and were far removed from diplomatic standards of the member states.

Building the Commission's external representation 1954–1993

The EU's fluid evolution has made it very hard to clearly time individual moments or steps of development. Usually for the EU, organisational and legal changes are catching up with established structures of practice. This is also the case when looking at EU diplomacy and in particular its external representation.

20 *The long road to EU diplomatic capacities*

Bruter (1999: p. 183) identified the first delegation as the office opened by the European Coal and Steel Community (ECSC) in London in 1956. The Commission's official history refers to the opening of a liaison office in Santiago de Chile, but also designates the London office as the 'first full diplomatic mission' (European Commission 2004: p. 12). The Commission's External Relations Directorate-General (DG RELEX) itself traced its roots back to the Washington information office established in 1954 (European Commission 2004). The opening of the then European Coal and Steel Community office (Burghardt 2004) deviated from established diplomatic practice in a variety of ways. First, the ECSC was not a state with all the ensuing consequences in diplomatic status and practice (Bruter 1999). Second, the head of the office was neither an ECSC official envoy, nor a diplomat from the member states, but a US citizen. Third, from the very beginning it was set out to be first and foremost an information office. Despite these categorical intricacies, it is clear that the intention of the then High Authority was to reciprocate the diplomatic recognition it had received from the United States of America. The US sent the first ambassador to the ECSC in 1952.

Irrespective of which office was first, 1954 is the starting point for the multiplication of offices representing the High Authority and later the European Commission abroad. The European Community was from the beginning an enterprise with links to the rest of the world and 'a complex set of external relations has been an integral part of its evolution' (Smith 2006: p. 313). This evolution is visible in the development of the delegation network as well as by changes in the headquarter organisation within the Commission in Brussels. The expansion of the network of external representations has continued to this day; the count of European Union delegations and offices reached 139 in 2017 (European External Action Service 2017). This growth has been structured over time largely by mirroring the domestic and external competences of the EU itself (Smith 2006: pp. 315–322). It has also been a reflection of the difficulty in determining the 'boundaries of external relations in terms of policy as much as in terms of organisational responsibility' (Smith 2006: p. 314). It has not, at least for most of the time, been the result of a deliberate strategy to develop a diplomatic network across the world. Or as Spence has put it: 'it has grown [...] with neither strategy nor even declared intention playing a serious role' (Spence 2006: p. 63).

The EC opened an office in Santiago de Chile in 1956 as the seat of the Economic Commission for Latin American (CEPAL/ECLA), which had set out to develop a potential Latin American common market. A strong presence in former colonies of the member states, in particular in African and Caribbean (ACP) countries, is another pattern that emerged early on in the development of the external service (Bruter 1999; Edwards 2005: p. 43). At headquarters level, the service that was most involved in the increase of the network of delegations was the Directorate General for Development (Spence 2006: p. 401). Overseas aid was managed via an agency at first, the European Agency for Cooperation (European Commission 2004: p. 15). The bulk of the Directorate General VII for Development retained the focus on project management and the disbursement of

The long road to EU diplomatic capacities 21

the European Development Fund, according to an official history of the European Commission (Dumoulin 2007: pp. 377–390). In the 1960s, the management of delegations was still outsourced to an agency, which reported to the Commission (Spence 2006: p. 402). An increase in numbers and in tasks beyond pure technical assistance under the revised external assistance framework of Lomé prompted administrative reforms (Spence 2006: p. 402; European Commission 2004: p. 19). Delegations started to include more permanent Commission officials and member states development officials (Spence 2006: p. 403).

Since trade took centre stage in the Community external relations (Smith 2006: p. 316), it also meant that some missions abroad were managed by the Directorate General for External Economic Relations, rather than DG Development (Spence 2006: p. 403). In 1965, this DG I acquired the central management of external representations, an essential part of the future organisation of external relations in the Commission. These later types of delegations were built according to a more diplomatic approach, focusing on information and representation as well as cooperation with member states (European Commission 2004: p. 24). This amounted over time to an 'extensive mechanism of international representation and reporting' (Smith 2006: p. 321). Two of DG I's directorates merged in 1967 to create a new Directorate-General DG XI for Trade and relations with the United States, Canada, South Africa, Australia, New Zealand, Japan, the Far East and the members of the COMECON (Bossuat and Legendre 2007: p. 341).

These wide responsibilities illustrate the internal organisational dynamics and the need for coordination between different parts of the European Commission. Smith has compared the role of DG I at the time to the US Trade Representative in that it was 'trying to coordinate and moderate the needs and interests of powerful internal baronies without possessing a great deal of coercive power' (Smith 2006: p. 321). In addition, member states were watching the increased visibility of these trade representatives with cautious eyes, and France in particular was opposed to strengthening the diplomatic influence of the delegations and their heads (Bossuat and Legendre 2007: p. 344).

But achieving full diplomatic status for its missions was still part of the Commission's objective for of this growing organisational structure (European Commission 2004: p. 36). The office in Washington DC and its staff were extended all diplomatic privileges and immunities by President Nixon through Executive Order 11689 (United States Code 2014). Clearly, also from a legal point of view, it is possible to speak of diplomatic representation by the predecessor of the EU from this point onward.

Still, the focus of both the staff concerned as much as headquarters was the execution of European external policies, trade, and in particular the implementation of the European Development Fund (Interview, Senior Commission official, 2011; Bruter 1999; European Commission 2004; Spence 2004). In the 1980s, however, a marked change was observed, inasmuch as delegations outside of the ACP were concerned. Spence described the shift of reporting lines towards the Commission's nucleus external relations Directorate-General DG I (2004: p. 66).

22   *The long road to EU diplomatic capacities*

In 1988, a unified system of administration for the delegation was merged from the two previous organisations (European Commission 2004: p. 33; Spence 2006: p. 404). Nuttall gives a detailed insight into the very limited organisational resources, specifically addressing European Political Cooperation within the Commission and the limitations placed on it in the 1980s (Nuttall 2006: p. 351).

In addition to the development and trade services, parts of an external relations headquarters service of the European Commission started to take shape in several Directorates-General. The Commission had a role to play in foreign policy as well, as Edwards observed: 'As a driver of foreign policy integration, it had the advantage, at least from the mid-1980s on, of being able to bring the economic and political aspects of policy together' (Edwards 2005: p. 52). The Commission's service dealing with European Political Cooperation was refashioned in 1993 as Directorate General DG Ia for political external relations (European Commission 2007: p. 407, Nugent 2001: p. 301). This DG also acquired the central management of delegations (European Commission 2007: p. 407).

After a wave of organisational reform regarding headquarters structure, staff rules and management of delegations at the beginning of the 1990s (European Commission 2004; Spence 2004, 2006; Smith 2006: p. 339), the European Commission's Directorate-General for External Relations, or DG RELEX, considered itself to be a European 'diplomatic service avant la lettre' (Interview, Senior Commission official, 2011). The official history of the Commission's external delegations underlines this self-image with a quote from a report written by Adrian Fortescue to the European Council from 1982: 'The Commission has the nucleus of a foreign service. Its external delegations are doing work directly comparable to Member State embassies' (European Commission 2004: p. 29). From 1995, there were still four external relations Directorates-General: DG1 Commercial Policy, DG IA External Relations, CFSP and missions, DG IB External Relations with the Southern Mediterranean, Middle East, Latin America, South-East Asia and DG VIII Development (Nugent 2001: pp. 301–302).

In 1996, the Williamson Report, or more accurately, the 'Report on the longer-term requirements of the External Service' proposed a unified structure of delegations and headquarters services including a rotation system for external relations staff (European Commission 1996). It was tellingly based on a comparative study of member states' diplomatic services (European Commission 1996: Annex I). The same year also marked the beginning of regular reports by the European Commission to both the European Parliament and the Council of the EU on the management and development of the external service (European Commission 2004: p. 50). Despite being inconsistently named, these regular communications on the 'multiannual plan to allocate External Service Resources' (European Commission 1998), 'The Development of the External Service' (European Commission 1999) and 'Concerning the development of the external service' (European Commission 2000) specified in considerable detail the reorganisation taking place in the external service. In line with general Commission administrative reform, this involved not only the rationalisation of staff

The long road to EU diplomatic capacities 23

numbers and delegations in relation to tasks (European Commission 1998: p. 3), but also a reorganisation to balance the Commission's representation in regions across the world and in particular in the former Soviet Union, Warsaw Pact countries and Yugoslavia (e.g. European Commission 1998: p. 5). The Commission also streamlined the administrative structure of the 'Unified External Service', e.g. by creating 'a single pool of posts' managed by 'a single department' (European Commission 2002a: p. 2; European Commission 2002b). From this department's purview only two types of staff were excluded: humanitarian aid staff in order to ensure that they would be perceived as neutral and apolitical in the field, and staff on loan to the external service by other directorates-general. A steering committee for the external service was endowed with a wider mandate (European Commission 2002a: p. 22). At headquarters level, and to a limited degree in delegations, the administrative distinction between development, trade, aid implementation and external relations remained within the so-called 'famille RELEX'.

The European Parliament may not have believed that the Commission was already in possession of a diplomatic service in the 1990s, but it certainly supported the expansion and reorganisation on the part of the Commission at the time. In the annual report on CFSP, the Matutes Report, in 1995, the EP expressed its position clearly:

> [the EP] believes that it is essential for the European Union to have a diplomatic apparatus of its own; is of the opinion that the Commission's delegations to non-member countries should be upgraded to embassies of the European Union.
>
> (European Parliament 1995a: p. 238)

In an opinion on the treaty reform debate held in the following year, the EP also stated its unequivocal support for a strong role of the Commission in the Common Foreign and Security Policy:

> The Commission should be fully integrated into the definition and elaboration of CFSP, with a right of initiative. It should be given implementing power. In order to rectify difficulties that have emerged in the field of policy design and formulation, a joint Commission-Council planning and analysis unit should be established.
>
> (European Parliament 1995b)

During the later stages of this evolution in the Commission's external service, political demands were made for stronger collaboration with national diplomatic services. Laursen and Vanhoonacker reproduced a Belgian proposal expressing an interest in developing 'a better mix between expertise and diplomatic information from the Member States and the Commission's experience' (Laursen and Vanhoonacker 1992: p. 273). Spence quotes a Belgian demand in 1996 for a coordinated use of diplomatic resources (Spence 2006: p. 408). From the late

24 *The long road to EU diplomatic capacities*

1990s, the Commission attempted to build stronger links to the diplomatic community of the member states by the inclusion of seconded diplomats (European Commission 1999: pp. 7–9). The Commission also noted that so far none of the nine staff participating in the scheme had been serving members of a member state diplomatic corps (European Commission 1999: p. 8). The Commission was thus actively looking for a stronger link to the member states' diplomatic services in the late 1990s, albeit with limited success.

The Commission was thus a first mover in terms of organising for external representation, and its increasingly unified external service was one core element of the EU's relations with the world. In addition to the Community fields of trade, development and other internal competences with relevance to other countries, member states were slowly collaborating in more traditional foreign policy. This cooperation in the Council also had administrative repercussions, which are the focus of the next section.

The organisation of European Political Cooperation

After the first decade of European integration the Community side of EU external policy was followed by increased attempts to coordinate so-called high politics of foreign policy and defence. From purely intergovernmental beginnings and at very slow pace, a second source of organisational structures at the EU level came into being. Once more formally established, European Political Cooperation and later the Common Foreign and Security Policy became the second organisational heritage of EU foreign policy.

Looking for the organisational roots of the EPC machinery seems futile at first as the process started out as intergovernmental ministerial and committee meetings (Nuttall 1992: pp. 52–73). Wallace and Allen describe clearly the absence of strong institutional characteristics at the beginning of political cooperation: 'it had no definite institutional basis; it had no secretariat; it had, at best, tenuous links with the existing institutions of the European Communities' (Wallace and Allen 1977: p. 227). The reasons for the lack of institutional underpinning of the foreign policy coordination process, however, are a good illustration of the typical conflicts the member states found themselves part of. Attempts in the 1950s to integrate more deeply on defence failed as the French parliament did not ratify the European Defence Community. While in the 1960s regular meetings between foreign ministers started to take place, underlying disagreement between the member states on these arrangements remained.

France in particular was a strong proponent of a purely intergovernmental arrangement with a political secretariat in Paris, not in Brussels (Allen and Wallace 1982: p. 22; Nuttall 1992: pp. 71–72). Smaller member states such as the Netherlands and Belgium supported the founding of such a secretariat, only in Brussels, in order not to lose the connection to the Community institutions (Allen and Wallace 1982: pp. 22–23; Nuttall 1992: p. 72). Disagreement between the two sides left the EPC in its early years without any permanent administrative support (Juncos and Pomorska 2010: p. 8). This disagreement persisted throughout the

The long road to EU diplomatic capacities   25

1960s and only in 1970 could a compromise be found and European Political Cooperation begin. The compromise itself found in the Davignon Report was based on very loose arrangements and was intergovernmental in nature (Davignon Report, 27 October 1970). It consisted of meetings of foreign ministers, the creation of a political committee of senior diplomats and, if necessary, working groups underneath this structure (Allen and Wallace 1982: p. 24). The meetings were to be held in the capital of the presidency rather than in Brussels (Allen and Wallace 1982: p. 24).

Diplomatic cables of the United States including diplomatic assessments of the US staff in host countries provide some additional anecdotal evidence for this development. One document indicates that a Belgian paper dealing with 'Administrative problems involved in exercising the Presidency' was making proposals towards the creation of a Secretariat (US Diplomatic Cable 1973c: No. 08154), after a German proposal had been presented and withdrawn that year (US Diplomatic Cable 1973a: No. 07202). A proposal to detach an official for purposes of administrative support in the embassy of the state holding the presidency was seen as the most feasible option. This 'Ersatz' or 'rolling' secretariat was also acceptable to the French, who otherwise staunchly separated the EC and political cooperation (US Diplomatic Cable 1973b: No. 07203). If leaked US diplomatic cables are to be trusted, the French blocked further discussion of a Secretariat, after its location in Paris had been rejected (US Diplomatic Cable 1973a: No. 07202). The French difficulty with a rapprochement between Community institutions and foreign policy is well documented (see e.g. Allen and Wallace 1982: pp. 24–25; Allen 1998). In 1973, the foreign ministers approved the Copenhagen Report setting out the practices already achieved, rather than genuine new proposals (Allen and Wallace 1982: pp. 25–26; Copenhagen Report, 23 July 1973). In addition to the 'rolling secretariat', the so-called 'Political Co-operation machinery' was described as consisting of a Political Committee, a 'Group of Correspondants' [sic], and other potential working parties. The 'Group of Correspondants' was specifically created to 'follow the implementation of political co-operation and of studying problems of organisation and problems of a general nature' (Copenhagen Report, 23 July 1973).

The attempt by the member states to keep the European Commission at arm's length, yet still relying on its input and recognising the need for coordination with it, formed part of the contradictions of European political cooperation from the very beginning (Nuttall 1992: pp. 59, 65, 74). Even in these beginnings of EU foreign policy, intergovernmental political and supranational economic aspects of relations with the rest of the world were not neatly separable. The Tindemans Report of 1975 called for ending the differentiation between foreign policy cooperation and regular Council meetings while maintaining the different policy preparation processes leading up to the council meetings (Allen and Wallace 1982: p. 26). But the report 'merely gathered dust on the shelf' (Edwards and Pijpers 1997: p. 6). Observers of EPC also hinted at another problem in the high politics side of EU foreign policy: that it merely created 'procedure as substitute for policy' (Wallace and Allen 1977). The ability to

26   The long road to EU diplomatic capacities

manage everyday foreign policy activities jointly for European countries was already then seen as requiring in the long run 'the establishment of both a common foreign policy and a common diplomatic service' (Allen 1982: p. 175). But the step-by-step approach to integration would also be followed in political cooperation.

In 1981, the 'London Report' strengthened the role of the rotating chair, the Presidency, in running European Political Cooperation. It also introduced a new type of administrative support in the form of the Troika Secretariat, i.e. seconded national officials from the preceding and succeeding Presidencies (London Report, 13 October 1981; Nuttall 1992: p. 179). This small team of officials almost immediately proved their worth in successive political crises (Nuttall 1992: p. 201). At the same time, the European Commission was to be 'fully associated' with the EPC. An initiative by the German and Italian Foreign Ministers, the Genscher-Colombo initiative, made the argument for stronger political cooperation in Europe and more Community involvement in external affairs, but led only to a limited 'Solemn declaration' in Stuttgart 1983 (Edwards and Pijpers 1997: p. 6). This is an example of a less successful step towards further institutionalisation and at the same time highlights the nearly continuous attempts at moving forward in this 'institutionalisation of cooperation' (Smith 2004). Foreign ministries in the member states had increasingly become enmeshed in a continuous dialogue, not only about policy (Hocking 2002: p. 277), but also about the organisation of this process. Without central offices that could develop independent proposals, it was the foreign ministries themselves that were responsible for coming up with reform proposals.

In 1985, yet another report prepared by former Irish Foreign Minister Dooge proposed a permanent secretariat for the EPC (Report of the Ad hoc Committee on Institutional Affairs 1985: p. 22), using the resources of the Council in order to support the Presidency in the management of the EPC (Nuttall 1992: p. 243, Report of the Ad hoc Committee for Institutional Affairs 1985: p. 22). While it was a joint report, not all members of the Committee agreed with all parts, entering reservations on individual proposal items. Consensus on the organisation of EU foreign policy administration was still hard to come by. Finally, the Single European Act in 1987, a reform treaty that covered both Community aspects and political cooperation, formalised EPC in a European treaty and set up a secretariat (Nuttall 1992: p. 243; Dijkstra 2008: pp. 152–153; da Costa Pereira 1988). In essence, it created a more permanent structure of seconded national officials with an administrative base in the Council Secretariat in Brussels. Observers judged the 'institutional innovation' decided in the Act to be 'half-hearted' (Rummel 1992: p. 298), even if it set off an institutional trajectory towards more Brussels-based decision-making, or 'Brusselisation' (Allen 1998).

In response to external shocks, such as the fall of the Berlin Wall and the ousting of Communist regimes in Central and Eastern Europe, the member states embarked on discussions about the reform of the European foreign policy structures. These were part of wider discussions leading up to a new treaty on creating a 'Political Union' to complete the economic integration of the member

The long road to EU diplomatic capacities   27

states. While always only one aspect of negotiations, external action and its impact always remained an element of the large-scale 'institutional relaunch' of the EC proposed by Belgium (Laursen, Vanhoonacker and Wester 1992: pp. 5–6). During the negotiations, a Belgian proposal also included an

> initial experiment in synergy by setting up a 'special task force' made up of some diplomats specialising in Eastern Europe and who would be seconded by the Member States and some Commission officials.
>
> (Laursen *et al.* 1992: p. 273)

An adapted Franco-German proposal for a Common Foreign and Security Policy went through several variations (Nuttall 2000: pp. 114f.) and in the negotiations for a new treaty member states were faced with widely varying objectives and interpretations of it. Some, including the UK and Denmark, wished for a continuation of EPC 'along existing lines' (Nuttall 2000: p. 150). Germany, the Benelux and Italy wanted to align it with Community procedures (Nuttall 2000: p. 150), while the French wanted an improved common policy but with stronger links to the European Council (Nuttall 2000: p. 150). In the end, the Treaty on the European Union built a Common Foreign and Security Policy, and brought the former EPC closer to the Community with a single institutional framework at ministerial level. It maintained the intergovernmental nature of decision-making as well as the apparatus below ministers in the Council (Nuttall 2000: p. 182).

In administrative terms, the Treaty on the European Union merged the Troika Secretariat of seconded officials with the Council Secretariat (Nuttall 2000: p. 183). In the Council Secretariat, the external relations tasks were joined in a Directorate General, the so-called DG-E, with two major elements: one the services for the Common Foreign and Security Policy, the other dealing with external economic relations (Nuttall 2000: p. 251; Juncos and Pomorska 2010: p. 9). It maintained a strong element of national seconded officials among its staff, but now also included a number of European officials (Dijkstra 2013: p. 54). While servicing the Council meetings and working groups like all other parts of the Secretariat, the CFSP section slowly began to take on more substantive tasks. Because of the limited role of the Commission in CFSP, it started to assist 'the Presidency to write its own proposals' (Nuttall 2000: p. 253). Despite these developments towards organisational unification on the Council side, European policy was still off the mark in terms of visibility and the ability of the EU to act not only jointly, but also effectively. In the mid-1990s the next round of institutional reform ideas circulated, this time focusing on institutional change at the top rather than on the machinery. The ideas floated, however, bore a close resemblance to those discussed in the early 1990s, in particular the idea of creating a Deputy Secretary-General of the Council for Foreign Policy found in the Belgian memorandum (Laursen and Vanhoonacker 1992: p. 273).

In order to look more closely at the discussion surrounding the leadership and structure of the EU foreign policy machinery, this section will analyse in more

28 *The long road to EU diplomatic capacities*

detail the positions expressed by member states and European institutions in the treaty reform discussions of the 1990s. It will also describe the administrative changes that these expansions of foreign policy architecture at the EU level brought with them. A clear overview of the views of member states and EU institutions in the 1990s will provide clues as to what shaped the opportunity structure for the decision to create the EEAS in the early 2000s.

Member states and the reorganisation of European foreign policy

Since the roots of European Political Cooperation lay in purely intergovernmental coordination meetings, the central role that member states played in the evolution is unsurprising and well documented in the literature (Allen *et al.* 1982; Edwards and Pijpers 1997). Changes in the organisational structure underpinning this cooperation needed agreement by all governments. Member states did not agree completely on objectives, methods, or the substance of policy. This is illustrated well by the professed preferences on the revision of EU foreign policy structures on the Council Secretariat's side in the run-up to the 1996 Intergovernmental Conference. The 1996 IGC, which was already foreseen in the Treaty of Maastricht, had a particular focus on institutional balance, foreign policy, economic union and enlargement. The organisational structure of future EU foreign policy was part of this negotiation.

In 1994, a high level group of experts on CFSP, at the request of European Commissioner for external relations Hans van den Broek, spelled out proposals with a clear integrationist twist (High Level Group 1994). With regard to the organisational structure, the High Level Group 'advocate[d] (without awaiting the outcome of the IGC) the immediate establishment of a genuinely independent permanent central analysis and evaluation capability in Brussels' (High Level Group 1994: p. 8). It should retain expertise from the Council, Commission and the Western European Union and should be led by a special advisor nominated by the European Council (High Level Group 1994: p. 9). A year later, another group of experts working under the sponsorship of the Bertelsmann Foundation in collaboration with the European Commission's planning staff came to similar conclusions: 'There is an urgent need, therefore, for a European Planning Staff, which should be a joint Commission-Council body' (Working Group 1995: p. 13).

In 1995, a reflection group mandated by the European Council and chaired by Carl Westendorp in its 'Progress Report from the Chairman of the Reflection Group on the 1996 Intergovernmental Conference' included a similar proposal: 'The Group agreed that an analysis, forecasting, planning and proposal unit or body should be set up for the common foreign policy' (Reflection Group 1995: p. 29). The group also discussed two options for the CFSP 'figurehead'. One option was 'locating the unit at the General Secretariat of the Council, with its facilities strengthened and the Secretary-General raised in rank to ministerial level'; an option favoured also because this solution would 'highlight the

The long road to EU diplomatic capacities   29

desirability of placing the unit at the Council, on account of the central role played by States within the CFSP' (Reflection Group 1995: p. 29). The second option was a new figure, a 'High Permanent Representative for CFSP, appointed by the European Council' (Reflection Group 1995: p. 29). This new figure would have the task of chairing the Political Committee and have at his/her disposal a 'tri-partite body, made up of Member States, the Council and the Commission' as a planning and analysis unit (Reflection Group 1995: p. 30). The concept of merging the three sources of organisations involved in foreign policy for joint planning and analysis had already made a strong appearance in the preparation for the 1996 IGC, but also highlighted the division of opinions over which approach to take. This division was a reflection of the diversity of views present in the member states at the time. Sources involved in the preparation of member states in 1995 give an impression of the diversity of views prevalent in the capitals at the time.

Table 2.1 shows the focus of member states on different organisational issues. As early as the mid-1990s Germany and Austria looked very much to an analysis and planning unit to improve the functioning of CFSP. Belgium, without being too overtly pro-integrationist as may be expected, was looking to enhance the role of the Commission. France on the other hand preferred a much stronger, almost hierarchical role for the European Council. After a first round of negotiation and continued consultation of the experts, the positions of governments shifted more closely around a partly integrationist centre, without losing their specific stance entirely.

Table 2.1 and Table 2.2 illustrate the diversity of opinions present among member states, from the maintenance of strict intergovernmental cooperation to more integrationist changes in the organisation and decision-making processes. After the first round of consultations, most member states supported the creation of an 'analysis and planning' organisation within the realm of the Council Secretariat General (see Table 2.2). Some member states also wanted the staff of this body to be drawn from a variety of organisations. Individual member states also noted the need for better external representation, or for diplomatic resources. France still sought to strengthen the European Council, even if it did agree to the 'face and voice' (European Parliament 1997) of a 'Mr CFSP' (Table 2.2, European Parliament 1997). These preferences were naturally only one element of the discussions and were also informed by the wider discussions about the EU's institutional architecture in the 1990s (Laffan 1997).

All the High Representative's men

The appointment of a figurehead for EU foreign policy, the High Representative for the Common Foreign and Security Policy, in 1999 after the Amsterdam revisions to the Treaties and the war in Kosovo, proved an administrative watershed for the Council Secretariat (Christiansen and Vanhoonacker 2008). Javier Solana, a former Spanish Foreign Minister, is credited with shaping not only his own job description but also the institutional features relating to it (Duke 2011).

Table 2.1 Selected member states' positions on CFSP integration.

Member state	Position CFSP integration + = more − = status quo/less	Organisational structure	Other
Finland	−	CFSP Secretary General would not help	Retain rotation of Presidency
Austria	(+)	'Creation of planning cell from representatives of Council Secretariat, Commission, and Member States', not new CFSP Secretariat	Possibly led by 'personality' nominated by European Council, retain rotation
Netherlands	−	CFSP unit in CSG to play greater role in policy preparation; a separate organisation would need to include Commission and member states	
Luxembourg	+	Analysis and planning capacity in CSG	
Ireland	−	Improved structure for policy analysis and preparation	Retain rotation
France	(+)	Extend presidency term and right of proposal	Chairman of the European Council for three years
Germany	+	Working unit for analysis and planning led by a political Secretary for CFSP/bring together the capacities in Commission, Council and WEU	
Belgium	+	Commission as catalyst and coordinator of external action, exchange of personnel with MS	
UK	−	Develop WEU	CFSP strictly intergovernmental

Source: own overview based on EIPA 1995.

The long road to EU diplomatic capacities 31

In the ten years after his appointment, administrative structures of European foreign policy grew noticeably (Duke 2011: pp. 35–37). The Policy Planning and Early Warning Unit (PPEWU, later known as Policy Unit) under the High Representative was often seen as epitomising this change. Staffed mostly with seconded officials, its role resembled more closely the tasks of policy staff in European foreign ministries. It was to identify risks, provide analysis and assessment of and for foreign and security policy at the EU level (Duke 2011: p. 42). The Policy Unit was also tasked with providing policy options for EU action in different countries or regions around the globe (Duke 2011: p. 44). The policy unit was an interesting organisational experiment, including national diplomats in an otherwise European institutional environment, the Council Secretariat.

The growing structure in EU foreign policy associated with the Council Secretariat also included growth in more defence- and security-related policy areas. In 1998, the St Malo British–French declaration gave the impetus for a build-up of more defence-related policy structures. The Nice Treaty revision included its message relating to 'progressive framing of a common defence policy' (Keukeleire and MacNaughtan 2008: p. 174), or the European Security and Defence Policy (ESDP). With the creation of military structures and linkages to NATO, the ESDP started to develop organisational structures at the Council Secretariat (Allen and Smith 2001: pp. 98–99; Keukeleire and MacNaughtan 2008: pp. 179–185). The Council Secretariat grew to include an EU Military Staff (EUMS), Civilian Planning and Conduct Capability (CPCC) for civilian crisis management, and a crisis management and planning directorate (Allen and Smith 2001: p. 99; Duke 2011: pp. 50–61, Juncos and Pomorska 2010: p. 11, Vanhoonacker *et al.* 2011: pp. 8–12). In addition, the Council Secretariat acquired administrative resources through the setting up of a Situation Centre out of the Policy Unit (Duke 2011: p. 45). The Situation Centre, an intelligence analysis and crisis monitoring body, also includes seconded staff from the member states' national intelligence services (Duke 2011: pp. 45–46). The development of these security and military structures was based on delicate negotiation and also necessitated adjustments in the physical organisation of the administration as these matters required higher standards of security than other elements of foreign policy. The military staff and several central systems were thus housed separately from the other Council structures and have remained so even after the creation of a new merged service (Allen and Smith 2001: p. 100).

The external relations part of the Council Secretariat was constituted from the very beginning by a different type of staff and had to fulfil functions that were fundamentally different from the ones executed in other parts of the Council Secretariat (Interview 2, Senior Council Official, 2011, Interview 15, Senior Council Official, 2012). They were usually seconded from national foreign services and considered more flexible and political (Interview 2, Senior Council Official, 2011, Interview 15, Senior Council Official, 2012; see also Juncos and Pomorska 2010). Later, they were to include military, intelligence and crisis management staff, making for an unusually diverse workforce for strategic analysis of and response to international political and security situations.

Table 2.2 Selected member states' views on organisation structures in CFSP

Actor	Stance on CFSP += more integration, −= less integration/Status quo	Organisational structure	Other
EP	+	Joint Commission-Council planning and analysis unit	Union diplomatic apparatus; 'Parliament rejects […] the idea that there should be a "High Representative" for the CFSP.'
Commission	+	Increased practical cooperation; joint troubleshooting machinery; joint analysis unit COM and MS	'Firm opposition to appointment of a Mr CFSP'
High Level Group 2nd report	+	'New structure, in the form of a tripartite central analysis and proposal capacity and a CFSP High Representative', functional link with COM	
Belgium	+	Analysis and planning unit with MS, COM and WEU, headed by senior official	
Denmark	−	Analysis and planning unit under Council of Ministers	
Germany	(+)	'Face and voice' for CFSP, permanent analysis and planning unit, headed by Mr/Mrs CFSP, staff from MS, COM and CSG	
Greece	+	Gradual approach, stronger COM role	
Spain	+	Analysis, foresight, early warning and planning cell in CSG without right of initiative.	

France	+	Appointed representative	Strong role European Council
Ireland	(+)	Central planning and analysis unit at the service of the Presidency and the Council	
Italy	+	Mr CFSP, permanent secretariat appointed by Council, or elected Presidency for 2–3 years	
Luxembourg	+	Analysis and planning unit, with MS, COM and WEU	
Austria	+	Planning unit in CSG, representatives of the Council secretariat, COM and MS, head appointed by Council	
Netherlands	+	Analysis and planning unit in CSG, with COM, MS and WEU, headed by Senior Official appointed by Council and agreed by COM	
Portugal	–	Policy planning staff for CFSP in CSG, without right of initiative	
Finland	–	Rejects Mr CFSP	
Sweden	+	Better analysis and planning by CSG, and limited COM	
UK	–	CFSP-Planning Cell through modest enhancing CSG; CFSP Representative of Secretary-General rank, appointed by and answerable to Council	

Source: own compilation based on European Parliament 1997.

34 *The long road to EU diplomatic capacities*

Because of this difference in staffing Solana could claim that the new 'elements have helped create a new culture of real time foreign policy making' (European Convention 2002 WG VII WD 8: p. 6).

With this administrative structure engaged in the high politics of foreign policy, the Council Secretariat and its officials as well as the seconded national diplomats must be considered the second core legacy on the administrative side of European external relations and foreign policy. The Secretariat grew in size and remit from a small support team, made up of seconded national officials, into a meaningful administrative presence of several hundred administrators. Table 2.3 illustrates the slow institutionalisation process, in which at first reports to the member states recommended an increase in the number and type of meetings at political level as well as organisational changes to the support structures. The organisational pinnacle in this instance is the creation of a permanent secretariat based in Brussels by the Single European Act.

The growth phases were influenced largely by two factors. On the one hand, they were shaped by the conflict between the intergovernmentalist and supranationalist views on European foreign policy prevalent in the member states. On the other hand, they were driven by external events such as the fall of the Berlin Wall and the wars in the Balkans, which helped to galvanise further integration. The underlying political disagreement between intergovernmentalists and supranationalists, but also the more nuanced differences between member states of each camp, are nowhere more apparent than with regard to organisational arrangements in EU foreign policy. It is the politics of organisational structure that determine to a large degree the development in EU foreign policy over the decades of EPC and CFSP. In many ways, the Council Secretariat's role in CFSP was already a merger of traditions considering the important role played by seconded officials. Looking at the member states is undoubtedly of greatest relevance for the evolution of Council structures as parliamentary scrutiny was virtually non-existent. The Commission's own internal evolution has been illustrated above. The Commission's interaction with the foreign policy mechanisms of the member states has been subject to repeated analysis with regard to the EPC (Nuttall 2006) and to the CFSP (Spence 2006). The EP's role is less directly relevant for changes in the beginnings of EU foreign policy, but understanding the view of the EP completes the picture of Brussels' actors.

Parliamentary activism over two decades

Member states were not the only actors voicing views on the need for change in the organisation of European foreign policy cooperation. European institutions were part of this debate as well. The European Parliament, with a low level of formal powers in this particular policy area, used the EU reform debates of the 1980s and 1990s to express its opinion on how the EU should proceed. In particular the first directly elected European Parliament in 1979 felt the need to press for a 'political union', which included stronger foreign policy cooperation (Alonso Terme 1992: p. 269). The following depiction of

Table 2.3 Progressive institutionalisation of European Political Cooperation 1970–1986

Year	Title	Political	Organisational
1970	Luxembourg (Davignon) Report	Ministerial meetings once every 6 months, Political Committee at least 4 times a year, Working Groups	Host state will provide secretarial services; nominate one foreign affairs official as correspondent
1973	Copenhagen Report	Ministerial meetings 4 times a year, Political Committee as frequently as necessary, Group of European 'Correspondents', Working Groups	–
1981	London Report	Ministerial meetings, informal Gymnich meetings, Political Committee, Correspondents' Group, Working Groups	'Presidency assisted by a small team of officials from the preceding and succeeding Presidencies', officials remain in home diplomatic service at the embassy in Presidency
1983	Solemn Declaration on the European Union (Stuttgart)	–	–
1985	Report of the Ad hoc Committee on Institutional Affairs (Dooge) Report	Regular EPC working meetings at the Community seat and meetings in capitals	'Creation of a permanent political cooperation secretariat (…); the secretariat would to a large extent use the back-up facilities of the Council and should help to strengthen the cohesion between political cooperation and the external policies of the Community'
1986	Single European Act	Ministerial meetings, also discussions in Council, Presidency of EPC = Presidency of Council, Political Committee, European Correspondents' Group, Working Groups	'A secretariat based in Brussels shall assist the Presidency in preparing and implementing the activities of EPC and in administrative matters. It shall carry out its duties under the authority of the Presidency', members have same status as members of diplomatic missions of member states

36 *The long road to EU diplomatic capacities*

selected EP reports on European Political Cooperation and CFSP illustrates the EP's strongly integrationist views.

Recurrently, the EP insisted on an expansion of political cooperation and an increase in capacity at the EU level. Table 2.4 gives an overview of the incessant engagement of the European Parliament in the organisation of EU external affairs, despite, or maybe rather because of, its lack of legislative power and its growing appetite to increase it. During the 1990s, the European Parliament was getting more involved in the structure of the Commission's external service via its budgetary powers and achieved an appearance before Parliament by new heads of delegations (Spence 2006: p. 408). Some evidence suggests that the more detailed demands were in fact derived from informal discussions between Members of the European Parliament and relevant Commission staff and represented what the Commission thought it needed in the first place (Interview 9, Senior Council official, 2011). By that time, an overhaul of the institutional system of the European Union was already on the horizon.

But the EP also expanded its vision of the organisation of EU foreign policy cooperation. The European Parliament in 2000 called for the first time for a 'common Community diplomacy' in the Galeote I Report of 2000 (European Parliament 2000). The report demanded a common training path, better cooperation between national diplomatic services and the EU level and a clearer role for Commission delegations. It also spelled out clearly some of the demands the EP has consistently made since then regarding a European diplomatic service: the creation of a European diplomatic service linked to the diplomatic services of the member states (European Parliament 2000: pp. 6, 12), a diplomatic college and increased diplomatic training for officials (European Parliament 2000: pp. 6, 12), an upgrade of Commission delegations to embassies and a hearing of heads of delegations before the EP (European Parliament 2000: pp. 7, 12–13). The EP sought political visibility in the nomination of heads of delegations:

> [the EP] proposes that provision be made for heads of delegations to appear before the European Parliament's Committee on Foreign Affairs as a matter of course before taking up their duties, in order to outline and discuss their work programme.
>
> (European Parliament 2000: p. 7)

This is a position it would maintain right through the negotiations on the creation of the European External Action Service (European Parliament 2000; European Parliament 2001; European Parliament 2009a, b; European Parliament 2010).

Just a year later, the Galeote II report (European Parliament 2001) reiterated some of these demands and expressed more strongly its position on the growth of the external service in size and powers (European Parliament 2001: p. 8). Most organisational innovations, such as a common diplomacy and a College of European Diplomacy, are accompanied by a clear expansion of EP rights in the area of CFSP. As in all cases, it is also important to recall the institutional

Table 2.4 Selected European Parliament positions on the organisation of Union external affairs 1978–2001

Year	Title	Organisational	Other
19 January 1978	EP Resolution on European Political Cooperation (Blumenfeld Report)	Strengthen Commission in EPC	Information and reporting request for EP on EPC; 'European Political Cooperation Office' proposal remained in Committee
25 June 1981	EP Report on EPC and the EP (Lady Elles report)	Creation of a permanent secretariat	Better information to EP
13 January 1983	Haagerup Report	No recommendation on new institutions (security)	Increased cooperation
17 May 1995	Bourlanges and Martin Report on the functioning of the European Union with a view to the 1996 IGC	Joint Commission-Council planning and analysis unit; own diplomatic apparatus for Union	Parliamentary supervision of CFSP
18 May 1995	Matutes (Own Initiative) Annual Report on progress in the field of CFSP	Risk Analysis and evaluation centre, diplomatic apparatus including European Union embassies	
21 February 1996	Opinion of the Committee on Foreign Affairs, Security and Defence Policy (draftsman: Mr Goerens) on the assessment of the work of the Reflection Group	Central analysis and planning unit; links with Council, COM and WEU; headed by the Commissioner responsible for external relations, responsible for external representation in the area of the CFSP	
13 March 1996	Dury and Marj-Weggen Report on the evaluation of the work of the Reflection Group	Joint analysis and planning unit (staff from CSG and COM) under authority of Commission, Commission should represent in CFSP/no Mr CFSP	
24 July 2000	EP resolution on the establishment of a common diplomacy for the European Union (Galeote I)	Professional, permanent Community diplomatic service, enhanced delegations	College of European Diplomacy; effective bridging system between MS and Community diplomatic services, hearing of heads of delegation in EP
30 May 2001	Report on the Commission Communication on the development of the External Service (Galeote II)	Supports COM reform of external service, more staffing, training	Delegation support MEPs, links to EP formalised

38 *The long road to EU diplomatic capacities*

characteristics of the actors involved and that unitary actions are only possible to a certain degree in such collective bodies such as the European Parliament. A close look at Table 2.4 also illustrates that the EP is not completely unitary, despite its clear integrationist leanings. From the Committee Opinion in 1996 and its subsequent plenary report, it is possible to deduce an internal divergence. The EP committee responsible for foreign affairs was more integrationist than the whole of the EP.

The development on both sides of the Rue de la Loi in Brussels, inside the European Commission's unified external service and the former EPC turned CFSP machinery in the Council Secretariat, was always just one element in a larger sequence of institutional reforms. In the later stages from the Single European Act onwards, organisational change in these areas was closely linked to overall Treaty reform. This remained equally the case in 1999 and later. An additional Treaty revision preparing for enlargement, the Nice Treaty was already in itself seen as temporary fix, setting the stage for a new attempt at grand institutional reform of the EU. The Treaties created to fix problems were found wanting and triggered the next phase of rethinking the institutional structures of the EU.

The member states' Heads of State and Government set off on a slightly different process of institutional revision in the Laeken declaration (European Council 2001) by setting up a Convention to prepare the next Intergovernmental Conference. This Convention on the Future of Europe turned out to be a milestone in the evolution of EU external affairs administration. The fact that the EP called in early 2000 for a common European diplomacy (European Parliament 2000, 2001) is of particular relevance to this analysis as members of the European Parliament played a relevant role in the European Convention on the Future of Europe. The Convention was a new version of treaty reform, which was called upon by the member states in December 2001 in order to provide for a wider political and societal discussion on the future of Europe and its organisation. The political views of the EP became relevant for institutional reform alongside those of the European Commission and the member states. Because of its profound, and at the time unexpected, impact on the EU external relations and foreign policy structures, the Convention merits a thorough analysis, which will be conducted in Chapter 4 with a specific focus on the organisational arrangements in external action.

Conclusion

From this broad overview of the external policy parts of the Commission and the Council Secretariat, as well as the views present in the member states and the European Parliament, a rich empirical ground for the study of institutional development and change becomes visible. The European Commission started developing a sort of external service fragmented across policy areas such as information services, development and trade, which was mirrored by its spread across different organisational sub-units. Over time, and most notably in

The long road to EU diplomatic capacities 39

mid-1980 and again in the 1990s, the Commission undertook reforms to create a 'Unified External Service' within the 'Famille RELEX', the departments responsible for the implementation of various external policies. Nevertheless, the multiple administrative power bases in the Commission remained divided with trade, development and humanitarian aid services remaining separate at head-quarters level from the general external relations directorate general.

The Council Secretariat's foreign policy organisation on the other hand started evolving more gradually, starting notably only after the Single European Act in 1986 as a secretariat to support the member states in their efforts to coordinate foreign policy. It slowly accrued stronger organisational units on foreign policy analysis and forecasting units, largely dominated by member states diplomats. Additional organisational resources were added to the Council Secretariat with the establishment of the European Security and Defence Policy. In 1999, a figurehead for EU foreign policy was created in the High Representative for Common Foreign and Security Policy. Nevertheless, Council resources always lagged considerably behind the number of staff and funding levels of the European Commission and were less focused on implementation and administration of tasks. The Council Secretariat's role was supporting foreign policy by developing proposals, analyses and compromise solutions.

The fundamentally divided administrative structure of EU external relations, with the Community side dominated by the European Commission and the foreign policy element dominated by the member states and supported by the Council Secretariat, has been a long-standing feature of the institutional arrangements in external policy. This chapter has shown that attempts to overcome these divisions have been the driving force of institutional developments for several decades. Member states' views on how foreign policy should be conducted differ greatly, as do their preferences on the type of administrative structure through which it should be channelled. The reform debates throughout the 1990s illustrate the divisions between those wanting stronger institutions at the EU level in Brussels, others who opposed it as well as a variety of views in between. As the overview of proposals and positions from the 1996 IGC showed, a small merged organisation derived from the Commission and the Council was on the table, but never managed to reach the threshold of unanimous agreement among the member states. Some member states were very resistant to any movement towards Community influence on foreign policy decisions. The view on institutional structure appears to correspond to the divisions between supporters of deeper integration and those more sceptical of overall European integration. Considering the need for unanimity among the member states for the introduction of such a significant change in the institutional structure of the EU, the most likely outcome from an institutionalist perspective would be to retain the status quo and make slow progress through an institutionalisation of informal practice. Nevertheless, the EU has repeatedly introduced organisational changes, despite disagreements. But if incremental additions of tasks to organisations are the main characteristics of the evolution of EPC and CFSP, as the overview of institutional reforms in this chapter suggests, why did a relatively large

40 *The long road to EU diplomatic capacities*

organisational change take place in EU foreign policy and EU external relations on the basis of the Lisbon Treaty?

A central question arising from the historical material is what exactly made this institutional change possible. The apparent change in institutional structure despite a tendency towards stability needs an analysis that can take into account the historical administrative divisions in EU external relations and foreign policy as well as the nature and process of change in general government organisations. It also needs to take into account the fact that the views among member states are in many ways primary, but it is at the same time not sufficient to merely consider inter-state bargaining as decisive. After a treaty revision, there are decisions to be taken at the EU level in terms of secondary legislation and administrative rules. Any decision at this level will receive input from and need an implementation by European institutions, bringing in a supranational element and the views of the European Commission and the European Parliament. This means that the institutional development of EU external action appears to include distinct decision-making phases, at the level of treaty making as well as at the level of EU legislation and administrative acts. These are still distinct from the actual operation of the new organisation when concrete political and policy pressures arise in earnest. An in-depth analysis of the institutional change must also take into account these changing dynamics across different stages of decision-making and administrative operation.

References

Allen, David 1982: Postcriptum. In Allen, David; Rummel, Reinhardt; Wessels, Wolfgang (Eds.), *European Political Cooperation*. Butterworth: London.
Allen, David 1998: Who Speaks for Europe? The search for an effective and coherent external policy. In Peterson, J. and Sjursen, Helene (Eds.), *A Common Foreign Policy for Europe? Competing visions of the CFSP*. Routledge: London.
Allen, David and Smith, Michael 2001: External Policy Developments. *Journal of Common Market Studies* Annual Review, September 2001, vol. 39, pp. 97–114.
Allen, David and Wallace, William 1982: European Political Cooperation: the historical and contemporary background. In Allen, David; Rummel, Reinhardt; Wessels, Wolfgang (Eds.), *European Political Cooperation.* Butterworth: London.
Allen, David; Rummel, Reinhardt; Wessels, Wolfgang 1982: *European Political Cooperation*. Butterworth: London.
Alonso Terme, Rosa Maria 1992: From the Draft Treaty of 1984 to the Intergovernmental Conference of 1991. In Rummel (Ed.), *Toward Political Union. Planning a Common Foreign and Security Policy in the European Community*. Nomos: Baden-Baden.
Bossuat, Gerard and Legendre, Anais 2007: The Commission's Role in External Relations. In Dumoulin, Michel (Ed.), European Commission, *The European Commission, 1958–72. History and Memories.* European Commission: Brussels.
Bruter, Michael 1999: Diplomacy without a state: the external delegations of the European Commission. *Journal of European Public Policy*, vol. 6, no. 2, pp. 183–205.
Burghardt, Guenther 2004: Speech on the occasion of the 50th anniversary of US-EU relations. Available online at: http://useu.usmission.gov/burghardt_050604.html.

The long road to EU diplomatic capacities   41

Christiansen, Thomas and Vanhoonacker, Sophie 2008: At a critical juncture? Change and continuity in the institutional development of the Council secretariat. *West European Politics*, vol. 31, no. 4, pp. 751–770.

da Costa Pereira, Pedro Sanchez 1988: The use of a Secretariat. In Pijpers, Regelsberger and Wessels (Eds.), *European Political Cooperation in the 1980s. A Common Foreign Policy for Western Europe?* Martinus Nijhoff: Dordrecht, pp. 85–103.

Dijkstra, Hylke 2008: The Council Secretariat's Role in the Common Foreign and Security Policy. In *European Foreign Affairs Review*, vol. 13, no. 2, pp. 149–166.

Dijkstra, Hylke 2013: *Policy-making in EU Security and Defense. An Institutional Perspective*. Palgrave: Houndmills, Basingstoke.

Duke, Simon 2011: Under the authority of the High Representative. In *The High Representative for the EU Foreign and Security Policy–Review and Prospects*, pp. 35–64. Nomos: Baden-Baden.

Dumoulin, Michel 2007: From 'overseas countries and territories' to development aid. In Dumoulin (Ed.), *The European Commission 1958–1972*, pp. 377–390. European Commission: Brussels.

Edwards, Geoffrey 2005: The pattern of EU's global activity. In Hill, C. and Smith, M., *International Relations and the European Union*, pp. 39–64, Oxford University Press: Oxford.

Edwards, Geoffrey and Pijpers, Alfred (Eds.) 1997: *The Politics of Treaty Reform. The 1996 Intergovernmental Conference and Beyond*. Pinter: London.

European Institute of Public Administration (EIPA) 1995: Common Foreign and Security Policy and the Positions of Main Actors. Documents from the Colloquium 'The European Union's CFSP: Challenges of the Future.' 19 and 20 October 1995. 1996 IGC: EIPA: Maastricht.

Hocking, Brian 2002: Foreign Ministries in the EU Conclusions. In Hocking and Spence (Eds.), *Foreign Ministries in the European Union. Integrating Diplomats*. Palgrave: Houndmills, Basingstoke.

Juncos, Ana E. and Pomorska, Karolina 2010: Secretariat, Facilitator or Policy Entrepreneur? Role Perceptions of Officials of the Council Secretariat. *European Integration online Papers*, vol. 14, pp. 1–26.

Keukeleire, Stephan and MacNaughtan, Jennifer 2008: *The Foreign Policy of the European Union*. Palgrave: London.

Laffan, Brigid 1997: The IGC and institutional reform of the Union. In Edwards and Pijpers (Eds.), *The Politics of Treaty Reform*. Pinter: London.

Laursen, Finn and Vanhoonacker, Sophie (Eds.) 1992: *The Intergovernmental Conference on Political Union. Institutional Reforms, New Policies and International Identity of the European Community*. Martinus Nijhoff Publishers: Dordrecht.

Laursen, Finn, Vanhoonacker, Sophie, and Wester, Robert 1992: Overview of the Negotiations. In Laursen, F. and Vanhoonacker, S. (Eds.), *The Intergovernmental Conference on Political Union. Institutional Reforms, New Policies and International Identity of the European Community*. Martinus Nijhoff Publishers: Dordrecht.

Lipgens, Walter (Ed.) 1986: 45 Jahre Ringen um die Europaeische Verfassung. Dokumente 1939–1984. *Von den Schriften der Widerstandsbewegung bis zum Vertragsentwurf des Europaeischen Parlaments*. Europa Union Verlag: Bonn.

Nugent, Neil 2001: *The European Commission*. Palgrave: Houndmills, Basingstoke.

Nuttall, Simon 1992: *European Political Cooperation*. Clarendon Press: Oxford.

Nuttall, Simon 2000: *European Foreign Policy*. Oxford University Press: Oxford.

Nuttall, Simon 2006: The Commission and European Political Cooperation. In Spence and Edwards (Eds.) 2006, *The European Commission*. John Harper: London.

42   The long road to EU diplomatic capacities

Riker, William 1998: The Experience of Creating Institutions. The Framing of the United States Constitution. In Knight and Sened (Eds.), *Explaining Social Institutions*. University of Michigan Press, Ann Arbor, MI, pp. 121–144.

Rummel, Reinhardt (Ed.) 1992: *Toward political union: planning a common foreign and security policy in the European Community*. Nomos: Baden-Baden.

Smith, Michael E. 2004: *Europe's Foreign and Security Policy. The Institutionalization of Cooperation*. Cambridge University Press: Cambridge.

Smith, Michael 2006: The Commission and External Relations. In Spence, D. and Edwards, G. (Eds.) 2006, *The European Commission*. John Harper: London.

Spence, David 2006: The Commission and the Common Foreign and Security Policy. In Spence, D. and Edwards, G. (Eds.) 2006, *The European Commission*. John Harper: London.

Vanhoonacker, Sophie, Dijkstra, Hylke, Maurer, Heidi 2011: Understanding the role of bureaucracy in the European security and defence policy: the state of the art. *European Integration online Papers* (EIoP), vol. 14, pp. 1–33.

Wallace, William and Allen, David 1977: Political Cooperation: Procedure as Substitute for Policy. In Wallace (Ed.), *Policy-making in the European Communities*. Wiley: London.

Official documents

EU Treaty

Treaty on the European Union. Consolidated version, Official Journal C 326, pp. 1–390.

European Commission 1996: Rapport sur les Besoins a Plus Long Terme du Service Exterieur de la Commission. [Report on the Longer-Term Requirements of the External Service] SEC(96)554. Brussels.

European Commission 1998: Communication from the Commission on the multiannual plan to allocate External Service resources. SEC(1998)1261final. Brussels.

European Commission 1999: Communication from the Commission: The Development of the External Service. COM(1999)180final. Brussels.

European Commission 2000: Communication from the Commission to the Council and the European Parliament. The External Service. COM(2000)40final. Brussels.

European Commission 2001: Communication from the Commission to the Council and the European Parliament. The Development of the External Service. COM(2001)381final. Brussels.

European Commission 2002a: Memorandum to the Commission on the administrative reform of the Unified External Service. SEC (2002) 745/4. Brussels.

European Commission 2002b: Commission Decision of 17 December 2002 on the administrative reform of the External Service. COM(2002)5370. Brussels.

European Commission 2002c: Communication from the Commission. A Project for the European Union. COM(2002)247final. Brussels, 22.05.2002.

European Commission 2004: Taking Europe to the World. 50 years of the European Commission's External Service. European Commission: Brussels.

European Convention

European Convention 2002: WG VII WD 8: Address of the Secretary-General/High Representative Mr Javier Solana at the meeting of WG VII on 15 October 2002. 15.10.2002.

The long road to EU diplomatic capacities 43

European Council

European Council 2001: Presidency Conclusions. European Council meeting in Laeken 14 and 15 December 2001. Brussels.

European External Action Service

European External Action Service 2017: Annual Activity Report 2016. EEAS: Brussels.

European Parliament

European Parliament 1995a: Annual report on progress in the field of common foreign and security policy. Own Initiative Report INI 1995/2058 (Matutes Report). In Official Journal C 151 of 19.06.1995, p. 0170–0223. Brussels.

European Parliament 1995b: Report on the Functioning of the Treaty on European Union with a View to the 1996 Intergovernmental Conference – Implementation and Development of the Union (Bourlanges and Martin Report). Brussels. A4–0102/95. Brussels. Final text available at http://eur-lex.europa.eu/LexUriServ/LexUriServ.do?uri=CELEX :51995IP0102:EN:HTML.

European Parliament 1997: Intergovernmental Conference Briefing on Common Foreign and Security Policy, No. 5. Retrieved from www.europarl.europa.eu/igc1996/fiches/ fiche5_en.htm (Last accessed 12 March 2014).

European Parliament 2000: Report on a common Community diplomacy. (Galeote I Report) A5–2010/2000.

European Parliament 2001: Report on the Commission Communication on the development of the External Service (Galeote II Report). A5–0199/2001. Brussels.

European Parliament 2009a: Committee on Constitutional Affairs Motion for a European Parliament Resolution on the institutional aspects of setting up the European External Action Service of 20 October 2009.

European Parliament 2009b: Report on the institutional aspects of setting up the European External Action Service. Own Initiative Report (Brok Report) INI 2009/2133. Brussels.

European Parliament 2010: Proposal for the Establishment of the EEAS. Working Document by Elmar Brok (AFET), and Guy Verhofstadt (AFCO), rapporteurs on EEAS. 20.04.2010. Brussels.

Member states reports

Copenhagen Report 1973: Second Report of the Ministers for Foreign Affairs (Copenhagen Report) on 23 July 1973. Bulletin of the European Communities, 1973, no. 9. Available online at: http://aei.pitt.edu/4539/1/epc_copenhagen_report_1973.pdf.

Davignon Report 1970: Report by the Foreign Ministers of the Member States on the Problems of Political Unification on 27 October 1970 (Davignon Report). Bulletin of the European Communities, November 1970, no. 11. Available online at: http://aei.pitt. edu/4543/1/epc_first_report_oct_1970.pdf.

Report of the Ad hoc Committee on Institutional Affair to the European Council 29–30 March 1985 (Dooge Report). European Community: Brussels. Available online at: http://aei.pitt.edu/997/1/Dooge_final_report.pdf.

44 *The long road to EU diplomatic capacities*

London Report 1981: Report on European Political Cooperation issued by the Foreign Ministers of the Ten on 13 October 1981 (London Report). Reproduced in: Press and Information Office of the Federal Republic of Germany (1988), European Political Cooperation. Bonn. Available online at: http://aei.pitt.edu/4546/1/epc_london_1981_report.pdf.

High Level Group 1994: European Security Policy towards 2000: ways and means to establish genuine credibility. Brussels, 19.12.1994.

Reflection Group 1995: Progress Report from the Chairman of the Reflection Group on the 1996 Intergovernmental Conference. Madrid, 01.09.1995.

Working Group 1995: Interim-Report of a Working Group on CFSP and the Future of the European Union. Bertelsmann: Guetersloh.

Other

United States Diplomatic Cable 1973a: No. 07202. Bonn station.

United States Diplomatic Cable 1973b: No. 07203. Bonn station.

United States Diplomatic Cable 1973c: No. 08154. Bonn station.

United States Code 2014: Ex. Ord. No. 11689, Presidential Extension of Diplomatic Privileges and Immunities. Ex. Ord. No. 11689, Dec. 5, 1972, 37 F.R. 25987.

3 Bureaucratic change in EU foreign policy

From classic studies on the Cuban missile crisis and the reforms of the State Department to more modern research into the role of ideas and bureaucratic survival in foreign policy making, the study of US foreign policy has always also had an eye on the bureaucratic structure that makes foreign policy possible. With a weaker and less traditional bureaucratic organisation to support and execute its foreign policy, the bureaucratic development of EU foreign policy and external relations receives less attention. The institutions in this area of EU activity have a long history of slow and incremental changes with steps of ever-increasing administrative structures, as shown in the previous chapter. How this administrative structure has come about is one of the central concerns of institutional analysis of the EU.

This chapter highlights how different approaches deal with the challenges of administrative organisation and reorganisation, on a general level and more specifically in (EU) foreign policy. First, the chapter discusses an institutional approach to bureaucratic change. Second, it outlines the role that other frameworks, specifically the politics of bureaucratic structure approach, bureaucratic politics and bureaucracy theory, play in understanding the creation of new institutions. Third, it suggests a framework that combines these approaches in a sequential manner in order to analyse three distinct phases of evolution for a bureaucratic organisation in EU foreign policy. Fourth, it shows that an application of these phases to the EU political system is possible and can give specific insights for the evolution of the EEAS.

Explaining the design, emergence and behaviour of a new bureaucratic organisation is the focus of a variety of approaches. One of the most pertinent frameworks is the new institutionalism, which is commonly divided into several sub-strands. It originally focused on institutional stability over time, and thus has been criticised for its lack of explanations for change. This later led its proponents to confront change within its theoretical framework in ever more detail. Its strength, however, compared to more pure rationalist approaches such as the rational design of institutions debate (Koremenos *et al.* 2001a, 2001b, 2004), has been its ability to discern political conflict, power, and the role these forces play in relation to institutional change. The new institutionalism is an adaptable framework that allows for some flexibility in the

46 *Bureaucratic change in EU foreign policy*

definition of institution ranging from party systems to individual administrative agencies. Historical institutionalism can thus provide an important temporal perspective on the evolution of an organisation, but at the same time may say less about the specifics of a government agency's behaviour. The bureaucratic politics paradigm developed in the 1970s has used the insights of the analysis of bureaucracies to explain their impact on foreign policy (Allison 1971; Allison and Halperin 1972, and later Allison and Zelikow 1999; Drezner 2000; Warwick 1975). This perspective allows for an acute observation of inter-organisational relations and conflict and thus presents an intermediary perspective between the high level institutional change of a political system and the functioning of a specific organisation.

Work on this narrower institutional focus, looking specifically at the emergence and operation of government administrations, has an even longer tradition. These bureaucracy theories deal mainly with the operation of new administrative organisations, or, in the terminology used in most of the studies, 'bureaucracies'. One of the central advances in studying bureaucracy was Anthony Downs' *Inside Bureaucracy* (1967), still a point of reference for the workings of these organisations some five decades later on. It is of limited concern to the study of inception and establishment of a new bureaucracy, but more relevant when it comes to its functioning and evolving relations with its environment.

In European Union Studies, institutional emergence is more commonly dealt with either at the grand level of the causes of European integration or at the level of major changes at the treaty level of the EU, such as changes in powers of the European Commission and European Parliament. Within the EU's institutional structure, the administrative literature focuses largely on the creation of more or less independent agencies at the EU level with some notable exceptions concerning work on the Council Secretariat and its civil servants, the emerging bureaucratic landscape in security and defence policy and an overall evolution of an EU executive. This eclectic analytical standpoint is expected to provide nuances on the different stages of evolution of an administrative organisation as different phases are interrogated with specific questions and the conceptual tools to provide specific answers. If the lessons of the historical evolution developed in Chapter 2 are any guide, the differences in these phases will not be captured by a single grand theory of institutional behaviour. This should hold true particularly where it concerns different actors taking decisions under varying institutional rules, and where these shifting conditions can be expected to result in different outcomes. With this approach, the book utilises an eclectic view of bureaucratic change in order to capture specific insights into processes of bureaucratic change.

The emergence and change of bureaucratic institutions

Before looking at the specificities of institutional and bureaucratic change in EU foreign policy and external action, the following section will set out general approaches to the emergence and change of institutions in political science and

Bureaucratic change in EU foreign policy 47

how these insights shape what we can learn about institutions in foreign policy. The 'new institutionalism' combines within it a variety of approaches to explaining politics by focusing on institutional arrangements, their emergence and evolution as well as their impact on actors and political outcomes. March and Olsen (1989) called for a new analytic approach to political science, which moved the focus from individuals and large social aggregates to the collective organisations that shape political life (March and Olsen 1989: pp. 4–6; Peters 2005: 18). Institutions, according to the 'new institutionalism', are a form of collective organisation created in order to achieve varying levels of predictable behaviour (March and Olsen 1989: pp. 4–6). And while the three main sub-branches of the new institutionalism: rational choice, sociological institutionalism and historical institutionalism, are distinct, they share a common focus and theoretical concepts (Immergut 1998: p. 5). All three branches depart from the notion that individual behaviour alone accounts for political outcomes (Immergut 1998: p. 6). They see institutions as an intermediary between behaviour and political outcomes, restricting and shaping the behaviour of people interacting with the institution. Their differences can be observed in the details of this conjecture. Rational choice institutionalism sees actors interacting with an institution and its rules strategically in order to satisfy particular interests. Sociological institutionalism models actors as boundedly rational and posits that their interests are structured by the institutions they interact with. Historical institutionalism puts the focus on the historical element of the structuring effect of institutions on actors' behaviour.

March and Olsen describe explicitly the duality of political institutions:

> Bureaucratic agencies, legislative committees, and appellate courts are arenas for contending social forces, but they are also collections of standard operating procedures and structures that define and defend values, norms, interests, identities, and beliefs.
>
> (March and Olsen 1989: p. 17)

While they do not give an exact definition of their understanding of what institutions are, they are rather clearer on the type of institution their focus rests on: '[we] wish to explore some ways in which the institutions of politics, particularly administrative institutions, provide order and influence change in politics' (March and Olsen 1989: p. 16). Their seminal contribution *Rediscovering institutions: the organizational basis of politics* (March and Olsen 1989) is often referred to as ushering in the 'new institutionalism', but its role as a study in administrative or bureaucratic change has been neglected:

> Administrative reorganizations are interesting in their own right. The effectiveness of political systems depends to a substantial extent on the effectiveness of administrative institutions, and the design and control of bureaucratic structures is a central concern of any polity.
>
> (March and Olsen 1989: p. 69)

48 Bureaucratic change in EU foreign policy

March and Olsen focus on change caused by institutions, but also present theoretical aspects of how institutions themselves change; 'an institutional perspective on institutional change' (March and Olsen 1989: p. 53). They argue that 'efforts to reform political institutions are often unsuccessful in accomplishing precisely what was intended' and stress the difficulty of 'intentionally transforming' state institutions (March and Olsen 1989: pp. 65–66). These observations are based on premises that differ from the other institutional approaches, such as assuming limited rationality of actors and a temporal and accidental approach to problem solving (March and Olsen 1989: pp. 11, 28–29). Tracing the attempts at the reorganisation of the US federal government in the 20th century, March and Olsen conclude that individual steps of reorganisation failed, while the collection of attempts actually led to fundamental changes in the bureaucratic landscape of the US political system (March and Olsen 1989: pp. 84–86). They find that 'the long run development of political institutions is less a product of intentions, plans and consistent decisions than incremental adaptation to changing problems with available solutions within gradually evolving structures of meaning' (March and Olsen 1989: p. 94). While this appears largely to contradict rational theories of institutions, it is not contradictory in all aspects. The normative institutionalism of March and Olsen does acknowledge the importance of resources and power in shaping outcomes (March and Olsen 1989: pp. 152, 163). Change in the bureaucratic landscape has not only been at the centre of the beginning of the new institutionalist research agenda, but is also a recurring debate within and between the sub-strands of the new institutionalism. This change does not take place in a vacuum: 'no institution is created de novo' or in some kind of 'institutional void' (Riker 1998: p. 123). Thus, change over time needs to take into account the historical legacies of institutions.

Institutional change and its insights for analysing bureaucracy in foreign policy

In order to highlight institutional change in foreign policy, it is necessary first to take a brief look at the institutions that exist in this particular area, and how their development can be considered in relation to the general study of institutional change. There is no unified approach to either of these issues in academic disciplines, and Historical institutionalism is not a unitary approach to the study of institutions. It has developed out of the analysis of large-scale structural transformations in societies and states, but now equally encompasses studies of political structures, and even individual institutions (Thelen and Steinmo 1992: p. 2). Ikenberry, in a study of American Foreign Economic Policy, identifies these three levels as 'institutional structures' encompassing a procedural level, a structural level within the state and a level of the 'normative order between state and society' (Ikenberry 1988: p. 227). The organisational level of the state, individual government departments or the 'centralization and coherence of bureaucracy' (Ikenberry 1988: p. 227) is thus largely confined to the mid-range of this scale. On all three levels, the focus of the analysis in historical institutionalism is on the constraints of past institutional arrangements on today's actors, or 'that policy choices made when an institution is being formed [...] will have a continuing and largely determinate influence [...] far into the future' (Peters 2005: p. 71). Warwick's influential study on the organisational changes in the State Department is another detailed US case for this type of study, highlighting many unintended consequences of reform (Warwick 1975).

The fact that choices at the beginning of an institution or policy have a major impact in the long run of the institution's life cycle is usually referred to as 'path dependence' or 'path dependent' processes (David 1985: p. 332; Hall and Taylor 1996: p. 941; Immergut and Anderson 2008: pp. 354f.; North 1990: p. 115; Pierson 2000a: pp. 251ff.). These arguments are aimed at backing particular assertions about political reality over time:

> Specific patterns of timing and sequence matter; starting from similar conditions, a wide range of social outcomes may be possible; large consequences may result from relatively 'small' or contingent events; particular courses of action, once introduced, can be virtually impossible to reverse; and consequently, political development is often punctuated by critical moments or junctures that shape the basic contours of social life.
>
> (Pierson 2000a: p. 251)

As these arguments are largely derived from economics and economic history (Pierson 2000a: pp. 253–256; North 1990), their underlying mechanisms are economic in nature. Pierson sees the main argument for path-dependent processes in 'increasing returns' (Pierson 2000a: p. 253). The abstract process is based on random and unpredictable individual events, combined with a decision rule, which leads to increased inflexibility as time passes (Pierson 2000a: p. 253). Events early in the process have a larger impact than similar events later on and may in the end lead to a less efficient outcome than other alternatives (Pierson 2000a). Douglas North (1990) first applied these concepts to the study of institutions from an economic perspective. Of course, 'politics differ from economics in many ways' (Pierson 2000a: p. 257), but once economic arguments are adapted to the realm of politics, they can and have been used as a productive source of theory in political science as well (Moe 1984: pp. 739, 758–762).

In the case of increasing returns, it is argued that the cost of creating an institution is high and that its benefits derive largely from repeated use and learning (Pierson 2000a: p. 254). Pierson also argues that it is precisely those aspects that make institutions useful in a political system, by overcoming collective action dilemmas that make them hard to change (Pierson 2000a: p. 259). Outside the realm of political science, David has pioneered this concept of path dependency to explain the success of the QWERTY keyboard over more efficient rival arrangements (David 1985). David's work also illustrates that path-dependent processes do not favour useful or ideal outcomes, but rather explain why established decisions stick irrespective of their subsequent evaluation (David 1985). Political institutions, and in particular government bureaucracies, are oriented

50 Bureaucratic change in EU foreign policy

towards the status quo (Pierson 2000a: p. 262; March and Olsen pp. 34–35), in turn increasing the static logic of the approach. When applying the increasing returns logic of economics to political science, the outcome is a theoretical approach focused firmly on stability and rigidity of institutional structures rather than dynamic changing ones. This 'overly static view' (Pierson 2000a: p. 265) has been debated within the historical institutionalist research agenda as a major difficulty for the approach (Hall and Taylor 1996: p. 942; Pierson 2000a: p. 265; Thelen and Steinmo 1992: pp. 13–14). In order to explain change, something must interrupt the 'increasing returns' (Pierson 2000a), 'mechanisms of reproduction' (Collier and Collier 1991: p. 30) or 'positive feedback loop' (Pierson 2000a: p. 265) observed in historical analyses of political institutions. This particular moment of change and the political processes within it are at the core of this analysis.

Starting the analysis with the moment of inception of a new administrative body, in this case the European External Action Service, should allow us to understand first how far institutionalist explanations hold and second how politics and political and bureaucratic conflict impact on any new organisation. However, because institutional stability and institutional change sit uneasily as concepts, it becomes essential to take a close look at what mechanisms connect them from an institutionalist perspective. After an analysis of why change is a difficult concept to capture for traditional historical institutionalism, the main arguments that had been levied against historic institutionalism's explanations of change will be discussed.

Critical junctures of bureaucratic change

The prevalent model of dealing with change in historical institutionalism, 'punctuated equilibrium', has been borrowed from evolutionary biology (Eldridge and Gould 1972). A 'punctuated equilibrium' in biology describes the assumption that evolution is generally in equilibrium but turns critical at certain moments in time when rapid change happens (Eldridge and Gould 1972). Krasner uses this concept as an analogy to illustrate the logic of institutional change (Krasner 1988: pp. 77–79). While he expresses caution about confounding institutional change too much with the biological concept (Krasner 1988: p. 79), he remains adamant that environmental factors as well as characteristics of the actor need to be considered in an explanation of change (Krasner 1988: p. 79). The concept and term of 'punctuated equilibrium' became the most accepted model of change in historical institutionalist research (Thelen and Steinmo 1992: p. 15) and has continued to be refined. As seen below in the conception of these critical moments, or junctures, the notion of external shocks or environmental factors in particular has been at the heart of the debate (Peters 2005: p. 77). A distinct line of thought, mainly outlined by Streeck and Thelen (2005) argued that a crisis is not necessary for 'transformative change', but that endogenous factors and gradual adaptations can have a similar effect (Mahoney and Thelen 2010). Mahoney and Thelen focus their analysis on combining

Bureaucratic change in EU foreign policy   51

factors of different groups of actors with an environmental context (Mahoney and Thelen 2010: pp. 15–32). While presenting an intriguing argument about how both structural and actor-centred factors of endogenous change combine towards a particular type of institutional change, their approach is more easily applicable in situations of domestic political systems. Adapting it to the variance in actors between different fora at the EU level, from convention to intergovernmental conference to inter-institutional decision-making would result in an overly complex model. At the same time, several of the insights of Mahoney and Thelen's work are relevant for this study, e.g. the notion that institutional rules within which decisions are taken are fundamentally ambiguous and the object of political contestation (Sheingate 2010: pp. 183–184). The particular environment of (re-)negotiation of existing rules at the EU level, or treaty reform, appears to be more fittingly captured by the concept of 'critical junctures' (Collier and Collier 1991) and the implied flexibility of institutional rules, in which decisions are taken. As this concept has been used very broadly, this study follows a more circumscribed version of it, outlined below.

When faced with change rather than stability, historical institutionalist scholars have resorted to introducing external factors into their equation for an explanation. These factors appear similar to what economists have called external shocks, i.e. forces with major impact on a given model but not conceptualised within it. These shocks provided an explanation of the impetus for change in many historical institutionalist studies. However, while external shocks are usually a single factor, in historical institutionalism a broader concept has come to the fore. Usually, these exogenous forces have been construed around a certain number of events, or at least periods of time considerably shorter than the observed time period of the study (Capoccia and Kelemen 2007). The term for these time periods is 'critical junctures', a concept elaborated by Collier and Collier (1991: pp. 27–39) in their large-scale study of Latin American states and their relation to the labour movements. Collier and Collier use the expression on the basis of work done by Lipset and Rokkan on 'crucial junctures' for the development of voting behaviour (Lipset and Rokkan 1967: p. 37) and see them as a 'period of significant change, which typically occurs in distinct ways in different countries (or in other units of analysis) and which is hypothesized to produce distinct legacies' (Collier and Collier 1991: p. 29). Because the use of the concept is tied largely to 'macrohistorical' analyses, the focus has often been on the period after the establishment of a new institution or policy rather than on the critical juncture itself (Capoccia and Kelemen 2007: p. 342). Often, these studies have explained the critical juncture itself by external factors, or 'antecedent conditions rather than from actions and decisions that occur during the critical juncture itself' (Capoccia and Kelemen 2007: p. 342; Hall and Taylor 1996: p. 942). Capoccia and Kelemen advance a new definition of critical junctures, which is considerably more focused towards institutional analysis:

In institutional analysis critical junctures are characterized by a situation in which the structural (that is, economic, cultural, ideological, organizational)

52 *Bureaucratic change in EU foreign policy*

influences on political action are significantly relaxed for a relatively short period, with two main consequences: the range of plausible choices open to powerful political actors expands substantially and the consequences for the outcome of interest are potentially much more momentous.

(Capoccia and Kelemen 2007: p. 343)

Capoccia and Kelemen also determine clear conditions for what characterises a critical juncture. The time period of the juncture must be short in relation to the period of observation and the options available to actors within the juncture must be larger, and the impact of choices stronger, during than before and after the classified time period (Capoccia and Kelemen 2007: p. 348).

Instead of focusing on the 'positive feedback loop' (Pierson 2000a: p. 265), or the 'mechanism of reproduction' (Collier and Collier 1991: p. 30), i.e. the mechanisms that lead to a path-dependent process (Pierson 2000a: p. 265), Capoccia and Kelemen shift the focus to tracing the process during the critical juncture (Capoccia and Kelemen 2007: p. 343). In particular, they stress the need to 'reconstruct, in a systematic and rigorous fashion, each step of the decision-making process, identify which decisions were most influential and what options were available and viable to the actors' (Capoccia and Kelemen 2007: pp. 354–355). These methodological concerns echo the importance of sequence and context, which had been voiced in earlier historical institutionalist research (Collier and Collier 1991; Pierson 2000a, 2004). This necessary attention to sequence and context is reflected in the methodological choices for this research as set out in Chapter 1. If both sequence and context are central to the argument of institutional evolution, process tracing becomes the observation method of choice (George and Bennett 2005; Hall 2012; Kittel and Kuehn 2012). Process tracing will allow the identification of influential actors, diverging opinions, and the role of the institutional environment in determining specific outcomes in the empirical part of this book.

Other modes of change

Despite the debates presented above, the question whether historical institutionalism can by itself account for change in an institutional setting, has been contested. Hall and Taylor argue that for historical institutionalist research existing institutions 'give some actors more power than others over the creation of new institutions' (Hall and Taylor 1996: p. 21). The approach does not, however, describe mechanisms to explain the relaxation of the existing power relations, nor does it determine in which direction change will move. Hall and Taylor also argue in their later work that historical institutionalist research has devoted too little effort to 'developing the micro-logic that links institutional structures to action' (Hall and Taylor 1998: p. 958; see also Immergut and Anderson 2008: p. 361). Historical institutionalism remains the approach most attuned to find effects of preceding institutional arrangements on current structures and thus provide the best starting point for an explanation

Bureaucratic change in EU foreign policy 53

of creating a new organisation out of a mixed institutional heritage. Peters has argued that despite not being explicit on the question about how institutions are designed, it is an essential element of historical institutionalism as so much focus is put on the effects of early decisions in an institution's life cycle (Peters 2012: pp. 84–85).

It is precisely in response to this difficulty of conceptualising change that the approach has generated a wealth of research on 'institutional genesis and change' (Immergut and Anderson 2008: pp. 354, 355f.). Streeck and Thelen (2005) have for example argued for a more sophisticated and gradual model of institutional change. While their discussion of change develops interesting conceptual categories, it follows a complex logic of actors and categories that appears difficult to transpose to the policy area and institutional structure under investigation. Closely related to this debate is the argument about the nature of change. Is change gradual and incremental, or is it large-scale and watershed-like? Both concepts have followers in the historical institutionalist camp. Mahoney and Thelen present a theory of 'gradual institutional change' (2010), which echoes the incremental adaptation already argued by North (1990: p. 83, pp. 86–87) to be the norm of institutional change. North, however, also analysed the potential for revolutionary, or discontinuous, change (North 1990: pp. 89–90), in a way similar to the concept of 'critical junctures' (see above). While empirical evidence can be found for both, the main difficulty is to determine the scope of both gradual and discontinuous change. In particular in the analysis of the development of the EU, discontinuous change is hard to find in its pure form, while gradual change might seem to preclude certain leaps of institutional development that have been identified in Chapter 2. At the same time, Chapter 2 also gives some indication that the creation of the EEAS appears to be a break from established institutional pathways. This would create additional difficulties for a gradual approach to change.

Recurring criticisms of historical institutionalism have been its use of an inductive logic (Aspinwall and Schneider 2000: p. 24; Thelen and Steinmo 1992: p. 12) as well as the fact that it is a theoretically eclectic approach, appearing at times to be either sociological or rational choice (Hall and Taylor 1996: p. 940; Peters 2005: p. 85). At the same time, it is this eclecticism that has allowed for adapting historical institutionalism to a variety of situations. The importance for a micro-logic and detailed narrative has more recently dominated the theoretical discourse about historical political research and its methods (Buethe 2002: pp. 482, 487f.; Capoccia and Kelemen 2007: p. 357). The strength of such an approach, methodologically tied closely to process tracing, has been settled as being able to identify 'causal mechanisms and proximate causal relationships and thus not falling prey to the correlation-causation fallacy' (Kittel and Kuehn 2012: p. 2). Since that is the central objective of the research question on the causes and mechanisms behind the creation of the EEAS, process tracing is the method used to varying degrees in all empirical chapters of this book (see Chapters 4 through 7).

54 *Bureaucratic change in EU foreign policy*

Rational choice and change

The lack of mechanisms available to historical institutionalist arguments about critical junctures, i.e. the processes during a critical juncture, has been approached in one line of research by inserting elements from rational choice institutionalism (e.g. Katznelson and Weingast 2005). In this line of argument, rational choice perspectives on decision-making, including the importance of decision-making rules on the outcome, the preferences of actors, as well as the role of veto-players in shaping outcomes, are central to overcoming historical institutionalism's lack of expected processes in a critical juncture. These elements are relevant for this analysis because of the attention paid to diverging preferences of actors and the processes by which these differences are overcome. Because historical institutionalism does not prescribe a particular logic to actors, it is open to be used with competing sets of logics. The focus of this debate has been between a logic of rational calculation of interests based on the actors' preferences and a cultural, or appropriateness logic. The latter focuses more strongly on concepts closer to those of sociological institutionalism, such as the influence on and shaping of preferences by institutions, and ideas as drivers for change. With regard to rational choice institutionalism, Thelen and Steinmo insisted still in 1992 that the fact that historical institutionalism includes the preferences of actors in the model remains a fundamental difference (p. 9). But later research has also addressed this distinction and shown the usefulness of a merged understanding of these two approaches (Aspinwall and Schneider 2000; Katznelson and Weingast 2005; Mahoney 2005; Peters 2005; Mahoney and Thelen 2010).

Historical institutionalism has a good conception of the constraints of actors at a given decision-making moment, based on the distribution of power among actors and institutions derived from past situations (Thelen and Steinmo 1992: p. 14). Rational Choice Institutionalism has a clearer conception of the interaction of actors with given preferences within those constraints (Aspinwall and Schneider 2000). Miller has shown that a rational choice view of institutions does not preclude institutional 'dysfunction, nor "unintended consequences" ' (Miller 2000). This is a relevant analytical feature when studying the decision-making processes of EU institutions. Adapted versions of rational choice like the 'rational design of international institutions' approach argue that negotiators can bargain for the type of features they desire in an international institution (Koremenos *et al.* 2001a, b). In this conception, there is less room for historical legacies shaping institutional outcomes as pointed out by Duffield (2003: p. 418), or indeed political compromises with outcomes only very partially desired by negotiators (Pierson 2000a: p. 477). But historical legacies weigh heavily in a treaty- and rule-based system such as the EU and it is thus necessary to include them in the analysis.

While historical institutionalism focuses the attention of institutional analysis on effects over time, rational choice institutionalism on the other hand focuses on the mechanisms or institutional rules for resolving political disagreement. In combination, they should be bringing together the evolution of political positions and the institutional rules leading to a particular institutional settlement. But because the nature of institutional decision-making rules differs so widely between treaty making on the one hand and inter-institutional decision-making on the other, a further specification is necessary. Also, approaches to the creation of a new institution have rarely taken into account the second-level establishment of detailed institutional rules. This is less a phase of critical juncture and more regular politics setting ground rules for the establishment of a new organisation. In order to answer that question of institutional design and the organisational characteristics more precisely a related institutional approach, the politics of bureaucratic structure, offers potential avenues.

The politics of structural choice

A wave of academic interest in public organisations and their role in the political process gave rise to an interdisciplinary approach to understand these organisations' creation and behaviour in the US political system. This analysis of the creation of new administrative organisations offers potentially relevant insights into the second phase of institutional creation when political actors interact in a given decision-making system to set up a new administration. Under the catchphrase of the 'new economics of organization' (Moe 1984), a group of scholars in the US went about analysing bureaucracies according to a (thoroughly adapted) economic understanding of organisations. Their main objective was to explain the existence of bureaucracies, how superiors in a bureaucracy control their inferiors but also how politicians could control bureaucracies (Moe 1984: p. 758). In their explanation, they turned a logic derived entirely from economics into politics. Bureaucracies, the proponents of this approach argued, are created not because they produce a public good or service, even though they may do that as well, but because they have a positive effect for those politicians that create it (Moe 1984: 761). They are expressions of 'special interest more than of general welfare' (Moe 1984: p. 762). Their efficiency was consequently based on political considerations, not the efficiency of the market (Moe 1984: p. 762): 'Structural choices have important consequences for the content and direction of policy, and political actors know it' (Moe 1989: p. 268). Within the debate, researchers have disagreed about who or what is the essential driving force of creation and control of an agency and have come to differing perspectives. Some have argued for the role of interest groups (Moe 1989), for the President's role (Bendor and Hammond 1992; Krasner 1972), and for Congressional control (Weingast and Moran 1983; Weingast 1984). Later research has focused on the dynamic interactions between different institutions in attempts to control bureaucratic agencies (Whitford 2005: p. 44).

What brings the research agenda together is the focus on the 'politics of structural choice' (Moe 1989), i.e. the awareness that decisions on administrative or bureaucratic arrangements are fundamentally political decisions. They represent

56 Bureaucratic change in EU foreign policy

a coalition of interests that win out over others, not all members of the coalition necessarily even sharing the intent to create the same thing (Moe 1984: pp. 328–329). William Riker in a study of the creation of US system of government also reminds us that 'there is no reason to expect internal consistency from a reform carried out by a group' (Riker 1998: p. 121). Similarly, Shepsle argued that it was necessary to dissect the notion of a unitary intent of Congress in laying down legislation (Shepsle 1992: pp. 241–242). Decisions to create a new body in the political system do not have a singular intent behind them, irrespective of what is claimed by politicians. As shown above, in observing these political processes of creating a new organisation, process tracing takes account of the plurality of preferences of the involved actors and a varying institutional framework.

It is the serious application of Kenneth Arrow's insights on the cycling of collective decisions outcomes (Arrow 1963) that makes the politics of bureaucracy literature a relevant part of the debate about institutional emergence and change over time. It highlights three particular issues of relevance for studying the emergence of bureaucratic structures. First, there is a need to distinguish different sets of interests in a decision to create a new administrative organisation, the distribution of power at the time, and the decision-making rules. Second, the contest over the agency's shape and function continues in different stages and with different actors:

> The game of structural politics never ends. An agency is created and given a mandate, but in principle at least, all of the choices that have been made in the formative round of decision-making can be reversed and modified later.
>
> (Moe 1989: pp. 284–285)

Third, a new bureaucratic body that is created in a political system acts as a new force in that system with particular interests. This approach distinguishes the individual political factors driving institutional design and is central to analysing the emergence and shape of a new body at the EU level.

At the same time, the literature on the politics of bureaucratic structure gives little indication of direction of these dynamics barring the knowledge of the interests of the actors involved. Beyond the fundamental rational choice assumption of self-interest applied to individual institutional settings, it is left to the individual case study to determine the opposing forces of political conflict (e.g. Moe 1984: pp. 300f.). Despite its focus on the political aspects of the creation of an administration, it is the historical institutionalist research that appears more sensitised to the distribution of power across actors in the existing system. In some ways, the politics of bureaucratic structure offer the mechanisms of interaction and lines of conflict without the preferences and structural limitations of the moment of bureaucratic creation. It also does not need the specific requirements of a critical juncture as environment, but rather operates on the assumption of regular political processes resulting in an organisation that is also a political outcome. Research into the establishment of EU bureaucratic actors has been informed by these insights (e.g. Kelemen 2002, 2011), but has needed considerable adaptation from the US model with its particular political set-up, as explained in more detail below.

The politics of bureaucratic structure offers insights into the creation of new organisations in a political process, but is less concerned with the analysis of the new organisation itself. While the politics of bureaucratic structure can be expected to inform the setting up of the administrative organisation, or the establishment, once the new administrative actor is created, the organisation will operate on different principles. In order to understand this functioning of a new organisation and its developing self-interest in a system replete with other actors, a third set of theoretical approaches offers deeper insights. Bureaucracy theories and bureaucratic politics are two approaches that focus on the inside of public organisations and on the relationships between different organisations of the state. They can be expected to provide insights into the third phase of institutional evolution, the consolidation of the new administration. Where the politics of structural choice are about decisions concerning institutions, bureaucracy theories are about the driving forces within these administrative organisations.

Bureaucracy and bureaucratic politics

The study of a particular type of institution, in this case public administration or bureaucracies, has its foundation in economic approaches to political science that took hold from the 1960s onwards. As a basic tool for analysing governmental organisations, however, bureaucracy theories can still deliver comparative tools to further our understanding of public bureaucracy across regional and national political peculiarities. The study of bureaucracy is considerably older than this wave of political economy studies; the origins of modern studies of bureaucracy go back as far as Max Weber's *Wirtschaft und Gesellschaft* (1922: pp. 650f.) and Woodrow Wilson's treatise on what he called the 'most obvious part of government' (1887, reprinted in 1997: pp. 197–222). But it was the first group of political economists like Anthony Downs (1967) and Gordon Tullock (1965) that asserted that bureaucracies are a specific type of institution governed by rules that differ fundamentally from a prototypical 'firm' of neoclassical economics. They also theoretically distinguished the bureaucracy from political bodies such as a parliamentary committee or the government. Despite being based on economic reasoning, this led to particular conclusions about the political role of bureaucracies and their behaviour in the political arena. The overall research agenda has been referred to as a 'public choice' approach to bureaucracy (Wade 1979: p. 344). Downs' seminal work on bureaucracies, *Inside Bureaucracy*, is often quoted and presented as simple rational choice analysis of the preferences, incentives and structures of bureaucracies in the US context (Downs 1967). On closer inspection, Downs develops much more than a basic model of bureaucrats and bureaucracies.

58   *Bureaucratic change in EU foreign policy*

Budget maximisation and bureau shaping

What is a bureaucracy according to this public choice approach? Anthony Downs (1967) reasoned that a bureaucracy is defined by the following characteristics: it is necessarily an (a) large, (b) professional and merit-based organisation whose 'output is not directly or indirectly evaluated in any market external to the organization' (Downs 1967: pp. 24–25). Downs was adamant that his usage of the word bureaucracy and his general conjectures about it were analytical and carried no pejorative or political implications with them (Downs 1967: p. 1). By contrast, Tullock's analysis in *Politics of Bureaucracy* (1965) was not only rhetorically harsher, but ended with a call for reform of the 'inefficient' bureaucracy in the US (Tullock 1965: p. 221). Both types of studies tell us little about the emergence of a bureaucracy as they fundamentally adopted a functionalist model (Downs 1967: p. 5) or were silent about the emergence of the organisation as such (Tullock 1965). Both took the bureaucracy as an established fact and were considerably more concerned with the mechanisms inside the organisation. Tullock focused on the hierarchical relationships between individuals in a bureaucracy (Tullock 1965: p. 11) and the relationship with politicians (Tullock 1965: pp. 51ff.). Nevertheless, they did establish assumptions for early behaviour of bureaucratic actors. Downs explained that upon establishment a bureau, i.e. an administrative organisation, was expected to 'go through an early phase of rapid growth' and 'immediately begin seeking sources of external support' (Downs 1967: pp. 5, 7). It would at the same time seek to develop a range for autonomous action (Downs 1967: p. 6). This high-wire act between autonomy and support would be an essential element of a new organisation's life, according to Downs. From the perspective of the political administrative system, these are questions of control. While the new organisation tries to establish itself, other organisations and political bodies will attempt to control its behaviour.

The fundamental assumption shared by other researchers of the rational choice tradition was that bureaucracy as an organisation and bureaucrats as individuals would be fundamentally self-interested and would maximise utility in given choices. What that utility would look like was not uniformly agreed among rational choice bureaucracy scholars. Tullock asserted the simplest career-centred assumption of self-interest (Tulloch 1965: p. 29), while Downs developed the image of groups of ideal type bureaucrats whose motivations differed greatly (Downs 1967: pp. 88ff.). Individuals in these groups 'maximize utility' (Downs 1967: pp. 81ff.) on the basis of different motivational characteristics. On this fundamental basis of self-interest, Downs developed several sets of hypotheses about bureaucracies' internal functioning (Downs 1967: pp. 49ff.) and their relations to other actors (Downs 1967: pp. 212ff). The sheer scale of the study and the number of issues addressed in the book and expressed in the form of hypotheses led to an immediate criticism: it was nearly impossible to observe and measure for any one case the immense amount of data necessary to test the hypotheses (Crecine 1968). While this holds true for the study in its entirety, the approach can be used to define expectations of bureaucratic

Behaviour, e.g. the drive to expand the size of the organisation, and to shape its structure, as well as the relationships with other actors in its policy area. Bureaucracy theories focus the analysis on the driving forces of the organisation proper and on the countervailing pressures from competing actors. It is these factors in particular which raise questions about how the organisation operates and attempts to develop autonomy. Bureaucracy theory also raises inter-linked issues about the possibility of control and how outside pressures affect the newly built organisation.

The search for the internal drivers of bureaucratic behaviour has led to competing visions. Some proponents of a public choice approach to public bureaucracies have operationalised the notions of organisational self-interest as meaning simply the maximisation of an organisation's budget, also called the 'budget maximization' thesis (Niskanen 1971: pp. 36–42). In many ways, this is similar to Downs' concept of the organisation's search to 'expand' (Downs 1967: p. 16). Because a new organisation needs support as much as it needs to expand, the basic expectation is that it will attempt to increase its budget as well as devote resources to the service of the budgetary authority. This also illustrates how external actors, i.e. those organisations that support or control the organisation, have an indirect impact on the internal structure of the new organisation. At the same time, the budget alone is a crude measure. It is also shaped by other drivers such as the type of task an organisation is involved in. Developing on this line of thought, Dunleavy later argued that budget maximisation does not include a realistic assumption of bureaucrats' motivation (Dunleavy 1991: pp. 200–208). Rather, bureaucrats in high echelons of the hierarchy are interested in shaping the set-up and tasks of their organisation to their liking; they engage in 'bureau-shaping' (Dunleavy 1991: p. 208). If bureau shaping is a process that determines the early life of bureaucratic organisations, it can be expected that the organisation's leaders attempt to change the organisation's structure in line with their preferences (Dunleavy 1991). Since it is not possible in an individual case to predict the preferences, they need to be deduced from the evidence gathered. This then needs to be checked against both successful and unsuccessful change processes within the organisation.

Competition and control: inter-organisational relationships

An additional external factor that adds to Downs' relevance for studying bureaucracy at the EU level is that he is also fundamentally concerned with the inter-relations that exist between different types of bureaus (Downs 1967: p. 212; see also Dunleavy 1991: p. 171). While this specific focus derives from the pluralist American political tradition and appears inherent in the US system, it is of equal relevance in an institutional environment replete with bureaucratic actors such as the European Union. These inter-relations between 'bureaus' are at the core of the study of bureaucratic politics. The debate about bureaucratic politics is also a central area where the study of bureaucracy and the study of foreign policy interact systematically for the first time.

60 *Bureaucratic change in EU foreign policy*

In addition to the internal functioning, 'a great deal of dynamic activity of nearly every bureau involves its relations with other bureaus' (Downs 1967: p. 211). These inter-relations between administrative organisations, or in the language of Downs, bureaus, are not seen as smooth and cooperative. It is rather a mix of cooperation and competition that characterises them. Bureaucratic politics refers to the central conflict as 'turf wars' (Allison and Zelikow 1999). Downs had already presented this spatial view of an organisation's autonomous remit, at the borders of which conflicts with other bureaus occur. He calls this view of the policy space and the actions of the bureaus within it 'bureau territoriality' (Downs 1967: p. 211). Because the need to occupy a specific policy space is ingrained in an organisation, if another actor becomes active in the same space, the outcome is conflict. Naturally, if relations with other bureaus are one aspect of the environment relevant to a new organisation, relations with political bodies and clients form another element of this environment. Bureaucratic politics uses these basic insights to connect the internal functioning of an organisation with its wider environment and relations with other 'bureaus'. Because a bureaucratic organisation is created to serve political bodies, it is likely that this conflict will focus on the ability to control the organisation.

Bureaucratic politics

At the heart of the bureaucratic politics approach lies an understanding that bureaucratic organisations act not as mere technocratic sources of advice. Rather, bureaucracies have their own organisational interests. This is at the same time one of the core insights of the rational choice strand of the new institutionalism. In its most famous incarnation, the three models of governmental decision-making by Allison and Zelikow (1999), several relevant insights for the EU decision-making system can be found. The recognition that administrations are by themselves actors in the decision-making process and its application to foreign policy led to a resurgence in bureaucracy studies in the US debate. The objective of these scholars was to break open the assumption that foreign policy outputs are the result of the actions of a unitary actor, i.e. the state. Rather, they saw the output of the decision-making process as largely determined by behaviour of organisations inside the state and driven by interests of different factions within these organisations (e.g. Allison 1971; Allison and Halperin 1972; Allison and Zelikow 1999; Destler 1972; Halperin 1974; Hilsman 1987).

Allison and Zelikow discuss three models in their book *Essence of decision* (1999). First, they discuss a rational actor model, which is a stylised version of typical scholarship in traditional international relations research. It treats the state as a unitary actor, or 'black box' whose decisions are often implicitly or explicitly equated with national interest (Allison and Zelikow 1999: pp. 5, 24–25). Their second model, the 'organizational behaviour' model, departs from these assumptions on a variety of levels. The behaviour of a state is conceptualised as an output provided by a large organisation that operates under certain habitual procedures (Allison and Zelikow 1999: pp. 143, 147–148). In many

Bureaucratic change in EU foreign policy 61

ways, the model draws on concepts of the sociological variant of the new institutionalism, such as routines and the logic of appropriateness as decision guide (March and Olsen 1989). It also stresses that the choice of available options is largely determined by the routines available to the organisations involved (Allison and Zelikow 1999: p. 164).

Allison and Zelikow's third model is based on the observation that foreign policy decisions are not fundamentally taken by an individual or even unitary actor, but rather that the interaction of several actors is needed for a decision and its implementation (Allison and Zelikow 1999: p. 257). This view of the decision-making process highlights the role of bargaining between actors with different interests, as well as the difference in power that each of these actors brings to the interaction (Allison and Zelikow 1999: p. 160). Allison and Zelikow argue that it is these 'governmental politics' or 'bureaucratic politics' that have a large impact on the eventual output (Allison and Zelikow 1999: p. 295).

This 'bureaucratic politics' model has been questioned in the US context on the basis of both substantive and conceptual concerns. Krasner argued as early as 1972 that the ability of bureaucratic politics to dominate foreign policy decision-making depended largely on the president's involvement (Krasner 1972 pp. 168–169). In the end, Krasner took issue with the lack of room for agency and moral responsibility in Allison's model (Krasner 1972: p. 179). Similarly, Bendor and Hammond argued that bargaining was not necessary for decision-making in US foreign policy (Bendor and Hammond 1992: pp. 313–314) and that the governmental politics model was too complex to be useful (Bendor and Hammond 1992: p. 318; see also Stern and Verbeek 1998). Art criticised the bureaucratic politics approach to foreign policy making for not specifying clearly enough how much difference the bargaining between bureaucratic actors actually made to the policy (Art 1973: p. 474), and noted that that it was unclear what role their bureaucratic position played in this compared to their policy orientation (Art 1973: pp. 472–473). While these lines of criticism are valid, they are fundamentally shaped by the discussion of US foreign policy and its decision-making process. Therefore, most of the substantive arguments centred on the role of the US President and Congress in this process do not apply once the model is lifted from its US context.

Observable bureaucratic politics? Inter-organisational competition and control

Most of the study in the 'bureaucratic politics paradigm' is concerned with individual decisions of foreign policy, e.g. the explanation of a crisis and its handling (Stern and Verbeek 1998). Rosati (1981) has argued that routine operations are the area where its tenets should be most observable. In addition to routine operations, the consolidation phase is also a period that should be strongly determined by bureaucratic politics as during this phase decisions on the resource base as well as its autonomous remit and relations to other organisations are settled for the first time. When an organisation is establishing its own policy

62   Bureaucratic change in EU foreign policy

space and building an organisational structure and standard operation procedures, it should be more concerned with its own position and power (Downs 1967). But how can these relations with other bureaus and other actors be observed and analysed from an institutional perspective?

Bureaucratic politics has never developed its own coherent set of indicators or even categories of observable behaviour that should enable researchers to clarify the expectations for the impact of bureaucratic politics on the institutional process of establishing a new bureaucracy. This lack of structured empirical evidence has been criticised as an expression of the still under-developed nature of the paradigm (Welch 1998; Stern and Verbeek 1998). In order to address this lack of operationalisation of bureaucratic politics, this book relies on a different subset of institutional politics with established categories of control relationship between political and bureaucratic actors. Principal Agent (PA) approaches have a long-standing history in institutional analysis of politics and are particularly apt at categorising control relationships between political and bureaucratic actors. As Moe has put it, at the core of PA are 'issues of hierarchical control in the context of information asymmetry and conflict of interest' (Moe 1984: p. 757). That these issues are of central importance for organisational change has been shown by Warwick for the US State Department in extensive detail (Warwick 1975). These issues of hierarchical control capture the essence of competition about resources and influence that this phase of the institutional emergence seeks to address.

These analytical categories, highlighted in more detail below, will give a clearer structure to the analysis of conflicts surrounding the establishment of a bureau and its struggle in relation to its political masters as well as its bureaucratic competitors. It will be able to show the development of bureaucratic politics as well as political conflict between political bodies and administrative organisations. But because of the specific focus on a delegation relationship, PA is not universally applicable to all relationships between organisations. This means that its direct applicability to the type of administrative system under investigation is limited. Nevertheless, it has the most established categories of control, which is a useful starting point for the analysis of inter-organisational relationships. On the basis of these indicators, it may also be possible to determine who retains control over an organisation, even if no delegation relationship exist.

In order to determine primacy in inter-organisational relationships, control and autonomy are analysed as central concepts to consider. PA is concerned largely with delegation, an uneven relationship between different types of political actors. It aims at explaining regular patterns of control and service between the principal and its agent. Congress, for example, was analysed as the principal that delegated specific tasks to the agencies as agents (McCubbins and Schwartz 1984). At the same time, PA assumes that self-interested agents, because of the specific nature of their tasks, gain an informational advantage over their principal and want to exploit this situation (Moe 1984: p. 756; McNollgast 1999).

PA has also developed indicators of power relations between political bodies, or principals, and administration, or agents, in the form of control mechanisms.

Bureaucratic change in EU foreign policy 63

These instruments of control are central to principal agent analysis. A number of mechanisms of control have been identified (e.g. McCubbins, Noll and Weingast 1987; McCubbins and Schwartz 1984). Detailed prescription of the agent's mandate or administrative procedures are among the most typical ex-ante control mechanisms to be observed (McCubbins, Noll and Weingast 1987, 1989; Balla 1998). In addition, the principal can use the nomination of staff as a means of controlling the direction an agent takes (McCubbins *et al.* 1989: p. 435). Among ex-post control mechanisms are scheduled and detailed reporting and review requirements, which may alert the principal to unintended activity (McCubbins and Talbot 1986: p. 177). Linked to this mechanism is the possibility of budget revisions, to reward agents who are seen to act appropriately and punish those who are not (McCubbins and Schwartz 1984: p. 166, McCubbins and Talbot 1986: p. 177). All of these are classical means of political oversight, known as 'police patrol'; they are very costly to the principal (McCubbins *et al.* 1987: p. 244). Another set of mechanisms identified by McCubbins and Schwartz is 'fire alarm' monitoring, which relies on outside groups to respond when they are harmed in their interests (McCubbins and Schwartz 1984: p. 177). With these tools of control, it will be more easily possible to categorise the different ways in which political masters may wish to assert themselves over bureaucratic organisations, and they may also be useful in analysing inter-bureau relationships at the same time. On the basis of this, bureaucratic politics would expect conflict between political and bureaucratic bodies and the new organisation alike. This conflict would be expressed in strong attempts to exert control over the new organisation and through increased formalisation of interaction.

In combination, bureaucracy theory gives a rational account of the internal functioning of bureaucratic organisations and some general concepts of a 'bureau's' relationship with other bureaucratic actors. Bureaucratic politics focuses on these relationships and the role and impact a bureaucracy has in political decision-making processes. Both share the assessment that new bureaucratic organisations seek to survive and establish autonomy from external control. Thus, both approaches are core to questions about the consolidation of a new organisation like the European External Action Service, and what drives its functioning and how it is embedded in relations with other actors.

The phases of emergence of the EEAS

On the basis of the institutionalist frameworks introduced above, a sequential analytical framework of institutional approaches to the creation of a new bureaucratic body can be assembled. An analytical framework covering three stages uses the strength and focus of each of these approaches for the appropriate phase in the institutional creation and in that way gives a more complete understanding of what forces shape a new administrative actor. The three phases consist of the *inception* of the new organisation, i.e. the general political decision that a particular new body will be created. Next, a more specific set of political decisions are part of a phase labelled *establishment* for the purpose of this analysis.

64   *Bureaucratic change in EU foreign policy*

Finally, once the new organisation takes up its work, a phase of *consolidation* will be the subject of inquiry, where the development of internal functioning and relations to other actors of this new organisation takes centre stage. Each of these phases gives rise to typical processes and alignments, which will be detailed below.

Inception and the enacting coalition

Institutional approaches to political science have shown the particular relevance of specific moments in the decision-making process. In order to understand the changes in institutional constraints that enabled this next step in institutionalisation, it is necessary to 'go back and look' (Pierson 2000a). In the case of creating a new institution, this means looking at the 'moment of institutional formation' (Capoccia and Kelemen 2007: p. 342) in order to 'reconstruct, in a systematic and rigorous fashion, each step of the decision-making process, identify which decisions were most influential and what options were available and viable to the actors who took them' (Capoccia and Kelemen 2007: pp. 354–355).

> Researchers must not stop with simply identifying the critical juncture but must instead deepen the investigation of the historical material to identify the key decisions (and the key events influencing those decisions) steering the system in one or another direction, favoring one institutional equilibrium over others that could have been selected. Particular attention should be paid to the alternative choices that were available to the decision makers, as those can be reconstructed from the available record.
>
> (Capoccia and Kelemen 2007: p. 369)

Because of the different processes in the stages of decision-making, Lindner and Rittberger (2003) analyse the creation of a new organisation by distinguishing two political coalitions. In the phase of institutional inception, the 'enacting coalition' is the set of actors that comes to the decision to set up the organisation (Lindner and Rittberger 2003: pp. 448f.). This process is referred to as inception in this study. It contains the decision to create a new rule or a new organisation. This takes the form of an agreement of abstract nature during the time in which institutional rules are sufficiently relaxed to open a window for the creation of a new rule by actors involved in the decision. In terms of historical institutionalisms, the first phase can be considered a 'critical juncture', which initiates a separate organisational path. As we have seen above, the critical junctures concept rests on specific essential claims, such as the limited duration of this period, the relaxation in decision-making rules, and the relative impact of the decisions taken (Capoccia and Kelemen 2007). The enacting coalition is in essence the political consensus that is needed to create a new organisation in this specific period. The difference between this first decision and later decisions is important for the analysis of an institution. For both phases, conflict over institutions exists:

Because institutions affect policy outcomes and the policy-making powers held by organizational actors, these actors not only have preferences over institutions, but also compete to bring about their preferred versions of them. Institutions are thus contested.

(Stacey and Rittberger 2003: p. 861)

In order to understand the dynamic and direction of a critical juncture, i.e. to explain why a new institution was set up and has taken a particular shape, tracing this contestation about preferences over institutions is key. Capoccia and Kelemen (2007) have specified the basic objectives of such an analysis and rational choice historical institutionalism provides us with the tools to analyse the involved actors, their preferences and the extraordinary decision-making process. Peters *et al.* (2005) have also highlighted the role of political conflict in determining change in a historical institutionalist framework. For this phase of inception, the expectation is thus one of political conflict which, if resolved by an agreement, will result in an institution reflecting the actors' preferences. The question why an institution was created or changed and why it took a particular shape can be answered by detailed analysis of the preferences of actors and process tracing of what happened in this decision period.

The level of detail of the first decision determines to a large degree the level of room for manoeuvre in the second phase, creating a link between the two. The higher the level of conflict in the first phase, the more vague the decision (Lindner and Rittberger 2003: pp. 450–451). This in turn will result in stronger distributional conflicts in the second phase. This theoretical distinction between these phases is very pertinent to the EU institutional structure, as will be shown below, where under normal circumstances governments negotiate a change in the basic rules and institutions and another set of collective actors adopt legislation on the basis of these rules. It is this second phase which involves another set of actors and processes to determine the details of institutional establishment.

Establishment and the executing coalition

In addition to these large-scale negotiations and renegotiations of the institutional rules as well as basic rules of policy, there is an additional layer in the creation of these rules. It consists of specifying detailed institutional rules, about the institutional set-up of a new organisation and its role and functioning. This process is characterised by a different context and decision-making process, and different actors. It centres on the formation of an executing coalition within a set of institutional constraints (Lindner and Rittberger 2003). The process also focuses on the practicalities of setting up the organisation, but nevertheless includes political decisions. Lindner and Rittberger refer to this process as implementation (Lindner and Rittberger 2003), but for the purpose of this study it will be referred to as establishment of the organisation. Because the organisation in question is not yet operating, this terminology more accurately reflects the stage in the organisation's evolution. In particular at the level of government

66   Bureaucratic change in EU foreign policy

department, a political decision to create an organisation only sets off a process (Lindner and Rittberger 2003). In this second stage, a different set of actors translates the first decision into an administrative reality. The new organisation is thus created in a political and administrative process (Lindner and Rittberger 2003: pp. 451ff.). These decisions are taken by a different set of actors, referred to as the 'executing coalition' (Lindner and Rittberger 2003: pp. 453–454).

While the awareness of the two stages of institutional creation provides for an essential analytical distinction, a further look into the second stage of establishment is necessary. Rule-setting change, as has been argued above, can be captured by the concept of 'critical juncture' when for a distinct period of time treaty reform is negotiated. The second phase of implementing these rules or institutions is likely to be dominated by different dynamics. This approach takes the analysis further away from an international organisation approach, where states bargain to create institutions (e.g. Koremenos *et al.* 2004), and instead moves the analysis towards a comparative politics approach. It describes the coalitions necessary for the adoption of detailed institutional rules, which allow for the operation of a new organisation. Like the first phase, the establishment phase is characterised by negotiation among actors, but it has more institutional constraints. First, it is constrained by the first-order decision to create the organisation. Second, it forms part of a pre-defined decision-making process based upon treaty rules much like any adoption of secondary legislation at the EU level. This process sets out who participates in the process, determines their relative influence and offers other means of achieving a decision than negotiation, e.g. voting (Elgström and Smith 2000). Precedent limits the implementation by the executing coalition, without pre-determining it. It is a narrower process, because some elements of decision are likely to have been taken in the earlier phase. How much narrower a process it is depends largely on the level of detail of the first decision. Lindner and Rittberger (2003: p. 451) argue that actors are likely to specify detailed rules where they are interested in specific redistributive policy outcomes and less so where they negotiate diverging ideas on a polity. Even so, some elements, such as the type of organisation, its location in the overall institutional structure and similar issues, may be pre-determined by the first decision.

This secondary nature of the establishment process ties neatly into a path-dependent framework as discussed above. At the same time, it is a decision-making process concerning the establishment of a new bureaucratic actor, following many of the same rules as regular decision-making. The analytical approach for this phase must take into account these two characteristics, i.e. a level of path dependence and new institutional rules that constrain or enable new actors. Because of this change in institutional constraints and actors, it is bound to differ in the concrete expression of its negotiation format. This is also the case as the 'effects of institutional decisions on distributive outcomes become more visible' (Lindner and Rittberger 2003: p. 452). Because of this more direct visibility of effects, i.e. the gain and loss of budget, legal instruments or other political resources, the interests of the institutions involved are likely to be more pronounced. This conflict about organisational *substance* is a characteristic that in this analysis distinguishes the process of institutional creation from policy processes. While individual decisions on policy may have large effects on business or social groups, decisions on organisational substance are most likely to have the largest effect on the other organisations in this decision-making process, the administrative organisations themselves. In order to take account of these effects, it is particularly relevant to consider theoretical approaches that focus on these types of decision-making processes and the actors within them.

The application of American approaches of the politics of structural choice to the EU, i.e. the politics of Eurocratic structure (see below, Kelemen 2002), has merged political and bureaucratic competition in a useful framework. The empirical questions can be answered again by a detailed tracing of processes leading up to decisions as well as the evolution of the opinions of constituent parts. Process tracing, as in the rule-making phase, is key to determining the origins of outcomes of the establishment phase, too. It will also allow for the distinction between bureaucratic interests and political ones, depending on the actor in question and their internal decision-making process. Lindner and Rittberger call this implementing stage the 'institutional operation' phase of an institution (Lindner and Rittberger 2003: p. 451). While consistent for their analysis, this study argues that an additional distinction needs to be made. The implementation of the new organisation is still a phase of creation, not operation. The new organisation arguably does not yet exist. Setting out the detailed rules of the organisation's functioning and structure, or the detailed substance of a piece of legislation on policy, cannot be considered regular operation. The phase of setting the detailed institutional rules remains a period of establishment. Once the organisation starts to operate, a new phase is ushered in.

Consolidation of a new bureaucracy: from coalition to competition

The politics of structural choice approach implies that the political system itself changes upon the creation of a new administrative body or bureaucracy. As soon as a new agency is created, it becomes a self-interested, active part of the political system into which it was born (Moe 1989: p. 282). This insight is particularly relevant for distinguishing the creation or implementation phase from what follows. Once an organisation is established and starts functioning, it is possible to speak of an operational public administration, or bureaucracy. This phase is the final building block for explaining the evolution of a bureaucratic organisation, in which its internal processes and external relations are set up and develop into routine (inter)actions. In order to avoid confusion, the final stage, which concerns the period of time immediately after the organisation's establishment and when it starts fulfilling its organisational mandate, will be called consolidation. In the case of the EEAS, consolidation covers the tenure of the first two political leaders of the service.

The consolidation phase signals a final stage in the creation of an organisation. This phase can be distinguished from the first two by the mere existence of the new organisation, but equally by the fact that it will take up the duties that

68 *Bureaucratic change in EU foreign policy*

have been ascribed to it in its mandate. Because this does not happen in an empty space, but in a political and administrative system, this phase will be characterised by factors both internal and external to the organisation: its relationships with already existing organisations and structures as well as its internal functioning. The literature on institutional emergence has largely overlooked this phase. Only in traditional studies of public bureaucracies do we find the early operation of a new organisation as a central analytical and empirical concern. Bureaucratic politics and bureaucracy theory both argue that there are specific organisational characteristics of 'bureaus' and that these have an impact on the policy outcome (Welch 1998: p. 213). Where bureaucracy theory looks at the internal organisation, bureaucratic politics focuses on the 'political interactions between organizations and officials' (Welch 1998: p. 216). This means that both perspectives contribute to a complete analysis of bureaucratic emergence and operation, one focusing more on the internal characteristics, the other more on the necessary relations with other actors.

Most institutional analyses focus on the reorganisation of governmental structures at the level of the political system. As the focus of this study is a specific part of government executive – a diplomatic service at the supranational level – it needs to continue the analysis on the level of government department. The study of bureaucracy is the main approach in this area, focusing on the operation of administrative bodies as much as their effects on public policy outcomes.

The three stages of institutional development in the EU

Institutional approaches to change and creation of new organisations have been used above to create a three-stage analytical framework of this process of institutional creation within an existing institutional and political structure. But how do these processes relate to the creation of a new body at the EU level? Applying the framework to the EU political system more specifically will highlight the value of the original institutional analysis in an eclectic and sequential model. Any approach to institution building at the EU level necessarily needs to be open to existing structures because of the long-standing evolution of external relations services at the EU level (see Chapter 2), the role of EU institutions in the institutional design process and the specific decision-making modes at the EU level. Stacey and Rittberger consequently argued for a rational choice historical institutionalism with a particular focus on the EU, focusing on inter-organisational decision-making at the EU level (Stacey and Rittberger 2003). How the three stages of an institution's creation relate to EU politics is detailed below.

Inception: treaty reform and the enacting coalition

The phase of treaty making is the one where the institutional structure of the EU is agreed and potentially a new organisation can be created. The distinction between treaty change versus inter-institutional decision-making has become an almost intuitive element of analysing the EU. The processes of intergovernmental

Bureaucratic change in EU foreign policy 69

treaty change have provided a steady strand of research (e.g. Beach 2003; Christiansen 2002; Christiansen and Reh 2009; Christiansen *et al.* 2002; Edwards and Pijpers 1997; Devuyst 1998; Falkner 2002a; Moravcsik 1998). Finke has shown the domestic determinants of government positions in intergovernmental conferences (IGCs) (Finke 2009a). In a later study, he also showed how IGCs represent a bargain between all member states, rather than merely the most influential ones (Finke 2009b). He went on to demonstrate the difference between regular IGCs and the European Convention reform process in the early 2000s (Finke 2009b). For EU foreign policy and external relations, the dual nature of the institutional environment outlined in Chapter 2 also remains a relevant factor in the process of institutional change. Arrangements in EU foreign policy developed first based on intergovernmental agreement alone and only later turned into institutional structures at the EU level (Chapter 2; Smith 2004). The development of EU external relations inside the European Commission was by nature based on EU treaties and legal bases for their action.

Despite the fact that treaty negotiations represent possibly the most intergovernmental setting of all the 'diversity of negotiation contexts' (Elgström and Smith 2000: p. 674), the study of treaty change has not focused exclusively on member states. The role and influence of EU institutions has also been scrutinised (Christiansen 2002; Beach 2004; Falkner 2002a, 2002b). Highlighting the avenues for influence from the EU institutions, however, does not negate the centrality of member states as negotiators. The member states and their interests remain the core feature of treaty-making decisions, largely sustained by the required unanimous agreement.

The European Convention has also received a lot of scholarly attention as something of an outlier of treaty reform mechanisms (Finke 2009b; Finke *et al.* 2012). The Convention and its changed procedural constraints on the treaty reform outcome were to play a central role in the inception phase of the EEAS, as shown in Chapter 4. The EU's internal process thus provides for a distinct process of institutional inception, the treaty revision process. The application of a critical juncture concept to EU treaty reform appears simple. By definition, treaty reform is a temporary phenomenon, which opens up the policy space available to the creation of new rules on new policies, or institutions. At the same time, it cannot be merely assumed to be a critical juncture but rather categorised as such according to the standards defined by Capoccia and Kelemen (2007). Nevertheless, EU treaty reforms are also linked to each other in sequence, and while there is a theoretical possibility of complete change, change usually occurs along the lines of the established institutional structure of the EU. Treaty change by definition also has an impact on the institutional constraints of the second-order decision, as it is the Treaties that determine the actors' roles in the EU decision-making process, making path dependence an additional analytical concern for this phase. The unanimous agreement needed also brings up the question why a new merged structure should have been created in the first place when traditionally EU foreign policy institutionalisation had been slow, piecemeal and kept at a distance from the Community's external relations operations.

70 *Bureaucratic change in EU foreign policy*

After the treaty-setting, the EU in its second-order decision also has its specific version of the establishment process for building a new EU-level organisation based on the general rules adopted through the treaty. This EU decision-making process is governed by standard rules of EU law-making and includes European-level actors as well as member states, thus considerably altering the dynamics of the political process from treaty change. What impact this has on the establishment of a new organisation will be explained with relevant institutionalist analytical tools. Using process tracing to detail the decisions that led to the adoption of the EEAS will thus show the political forces that had an impact on the shaping of the organisation and what effect this had on later stages of the creation of the organisation.

Establishment: EU decision-making and the 'politics of Eurocratic structure'

Even before Trondal diagnosed the 'public administration turn' in studying the EU (Trondal 2007), it had developed into a relevant stream of EU research. While the terminology differs from US research into 'bureaucracy', the abstract focus and object of inquiry is very much shared between the different traditions: the organisation of public administration. Under different key terms and foci, researchers have looked at administration in the EU and at the EU level. Kelemen argued that the

> institutional structure of the EU differs from that of the US in important respects [but], many of the same factors influence the politics of agency design in both polities.
>
> (Kelemen 2002: p. 94)

Trondal also identified the core areas of interest: the focus has been on the Commission and its internal administrative reform (Kassim and Menon 2003; Balint *et al.* 2008; Schoen-Quinlivan 2011) or on regulatory agencies at the EU level (e.g. Kelemen 2002; Majone 1997, 2001; Thatcher 2002; Wonka and Rittberger 2010), because of the specific nature of EU integration. Moving beyond a dominant functionalist explanation for delegation at the EU level (Pollack 1997), Kelemen identified the specific politics of 'Eurocracy', or 'politics of Eurocratic structure' (Kelemen 2002). The 'politics of Eurocratic structure' approach is a European adaptation of a rational choice approach to institutional behaviour and control of institutions, the 'politics of structural choice' (Moe 1989). Looking at the politics between the European Commission, the European Parliament and the member states and how their interactions shape the nature of EU regulatory agencies (Kelemen 2002: pp. 97–99), Kelemen stressed that there was a specific distribution of preferences between the EU decision-makers, the Commission, the Parliament and the Council, and that these were largely stable. He argued that the European Commission generally sought to expands its powers and resources. Kelemen stated this clearly: 'The Commission is a well-known self-aggrandiser' (Kelemen 2002: p. 98).

Bureaucratic change in EU foreign policy 71

The European Parliament sought to expand its area of legislative influence and opportunities for oversight. The EP has, however, undergone a significant transformation, from an ally of the Commission for more integration, to a more assertive role as overseer (Kelemen 2002: p. 97). This is only likely to have become stronger with the transfer of additional legislative powers by the Lisbon Treaty. Meanwhile, the Council seeks to minimise the bureaucratic independence of supranational institutions and maintain control over their actions (Kelemen 2002: p. 97). This means that for the phase of institutional creation at the EU level, the analytical framework based on the politics of Eurocratic structure will be the dominant framework for explaining the outcomes of the inter-institutional decision-making. As an EU-specific application of a general institutionalist research agenda, it appears the strongest approach for this particular phase.

Consolidation: bureaucracy, bureaucratic politics, and the EU

The most pertinent approach to explain the behaviour of a new organisation at the EU level will be the one looking at its most basic and dominant characteristics. In this case that is first and foremost the organisation's characteristic as a bureaucracy. It is bureaucracy theory, taken from a US context and transferred to the EU, which will be the first point of call for identifying dominant factors for the new organisation's functioning and behaviour. Competition and control as environmental factors become central concepts of the consolidation phase of organisational change (Warwick 1975). Control can in many ways be seen as an indicator for autonomy of the organisation and its success in shaping its environment. The stronger the control exercised over a bureaucratic organisation, the less autonomously the organisation is able to act. In a mix of political and inter-organisational relationships, a knowledge of which relationships establish control over the new organisation is relevant in understanding the way the organisation functions.

In a sense, what makes bureaucratic politics and bureaucracy theory difficult to apply in a purely American context – the central unifying role of the President – could make it rather more useful in a European environment where leadership and executive power are dispersed more widely. European decisions are almost always collective in nature and will be even more prone to incorporate contradicting interests of politicians and implementing officials. This is the case in regular decision-making of the implementation phase in particular, with central involvement of the European Commission, i.e. an independent collegiate body drawing up legislative proposals and implementing policies, an independently elected European Parliament without right of legislative initiative and the Council, which assembles the representative of the member states. Without the ultimately unifying decision capability of the US Presidency, which itself is of little relief to departmental reorganisation as demonstrated by Warwick (Warwick 1975), insights from bureaucratic politics cover the inter-organisational relationships within the EU's decision-making process. In other words, because there are no single unitary actors, each position must be the

72 Bureaucratic change in EU foreign policy

outcome of an internal decision-making process as well as a decision-making process that needs the agreement of all these collective bodies.

Because of the general applicability of these control mechanisms to public organisations – international, supranational or national, the control mechanisms of principal agent approaches have been imported into a variety of other sub-fields including European politics (Pollack 1997; Thatcher 2002; Kassim and Menon 2003; Dehousse 2008). They have proven useful in grappling with the relationships between European actors as well as between member states and the EU institutions. They have also been used to describe the institutional characteristics of EU external relations and foreign policy (Damro 2007; Dijkstra 2008, 2009; Wagner 2003), providing a reference point to the previous institutional structure. This previous research has illustrated the compatibility of PA analysis with the EU political system and led to some research analysing the PA relationships of the EEAS (Furness 2013; Kostanyan and Orbie 2013). At the same time, principal agent approaches have specific requirements, i.e. an act of delegation that not all of the EEAS's relationships fulfil. PA indicators can thus partially plug a gap in the observable relationships of the EEAS, but are not the only expression of control and competition in this environment. Together with the categories developed in PA, bureaucratic politics will provide the basis to analyse the competitive relations of a newly emerging administrative actor and will allow comparison with other administrative arrangements.

Conclusion: the three stages of bureaucratic emergence

Institutional approaches to building a new administrative organisation have identified several phases of creation, as shown above. The first is an inception phase taking place at a critical juncture, relaxing the constraints on policy-makers and opening up the possibility for institutional change. The outcome of this phase leads to a second phase of institutional creation where the detailed rules and structure of the new organisation are decided upon by a different set of actors. Here the struggle for influence and resources, as explained by bureaucratic politics and elements of negotiation theory, comes to the fore. This study argues that an additional third phase needs consideration, which is the consolidation phase. During this phase, internal and external operation of the new bureaucratic actor is explained by two approaches: the internal operation is characterised by public choice bureaucracy theory, while the relations of the new actor to the existing institutional environment will be determined by bureaucratic politics. In combination, they provide a framework attuned to the changing set of rules applicable to each stage of the emergence.

In the first phase, historical institutionalism expects a relaxation of institutional constraints at a critical juncture that leads to the (potential) forming of an enacting coalition, which agrees to create a new organisation. An analytical focus on the critical juncture and the specific role of actors in it, will make it possible to explain the 'why' of the creation of a new organisation in a much more nuanced way. Rather than retreating to a functional explanation of why an organisation exists, this method can uncover the political mechanisms that lead to the decision to create an organisation. It can also answer why one kind of organisation was chosen over another. In the case of the EEAS, it looks at the European Convention and its variety of members. Chapter 4 will investigate this moment of inception of the EEAS with the focus on the actors who created the EEAS, the process by which they reach agreement as well as the institutional framework in which they take decisions.

In a second phase, the focus turns to the executing coalition, i.e. another group of actors that negotiate the implementation of the decision. The executing coalition implements the decision by agreeing to the detailed institutional set-up of the new organisation and is thus constrained by its framework. The analytical focus on the actors involved and their preferences within an EU-specific set of decision-making rules makes it possible to trace the political motives behind the organisation's set-up. With respect to the questions guiding this study, this approach is used to answer how the new organisation is created, what forces drive the setting up of the organisation and to what extent it is (path)-dependent on the set of decisions taken earlier. For the EEAS, this means looking at the Council of the EU and the member states, the European Parliament and the European Commission. Chapter 5 will proceed to apply this in the analysis of the administrative set-up of the EEAS, in particular its status, scope and staffing. By looking at the actors involved, what their preferences for the service are, and how they manage – or not – to imprint their vision on the new organisation, it addresses the second set of questions.

Finally, in the third phase, the new organisation is established and begins operating as a new bureaucratic actor. In this phase, bureaucratic politics or inter-organisational competition about resources and power become the dominant dynamic of operation between the organisations involved, as discussed above. The focus of analysis here shifts from the setting up of an organisation to its operation and how emerging relationships with other political and bureaucratic actors shape its own structure and ability to act autonomously. This consolidation is at the heart of the last empirical chapters. The EEAS consolidates in an environment dominated by the European Commission, but also relates to the European Parliament, the Council of the EU as well as the President of the European Council. Chapter 6 thus has at its core the analysis of how far the EEAS behaves like a bureaucracy, as well as what impact outside pressure had on its organisation and operation under High Representative Ashton. Chapter 7 continues the investigation of the contested consolidation into the tenure of the second High Representative Mogherini.

References

Allison, Graham 1971: *The essence of decision: Explaining the Cuban missile crisis*. Little, Brown: Boston.

Allison, Graham and Halperin, Morton 1972: Bureaucratic politics: a paradigm and some policy implications. *World Politics*, vol. 24, no. 1, pp. 40–79.

74 *Bureaucratic change in EU foreign policy*

Allison, Graham and Zelikow, Philip 1999: *The essence of decision: Explaining the Cuban missile crisis*. Longman: New York.

Arrow, Kenneth 1963: *Social Choice and Individual Values*. Wiley and Sons: New York.

Art, Robert 1973: Bureaucratic Politics and American Foreign Policy: A Critique. *Policy Sciences*, vol. 4, pp. 467–490.

Aspinwall, Mark and Schneider, Gerald 2000: Same menu, separate tables: The institutionalist turn in political science and the study of European integration. *European Journal of Political Research*, vol. 38, pp. 1–36.

Balint, Tim, Bauer, Michael W. and Knill, Christopher 2008: Bureaucratic change in the European administrative space: The case of the European commission. In *West European Politics*, vol. 31, no. 4, pp. 677–700.

Balla, Steven J. 1998: Administrative Procedures and Political Control of the Bureaucracy. *American Political Science Review*, vol. 92, no. 3, pp. 663–673.

Bauer, Michael and Knill, Christoph 2007: *Management reforms in International Organizations*. Nomos: Baden-Baden.

Beach, Derek 2003: Towards a new method of constitutional bargaining? The role and impact of EU institutions in the IGC and convention method of treaty reform. *Federal Trust Constitutional Online Paper Series* No. 13/03.

Beach, Derek 2004: The unseen hand in treaty reform negotiations: the role and influence of the Council Secretariat. *Journal of European Public Policy*, vol. 11, no. 3, pp. 408–439.

Bendor, Jonathan and Hammond, Thomas H. 1992: Rethinking Allison's Models. *American Political Science Review*, vol. 86, no. 2, pp. 301–322.

Buethe, Tim 2002: Taking Temporality Seriously: Modeling History and the Use of Narrative as Evidence. *American Political Science Review*, vol. 96, no. 3, pp. 481–493.

Capoccia, Giovanni and Kelemen, R. Daniel 2007: The Study of Critical Junctures: Theory, Narrative and Counterfactuals in Historical Institutionalism. *World Politics*, vol. 59, pp. 341–369.

Christiansen, Thomas 2002: The role of supranational actors in EU treaty reform. *Journal of European Public Policy*, vol. 9, no. 1, pp. 33–53.

Christiansen, Thomas, Falkner, Gerda, and Jorgensen, Knud Erik 2002: Theorizing EU Treaty Reform: beyond diplomacy and bargaining. *Journal of European Public Policy*, vol. 9, no. 1, pp. 12–32.

Christiansen, Thomas and Reh, Christine 2009: *Constitutionalizing the European Union*. Basingstoke: Palgrave Macmillan.

Collier, R. and Collier, D. 1991: *Shaping the Political Arena: Critical Junctures, the Labor Movement and Regime Dynamics in Latin America*. Princeton University Press: Princeton.

Crecine, John P. 1968: Book review: Inside Bureaucracy by Anthony Downs. *RAND Corporation Paper Series* P-3879: Santa Monica.

Damro, Chad 2007: EU Delegation and Agency in International Trade Negotiations: A Cautionary Comparison. *Journal of Common Market Studies*, vol. 45, no. 4, pp. 883–903.

David, Paul A. 1985: Clio and the Economics of QWERTY. *Economic History*, vol. 75, no. 2, pp. 332–337.

Dehousse, Renaud 2008: Delegation of Powers in the European Union: The Need for a Multi-principals Model. *West European Politics*, vol. 31 no. 4, pp. 789–805.

Destler, I. M. 1972: *Presidents, Bureaucrats and Foreign Policy: The Politics of Organizational Reform*. Princeton University Press: Princeton.

Devuyst, Yves 1998: Treaty Reform in the European Union: The Amsterdam Process. *Journal of European Public Policy*, vol. 5, no. 4, pp. 615–631.

Dijkstra, Hylke 2008: The Council Secretariat's Role in the Common Foreign and Security Policy. In *European Foreign Affairs Review*, vol. 13, no. 2, pp. 149–166.

Dijkstra, Hylke 2009: Commission versus Council Secretariat: an analysis of bureaucratic rivalry in European foreign policy. *European Foreign Affairs Review*, vol. 14, pp. 431–450.

Downs, Anthony 1967: *Inside Bureaucracy*. Little, Brown: Boston.

Drezner, Daniel W. 2000: Ideas, Bureaucratic Politics, and the Crafting of Foreign Policy. *American Journal of Political Science*, vol. 44, no. 4, pp. 733–749.

Duffield, John S. 2003: The Limits of Rational Design. *International Organization*, vol. 57, no. 2, pp. 411–430.

Dunleavy, Patrick 1991: *Democracy, Bureaucracy and Public Choice. Economic Explanations in Political Science*. Harvester: New York.

Edwards, Geoffrey and Pijpers, Alfred (Eds.) 1997: *The Politics of Treaty Reform. The 1996 Intergovernmental Conference and Beyond*. Pinter: London.

Eldridge, Niles and Gould, Stephen Jay 1972: Punctuated Equilibria: An Alternative to phyletic gradualism. In Schopf, Thomas (Ed.), *Models in Paleobiology*. Freeman: San Francisco.

Elgström, Ole and Smith, Michael 2000: Introduction: Negotiation and policy-making in the European Union – processes, system and order. *Journal of European Public Policy*, vol. 7. no. 5, pp. 673–683.

Falkner, Gerda 2002a: How intergovernmental are Intergovernmental Conferences? An example from the Maastricht Treaty reform. *Journal of European Public Policy*, vol. 9, no. 1, pp. 98–119.

Falkner, Gerda 2002b: EU Treaty Reform as a Three-Level Process. In *Journal of European Public Policy*, vol. 9, no. 1, pp. 1–11.

Finke, Daniel 2009a: Domestic Politics and European Treaty Reform. *European Union Politics*, vol. 10, no. 4, pp. 482–506.

Finke, Daniel 2009b: Challenges to Intergovernmentalism: An Empirical Analysis of EU Treaty Negotiations Since Maastricht. *West European Politics*, vol. 32, no. 3, pp. 466–495.

Finke, Daniel; König, Thomas; Proksch, Sven-Oliver; and Tsebelis, George 2012: *Reforming the European Union: Realizing the Impossible*. Princeton University Press: Princeton.

Furness, Mark 2013: Who controls the European External Action Service? Agent Autonomy in EU External Policy. European Foreign Affairs Review, vol. 18, no. 1, pp. 103–126.

George, Alexander L. and Bennett, Andrew 2005: *Case Studies and Theory Development in the Social Sciences*. MIT Press: Cambridge, MA.

Hall, Peter A. and Taylor, Rosemary C. R. 1996: Political Science and the Three New Institutionalisms. *Political Studies*, vol. 44, pp. 936–957.

Hall, Peter A. and Taylor, Rosemary C. R. 1998: The Potential of Historical Institutionalism. A response to Hay and Wincott. *Political Studies*, vol. 46, pp. 958–962.

Halperin, Morton, with Clapp, Priscilla and Kanter Arnold 1974: *Bureaucratic Politics and Foreign Policy*. Brookings: Washington, DC.

Hilsman, Roger 1987: *The politics of policy making in defense and foreign affairs: conceptual models and bureaucratic politics.* Prentice-Hall: London.

Ikenberry, G. John 1988: Conclusion: an institutional approach to American foreign economic policy. *International Organisation*, vol. 42, no. 1, pp. 219–243.

76 Bureaucratic change in EU foreign policy

Immergut, Ellen 1998: The Theoretical Core of the New Institutionalism. *Politics&Society*, vol. 26, no. 5, pp. 5–34.

Immergut, Ellen and Anderson, Karen 2008: Historical Institutionalism and West European Politics. *West European Politics*, vol. 31, no. 1, pp. 345–369.

Katznelson, Ira and Weingast, Barry 2005 (Eds.): *Preferences and Situations. Points of Intersection Between Historical and Rational Choice Institutionalism*. Russel Sage: New York.

Kassim, Hussein and Menon, Anand 2003: The principal–agent approach and the study of the European Union: promise unfulfilled? In *Journal of European Public Policy*, vol. 10, no. 1, pp. 121–139.

Kelemen, R. Daniel 2002: The Politics of 'Eurocratic' Structure and the new European agencies. *West European Politics*, vol. 25, no. 4, pp. 93–118.

Kelemen, R. Daniel and Tarrant, Andrew 2011: The political foundations of the Eurocracy. *West European Politics*, vol. 34, no. 5, pp. 922–947.

Kittel, Bernhard and Kuehn, David 2012: Introduction: reassessing the methodology of process tracing. In European Political Science, vol. 12, no. 1, pp. 1–9.

Koremenos, Barbara, Lipson, Charles and Snidal, Duncan 2001a: The Rational Design of International Institutions. *International Organization*, vol. 55, no. 4, pp. 761–799.

Koremenos, Barbara, Lipson, Charles and Snidal, Duncan 2001b: Rational Design: Looking Back to Move Forward. *International Organization*, The Rational Design of International Institutions, vol. 55, no. 4, pp. 1051–1088.

Koremenos, Barbara, Lipson, Charles and Snidal, Duncan (Eds.) 2004: *The Rational Design of International Institutions*. Cambridge University Press: Cambridge.

Kostanyan, Hrant and Orbie, Jan 2013: The EEAS' discretionary power within the Eastern Partnership: in search of the highest possible denominator. *Southeast European and Black Sea Studies*, vol. 13, no. 1, pp. 47–65.

Krasner, Stephen 1972: Are Bureaucracies important? (Or Allison Wonderland). *Foreign Policy*, no. 7, pp. 159–179.

Krasner, Stephen 1988: Sovereignty: An Institutional Perspective. In *Comparative Political Studies*, vol. 21, no. 1, pp. 66–94.

Lindner, Johannes and Rittberger, Berthold 2003: The Creation, Interpretation and Contestation of Institutions – revisiting Historical Institutionalism. *Journal of Common Market Studies*, vol. 41, pp. 445–473.

Lipset, Seymour Martin and Rokkan, Stein 1967: Cleavage structures, party systems, and voter alignments: An introduction. In Lipset and Rokkan (Eds.), *Party Systems and Voter Alignments: Cross-National Perspectives*, pp. 1–64, Free Press: New York.

Mahoney, James 2005: Combining Institutionalisms: Liberal Choices and Political Trajectories in Central America. In Katznelson and Weingast (Eds.): *Preferences and Situations. Points of Intersection Between Historical and Rational Choice Institutionalism*. Russel Sage: New York, pp. 313–334.

Mahoney, James and Thelen, Kathleen 2010: *Explaining Institutional Change. Ambiguity, Agency and Power*. Cambridge University Press: Cambridge.

Majone, Giandomenico 1997: From the Positive to the Regulatory State: Causes and Consequences of Changes in the Mode of Governance. *Journal of Public Policy*, vol. 17, no. 2, pp. 139–167.

Majone, Giandomenico 2001: Two Logics of Delegation: Agency and Fiduciary Relations in EU governance. *European Union Politics*, vol. 2, no. 1, pp. 103–122.

March, James G. and Olsen, Johan P 1989: *Rediscovering Institutions. The organizational basis of politics*. Free Press: New York.

Bureaucratic change in EU foreign policy   77

McCubbins, Mathew D.; Noll, Roger and Weingast, Barry 1987: Administrative Procedures as Instruments of Political Control. *Journal of Law, Economics and Organization*, vol. 3, no. 2, pp. 243–277.

McCubbins, Mathew D., Noll, Roger and Weingast, Barry 1989: Administrative Arrangements and the Political Control of Agencies. In *Virginia Law Review*, vol. 75, no. 2, pp. 431–482.

McCubbins, Mathew D. and Schwartz, Thomas 1984: Congressional Oversight Overlooked: Police Patrols versus Fire Alarms. *American Journal of Political Science*, vol. 28, no. 1, pp. 165–179.

McCubbins, Mathew D. and Page, Talbot 1986: The congressional foundations of agency performance. *Public Choice*, vol. 51, pp. 173–190.

McNollgast 1999: Political Control of the Bureaucracy. In Newman (Ed.), *New Palgrave Dictionary of Economics and the Law*, Palgrave Macmillan: London.

Miller, Gary 2000: Rational Choice and Dysfunctional Institutions. *Governance*, vol. 13, no. 4, pp. 535–547.

Miller, Gary 2005: The Political Evolution of Principal-Agent Models. *Annual Review of Political Science*, vol. 8, pp. 203–25.

Moe, Terry 1984: The new economics of organization. *American Journal of Political Science*, vol. 28, no. 4, pp. 739–777.

Moe, Terry 1989: The Politics of Bureaucracy. In Chubb and Peterson (Eds.): *Can the Government Govern?* Brookings: Washington, DC.

Moravcsik, Andrew 1998: *The Choice for Europe. Social Purpose and State Power from Messina to Maastricht*. Cornell University Press: Ithaca, New York.

Niskanen, William A. 1971: *Bureaucracy and Representative Government*. Atherton: Chicago.

North, Douglas 1990: *Institutions, Institutional Change, and Performance*. Cambridge University Press: Cambridge.

Peters, Guy; Pierre, Jon; King, Desmond 2005: The Politics of Path Dependency: Political Conflict in Historical Institutionalism. *The Journal of Politics*, vol. 67, no. 4, pp. 1275–1300.

Peters, Guy 2005: *Institutional Theory in Political Science: The 'New Institutionalism'*. Continuum: New York.

Peters, Guy 2012: *Institutional theory in Political Science*. 3rd ed. Continuum: New York.

Pierson, Paul 2000a: Increasing Returns, Path Dependence, and the Study of Politics. *American Political Science Review*, vol. 94, no. 2, pp. 251–267.

Pierson, Paul 2000b: The Limits of Design: Explaining Institutional Origin and Change. *Governance*, vol. 13, no. 4, pp. 475–499.

Pierson, Paul 2004: *Placing Politics in Time*. Princeton: Princeton University Press.

Pollack, Mark A. 1997: Delegation, agency and agenda-setting in the European community. *International Organization*, vol. 51, no. 1, pp. 99–134.

Riker, William 1998: The Experience of Creating Institutions. The Framing of the United States Constitution. In Knight and Sened (Eds.), *Explaining Social Institutions*, pp. 121–144. University of Michigan Press: Ann Arbor, MI.

Rosati, Jerel A. 1981: Developing a systematic decision-making framework. Bureaucratic Politics in perspective. *World Politics*, vol. 33, no. 2, pp. 234–252.

Schoen-Quinlivan, Emmanuelle 2011: *Reforming the European Commission*. Palgrave Macmillan: Basingstoke.

78 Bureaucratic change in EU foreign policy

Sheingate, Adam 2010: Rethinking rules: creativity and constraint in the US House of Representatives. In Mahoney, James and Thelen, Kathleen (Eds.), *Explaining Institutional Change. Ambiguity, Agency and Power.* Cambridge University Press: Cambridge.

Shepsle, Kenneth 1992: Congress is a 'They', not an 'It': Legislative Intent as Oxymoron. *International Review of Law and Economics*, vol. 12 no. 2, pp. 239–256.

Smith, Michael E. 2004: *Europe's Foreign and Security Policy. The Institutionalization of Cooperation.* Cambridge University Press: Cambridge.

Stacey, Jeffrey and Rittberger, Berthold 2003: Dynamics of formal and informal institutional change in the EU. *Journal of European Public Policy*, vol. 10, no. 6, pp. 858–883.

Stern, Eric and Verbeek, Bertjan 1998: Whither the Study of Governmental Politics in Foreign Policymaking? A Symposium. *Mershon International Studies Review*, vol. 42, pp. 205–255.

Streeck, Wolfgang and Thelen, Kathleen 2005: *Beyond Continuity: Institutional Change in advanced Political Economies.* Oxford University Press: Oxford.

Thatcher, Mark 2002: Regulation after Delegation: Independent regulatory Agencies in Europe. *Journal of European Public Policy*, vol. 9, no. 6, pp. 954–972.

Thelen, Kathleen and Steinmo, Sven 1992: Historical institutionalism in comparative politics. In Steinmo, Thelen and Longstreth (Eds.), *Structuring Politics: Historical Institutionalism in Comparative Perspective.* Cambridge University Press: Cambridge.

Trondal, Jarle 2007: The Public Administration turn in Integration Research. *Journal of European Public Policy*, vol. 14, no. 6, pp. 960–972.

Tullock, Gordon 1965: *The Politics of Bureaucracy.* Public Affairs Press: Washington, DC.

Wade, L. L. 1979: Public Administration, Public Choice and the Pathos of Reform. *The Review of Politics*, vol. 41, pp. 344–374.

Wagner, Wolfgang 2003: Why the EU's common foreign and security policy will remain intergovernmental: a rationalist institutional choice analysis of European crisis management policy. *Journal of European Public Policy*, vol. 10, no. 4, pp. 576–595.

Warwick, Donald P. in collaboration with Meade, Marvin and Reed, Theodore 1975: *A Theory of Public Bureaucracy. Politics, Personality, and Organization in the State Department.* Harvard University Press: Cambridge, MA.

Weber, Max 1947 (reprint from 1922): *Wirtschaft und Gesellschaft.* Siebeck: Tübingen.

Weingast, Barry 1984: The congressional-bureaucratic system: a principal-agent perspective. *Public Choice*, vol. 44, pp. 147–191.

Weingast, Barry and Moran, Mark J. 1983: Bureaucratic Discretion of Congressional Control? Regulatory Policy-Making by the Federal Trade Commission. *Journal of Political Economy*, vol. 91, no. 5, pp. 765–800.

Welch, David A. 1998: A Positive Theory of Bureaucratic Politics? *Mershon International Studies Review*, vol. 42, pp. 205–255.

Whitford, Andrew B. 2005: The Pursuit of Political Control by Multiple Principals. *Journal of Politics*, vol. 67, no. 1, pp. 29–49.

Wilson, Woodrow 1997 (reprinted): The Study of Administration. *Political Science Quarterly*, vol. 2, no. 2, pp. 197–222.

Wonka, Arndt and Rittberger, Berthold 2010: Credibility, Complexity, and Uncertainty: Explaining Institutional Independence of 29 EU Agencies. *West European Politics*, vol. 33, no. 4, pp. 730–752.

4 The shape of things to come

The inception of the European External Action Service

As of the early 2000s, the dynamics of conflicting interests in creating joint structures at the EU level and in Brussels had not changed dramatically since the mid-1990s despite the presence of new actors (see Chapter 2, Edwards and Pijpers 1997). Already in the early to mid-1990s a small 'merger' of Commission staff into a Council foreign policy structure was seen as a possible solution to Europe's foreign policy problems, but could not in the end be agreed on. What then created the conditions for the creation of a new service that was based in Brussels and combined within itself the foreign policy structures developed in the Council Secretariat and the Community external relations? And how did we arrive at this organisation merged from three sources in the Commission, the Council Secretariat and the member states' diplomatic services?

This chapter traces the inception of the EEAS and its most basic organisational structure across the debates of the European Convention from 2001 to 2003. After highlighting the background and organisation of the European Convention, it analyses the various actors and positions through the working group and then the plenary of the Convention. It then shows how the EEAS was conceived in an environment of large-scale renegotiation of the EU's structure. The chapter concludes with an analysis of how the events of the Convention shape the EEAS in the later stages of its development and how far institutional logic explains the inception of the service.

For the EEAS, this institutional formation is to be found in the political processes at the European Convention. It was the decisions taken at the Convention that provided for a sea change in the process of connecting external relations and foreign policy in the EU and the creation of a new, third body between the European Commission and the Council Secretariat. In order to answer the first of the key questions for this study as outlined in the introduction, i.e. to answer why the EEAS was created, and why it took a specific form (see Chapter 3), it is essential to look at the Convention in more detail. What happened at the Convention with regard to the external action of the EU? Was there political conflict and how was an enacting coalition built in the process? By working out the role of the deliberations of the Convention, how and when the EEAS was entered into the text of its Treaty proposal, we will get a better understanding of the first stage of institutional creation.

80   *Inception of the EEAS*

The European Convention: background, organisation and objective

In order to trace the process of the creation of the basic structure of the EEAS at the European Convention, it is important to understand the political environment as well as the institutional organisation of the European Convention itself. Institutional structures, such as decision-making procedures, favour some actors over others and allocate resources differently between groups. This section introduces the Convention with a view to highlighting the different actors and the institutional rules applicable to their decision-making, the political orientation of the overall constitutional debate, and the substantive focus of reform debate in external action.

The Convention on the Future of Europe did not come out of nowhere. The European Union in the late 1990s and early 2000s was in a process of continual discussions on its institutional structure. Because of the prospect of enlargement, a number of new treaties never quite provided the institutional answer to the political challenges of the time, such as enlargement. The Treaty of Nice was to change the institutional set-up, and resolve the 'Amsterdam leftovers' (Shaw 2003: p. 219). It did not live up to its expectations and in a declaration to the treaty, the Heads of State and Government called for a more fundamental debate 'on the future of the Union' (Declaration no. 23, Treaty of Nice 2001). This was to include a process wider in participation than an intergovernmental conference and ultimately lead to a new intergovernmental conference in 2004. In 2001, the member states would agree in more detail on what this process should look like. The Laeken declaration (see below) was in many ways already foreseen and postponed by the Nice Treaty. The way the Convention was set up and organised contributes to the weight its decisions continued to have even after it had disbanded and its end product, the Constitutional Treaty, had been rejected.

The European Convention was a new mechanism of Treaty reform for the European Union. At least, in its form, it attempted a 'grand bargain' of European Treaty reform, which was to be the basis of all future development of the EU institutional and policy set-up. Prior to the Convention, reform discussions had taken place in a 'Group of Wise Men' nominated by the European Council (Group of Wise Men Report 1999). On the basis of this report, the Commission had contracted the European University Institute to draw up a revised Treaty addressing some of the issues such as lack of clarity in the treaty structure (European University Institute 2000: p. 1). Its proposal of a revised treaty structure with one Basic Treaty of the European Union and a consolidated Treaty on establishing the European Community has some resemblance to the outcome of the treaty changes to come, even if its authors could hardly have foreseen all of the political reverberations of the time.

Institutional reform was clearly on the agenda of the Heads of State and Government of the time. It was the European Council which called for the Convention to be established in the Laeken declaration of 2001 (European Council 2001). The Laeken European Council saw the EU as in need of changing in

Inception of the EEAS 81

order to face internal and external challenges (Allen 2004: p. 19). It was to re-constitute the EU in a time when frictions between integrationists and intergov-ernmentalists were added to by disputes along the lines of smaller versus larger member states (Allen 2004: p. 21). It was also seen as a new way to find a com-promise, where the old ways in the form of the Intergovernmental Conference had failed: 'we had to succeed where the 27 Foreign Ministers had failed and even the 15 Ministers had failed in 2000 [...] it is because they failed to get unanimity among themselves that the Convention was set up' (Interview 05, Convention member, 2011). And while the reality of the Convention for proced-ural reasons was not an exercise in a genuine deliberative setting (Allen 2004: pp. 23–24), it allowed for the negotiation of a broader consensus than an inter-governmental conference. Some scholars have called this the 'Convention paradox' (Magnette and Nicolaidis 2004: p. 382).

The Convention's mandate was deliberately left open to leave room for a variety of interpretations in order to allow for the diverse opinions of the member states on what it should do (Magnette and Nicolaidis 2004; Magnette 2005). For those member states sceptical of the Convention method for treaty reform, its objective was to present several options to governments before the intergovernmental conference. For those seeking a grand bargain, it was to present clear, legally framed recommendations to the European Council (Magnette 2005). It was part of a two-stage process and tasked with 'pav[ing] the way for the next Intergovernmental Conference as broadly and openly as possible' (European Council 2001: p. 24). Magnette and Nicolaidis illustrate how the broad mandate and reference to an intergovernmental conference were intended as safeguard against any 'constitutional ambition' of the Con-vention (Magnette and Nicolaidis 2004: p. 388). The final outcome of the Convention would still represent a step forward rather than a grand federal bargain. The questions it was to address were by nature of the Convention much larger than the organisational set-up of EU external relations, but insti-tutional questions in external relations were on the agenda of the Convention. It is necessary to take a closer look not only at the distribution of views, but also the institutional advantages and resources across actors.

Actors of the Convention

The Convention's delegates included 15 representatives of the member states' governments, 13 representatives of the governments of the candidate states, 30 members of national parliaments, 16 members of the European Parliament and two representatives from the European Commission (see Figure 4.1). The Con-vention operated under the leadership of a praesidium, the three members of which were nominated in the Laeken declaration: Valery Giscard d'Estaing as chairman, and Giuliano Amato and Jean-Luc Dehaene as deputies. The praesid-ium exercised a strong and central role over the course of the Convention (Inter-view 16, Convention Secretariat Official, 2012), but research has suggested that as the Convention continued the room for substantive influence was reduced

82 Inception of the EEAS

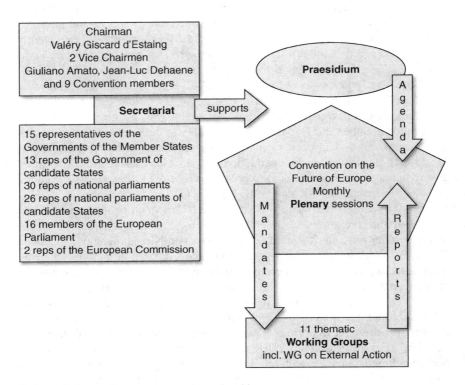

Figure 4.1 Convention structure and membership.

(Kleine 2007). This praesidium was supported in its task by a Secretariat whose officials were European and national officials and did most of the drafting of the legal text.

These procedurally privileged actors clearly envisioned a much stronger role for the Convention than did some member states' governments and even some members of the Convention. One senior Convention member described the objective as follows:

> Namely that the group as such decided, notwithstanding the fact that the mission statement mentioned that we could express different opinions, the group from the beginning said, no, we will to have consensus. Rather than give two or three contradictory schemes of concepts we will try to have consensus. And even more we will try to translate it into proposal for a Treaty. The result of that is that – and that is also the reason why we did it – we knew very well that we would have to report to the Council and that then the classical intergovernmental conference would start. But we also knew if we delivered by consensus a Treaty text, they would have no other choice then to say well we start the IGC on the basis of that text. And from that

Inception of the EEAS 83

moment you can change some elements but you are in the framework that you don't come out – and that's what happened.

(Interview 05, Convention member, 2011)

This approach narrowed the objective of the Convention considerably towards presenting at least a draft of treaty text in order to lock in as many changes as possible before the draft would be returned to the exclusive negotiation of the member states. In the end, it locked in substantive changes to the EU structure not only for the subsequent IGC, but also for the treaty review period after the rejection of the Constitutional Treaty by referendum in two member states. In many ways it framed the Lisbon Treaty, which was to be the basis of creation of the EEAS (see below and Chapters 5 and 6).

The Convention was of course not just an idealised deliberative setting, but a political body with some of the same pressures regarding time, information and political influence as other assemblies. The praesidium played a large role because it represented a clearinghouse of constant negotiations alongside the public negotiations in the Convention plenary and working groups (Finke *et al.* 2012). Because of the diverse nature of the conventioneers, the role of more experienced international politicians and permanent members of the Secretariat was augmented (Interview 01, 03, Secretariat Officials, 2011; Interview 16, Secretariat Official, 2012; Interview 05, Convention Member, 2011; see also Deloche-Gaudez 2004). Magnette and Nicolaidis have pointed out that in addition, the Convention was working 'in the shadow of the IGC' and yet managed to push the boundaries of compromise (Magnette and Nicolaidis 2004: p. 382). The Secretariat in turn did most of the drafting and even prepared the background documents on which the debates, e.g. on external action, would be based (Interview 03, Secretariat Official, 2011). A Secretariat official also noted that 'it had a certain dynamic, we had to go through the motions, but we started writing the articles very early on', lending support to the idea that the Secretariat had an influence on the outcome of the Convention (Deloche-Gaudez 2004). At the same time, they could not oppose an emerging consensus, as the case of the double-hatted High Representative illustrates below.

Among the Conventioneers, there was not only division among those with a formative role in the Convention, i.e. members of the praesidium or chairmen of the working group, but also varying levels of expertise. It was perceived by both members of the Convention as well as officials in the Secretariat that Members of the European Parliament played a dominant role in the discussions, in particular at the beginning of the Convention.

There was a serious imbalance in the level of expertise in the Convention, in that the block of MEPs were far more knowledgeable about the way the European Union worked and as a consequence far more able to propose far-reaching proposals and be able to justify them than certainly national parliamentarians.

(Interview 16, Secretariat Official, 2012)

84 *Inception of the EEAS*

The Members of the European Parliament also seemed a relatively cohesive group in terms of their outlook on the reforms debated: 'The Convention was, in terms of content, often driven by MEPs (who) were well prepared, those actually all had a very communitarian approach' (Interview 05, Convention Member, 2011). However, this advantage appears to have diminished over time, and MEPs were making particular efforts to include national parliamentarians in the deliberations (Interview 25, Convention member, 2012).

Overall, 28 Conventioneers were direct government representatives for the member states in order to ensure that consensus on the Convention floor would also reflect their wishes. At the same time, the Convention also operated under the 'shadow of an IGC' (Magnette and Nicolaidis 2004) and member states did actively shape its outcome (Allen 2004). In addition, member states' representatives could rely on institutional support from national ministries, often putting them into a better resourced position than national parliamentarians and even MEPs. Their role in the Convention increased over time, as the outcome of the Convention turned into more concrete treaty proposals and evaluations of the ability to renegotiate changed. Early in the Convention, a lot of member states operated under false assumptions:

> A number of member states felt from the outset that there is no point in creating too many waves on this or raising too many questions on how this is all going to work, (...) in any case, we can change it all later when we get to the Intergovernmental Conference, which of course turned out not to be the case at all.
>
> (Interview 16, Secretariat Official, 2012)

The appearance of foreign ministers, e.g. of France and Germany, at the Convention plenary illustrated that the stakes had increased.

With this variety of actors, it is clear that while not perfectly coherent, certain groups had stronger status than others. MEPs were a driving force behind many of ideas of the Convention and while they lost some of their advantage over the duration of the Convention, individual MEPs were at the centre of the debate on external action till the very end of the Convention. Member state representatives varied in relevance and gained stronger influence over time as the Convention continued. Even with largely cohesive groups, the debates in the Convention were shaped largely by divisions on the views on the purpose and *finalité* of European integration. These views translated into concrete manifestations in terms of institutional preferences, or what some have called 'polity ideas' (Lindner and Rittberger 2003: p. 450). The next section analyses the fundamental disagreements in the Convention and how they shaped the debates around the institutional structure in external action.

Fault lines of the Convention: solutions to the EU's external action dilemma?

The deliberations in the Convention alternated between debates in the plenary and work in working groups. The first plenary debate on external action took place on 11 July 2002. Many options for reorganising EU external relations and foreign policy were put on the table, even if often in very general and ad hoc terminology. The divisions in the Convention resembled the spread of views in an Intergovernmental Conference, but included more variety in terms of backgrounds and experience. The divisions were generally perceived as conflicts between intergovernmentalists, or sovereignists (Magnette and Nicolaidis 2004: p. 388), and federalists (Allen 2004; Magnette and Nicolaidis 2004; Magnette 2005; Rueger 2011). This is not merely an academic analysis, but represented the experience of the people actively involved in the Convention as well:

> it was not according to the spectrum of the traditional political parties, it has more to do with the division between people who saw European integration as an objective itself and those who saw European integration as a means to act better.
>
> (Interview 03, Secretariat Official, 2011)

With regard to external action, this division between these two views on European integration expressed itself in various levels of abstraction in the discussions about foreign policy and external relations policy-making, the design of the office of the High Representative, and in the administrative arrangement in this policy area. Relations between the High Representative and the Commissioner for External Relations turned out to be a focal point for the institutional debate.

In the foreign policy debates, focusing on the EU's problems of consistency and coherence in external action, this divergence of views alongside the integrationist–intergovernmentalist spectrum was very visible. One recurring proposal to increase coherence was the introduction of a qualified majority in foreign policy decision-making. An alternate member of the Convention made several proposals in order to 'promote the Community method in the External actions of the EU' (Working Group VII, Working Document 11 WG VII WD 11). These proposals were met with scepticism not only by other members of the Convention, who attempted to make the member states central to EU external action (e.g. WG VII WD 40), but also by the advisory backbone of the Convention:

> Many people in the Convention thought, CFSP doesn't work because it is intergovernmental, so if there is more decision by the EU, then everything will be fine. But, of course, it's not like that.
>
> (Interview 03, Secretariat Official, 2011)

This illustrates the division on a more general matter of decision-making, but the divergences continued all the way through to the institutional structures of EU

86 *Inception of the EEAS*

external action. The central argument in both Working Group and Plenary was about how to connect the institutionally divided policy arenas of foreign policy and EU external relations for more political impact in the world. The main focus turned out to be the role and status of the High Representative in the new Treaty.

Linchpin in external action? The High Representative's hats?

The debate around the highest external representative of the EU, following in the footsteps of the High Representative Javier Solana, was at the heart of institutional reorganisation. Most contributors to the debate focused on the relations between the High Representative and the European Commissioner for External Relations. Also in the role of the HR, reform offers varied between federalist and intergovernmentalist visions in the Convention. The most common proposal for change was some form of merger of the two posts, varying in detail and in final location of the office. A good number of MEPs, e.g. Elmar Brok and Rene van der Linden from the European People's Party (EPP), proposed a merger into the Commission. Brok and the Swedish Parliament's representative Lennmakers also insisted on a single administrative centre:

> When it comes to the decision-making procedures, it is time we no longer had three units: the Commission, the Council and the foreign office of the presidency. It is time to merge them into one. We cannot have three foreign ministries or state departments.
> (Goeran Lennmaker, Verbatim Record, European Convention, 7 July 2002)

The German government's representative later in the debate also suggested this and stated the need for an 'effective diplomatic service' forged from three elements (Verbatim Record, European Convention 7 July 2002).

MEP Bonde, on the other side of the spectrum of the debate, insisted on the continuation of cooperation procedures between 'sovereign nations' (Verbatim record, European Convention, 7 July 2002). Even Peter Hain, the British government's representative, proposed that the High Representative chair the Foreign Affairs Council and be given the right of initiative. While this did not amount to a fundamental change, it was nevertheless a reserved step towards integration. The French representative Moscovici insisted that the diplomatic arrangement be located in the Council.

Despite the nuances, the majority of contributors to the debate supported a stronger push towards a reorganisation of EU external action structures, at least at the highest level. In this overall climate of the debate, it was up to a working group to develop a more structured and coherent proposal that could be the basis of a compromise. Working Group VII under the chairmanship of former Belgian Prime Minister Jean-Luc Dehaene was concerned with External Action and thus covered not only external action policy and its legal framework but also institutional questions. It met for the first time on 24 September 2002 after having been given a mandate by the plenary (European Convention CONV 252/02). The

Inception of the EEAS 87

working groups, after the first round of plenary discussions, worked independently on a report with specific suggestions for changes in EU external action.

Agents at work? Working Group VII on External Action

Working Group VII on External Action was expected to give recommendations that might remedy perceived shortcomings in this policy area, for example the perceived incoherence and ineffectiveness of EU external action. Its remit did exclude security and defence policy, which was to be considered in another working group. The big debates in the Working Group were clearly more about the decision-making process in external relations and about the apex of the administrative bodies, the future shape of the office of High Representative for Common Foreign and Security Policy. But discussions about organisational structure were predominantly held in Working Group VII. As the concept of a European External Action Service appeared in a draft report of this group, the analysis of the Convention in external relations will focus on this particular part and the actors in it.

After a first deliberation in plenary, a mandate gave the group the general outline of its expected output to be referred back to the plenary (European Convention 252/02). It included questions on how to define the Union's interest in EU external affairs, how to ensure coherence of its diverse actions in trade, development and other international policy areas and how to improve the external representation of the EU abroad (European Convention 252/02: pp. 2–4). Even though this appears more abstract than the administrative set-up in EU external affairs, the issue of administrative organisational structure formed a substantive part of this reform debate. It features on the one hand in debates about the High Representative; in the discussions about the administrative support this role should have, but also in the debate about the Unions external representation (see Appendix 1). In the summaries of the first debates written by the Convention's Secretariat, the diplomatic service is actually only mentioned explicitly once (European Convention 342/02). But this is not a good measure of the saliency of the issue. Looking at the contributions to the debate gives a better picture of the variety of opinions and contributions on structuring the EU's diplomatic efforts in the future.

In the working group debates in autumn 2002, a full range of options appears. Elmar Brok, the conservative German MEP, contributed first in a letter to the Chairman of the group, proposing a 'Commissioner for Foreign Relations' (Working Group VII (WG) Working Document (WD) 2). As one of the most outspoken MEPs participating in the Convention, he then also advocated in debates a merger of the High Representative office with the External Relations Commission into the Commission (WG WD 17). This new 'double-hatted' figure would be supported by the European Commission (WG WD 17). This arrangement was supported by other members of the group, e.g. Adrian Severin, a Romanian parliament representative who advocated a transfer of the Council Secretariat staff and establishment of a 'diplomatic service inside the Commission' (WG WD 11). The

88 *Inception of the EEAS*

former Belgian Foreign Minister, Louis Michel, called for a reinforced Policy Unit of the Council at the service of both institutions. It would serve a High Representative who had been integrated into the Commission (WG WD 4).

The proposal of the double-hat position attracted criticism from the Convention Secretariat. The seconded diplomats had experience in member states diplomacy and European foreign policy and were thus acutely aware of the differences in methods and tools in comparison to the Commission (Interview 03, Convention Secretariat official, 2011). Across all debates in the Working Group, the Secretariat was still an actor in its own right (Allen 2004: p. 24; Deloche-Gaudez 2004; Interview 03, Convention Secretariat Official, 2011), largely also because the Secretariat did most of the drafting. Despite this initial opposition in the Secretariat, German representatives Pleuger and Bury are on record as repeatedly expressing the strong support of the German government for the double-hatted position leading the EU's external action while maintaining separate administrative structures (European Convention 2002 WG VII WD 17: p. 3). But the German government also wanted a reinforcement of the existing Council structure, in the form of a 'European Foreign Policy Unit' (WG WD 17). Irish delegate Bobby McDonagh voiced a similar position, but also mentioned the need for common services between Commission and Council Secretariat (WG WD 16). Between these options, a preliminary draft report outlined three choices for the question of the High Representative post: practical measures to improve coordination, full merger into the Commission or a 'double-hat' EU Minister of Foreign Affairs (WG WD 21).

The group also heard evidence from the individuals holding the offices in question at that time, i.e. the High Representative Javier Solana, the Deputy Secretary-General of the Council Pierre de Boissieu, the Commissioner for External Relations Chris Patten, and Commissioner for Trade Pascal Lamy and Commissioner for Development Poul Nielsen. Neither the HR and his Deputy, nor the RELEX Commissioner showed any support for the integrationist position, nor did they support the merger of the tasks of HR and RELEX Commissioner:

> The Commission and High Representative have distinct responsibilities: merging these functions would, in my view, create more confusion than synergy.
>
> (Javier Solana, Speech before the External Action
> Working Group 15 October 2002)

While Solana may not have entirely disagreed with the ultimate aim of some of the more federalist members of the Convention, he voiced his preference for a more moderate approach to development by 'such pragmatic pooling of resources (that) offers the potential to develop a "European Foreign Ministry" at a pace and in a manner the Member States feel comfortable with' (European Convention 2002 WG VII WD 8: pp. 9–10). In contrast, the Commissioners for both Trade and Development supported the creation of 'one centre of gravity' in EU external relations (European Convention 356/02), Nielson even going so far

Inception of the EEAS 89

as to place that centre in the European Commission. The 'one centre of gravity' expression was also the key message of the Commission's first input to the Convention (European Commission 2002c). Only in December 2002 would the Commission's position include an explicit reference to a 'single administration resourced from the General Secretariat (...), the Commission and the Member States' (European Commission 2002d: p. 13).

Despite developing these options, the debate continued on a similar spectrum in November. MEP Brok reiterated his position with the catchphrase 'one person, one administration' (WG WD 26). Together with Convention members Severin, Lamassoure and van der Linden, he proposed an integrationist solution, creating a 'Foreign Minister of the European Union FMEU' (WG WD 30). A day after this contribution Czech government representative Jan Kohout repeated the more moderate improvement of the Policy Unit in the Council (WG WD 33), which was also still maintained by German government representatives (WG WD 28). Portuguese representative Ernani Lopes issued the most strongly worded caution from the intergovernmentalist side, considering 'premature the setting up of a EU diplomatic service' (WG WD 34). Lopes equally had 'reservations on the idea that delegations of the Commission should become EU embassies' (WG WD 34). UK government representative Hain also contributed to a more intergovernmental view of the reforms by asking to delete references to a foreign minister and the idea that delegations would service the member states (WG WD 40). The British position included the need to use 'existing resources' and 'avoid duplication' (WG WD 40), stipulations which were to reappear in later stages of the discussions even long after the Convention.

Several variations existed between these different poles. A French parliament representative proposed a foreign minister post but with separate structures in the administration (WG WD 49). The Dutch government representative did not want references to a foreign minister, but supported opening the diplomatic service of the Commission to staff from the Council Secretariat (WG WD 47). An Austrian proposal included the merger of either 'some substructures' of the administrations of Council and Commission (WG WD 36) with a view to creating a 'Foreign Service' (WG WD 36). Danuta Huebner, who represented the Polish government, saw it as an opportunity:

> I would also like to stress that the double-hatting exercise will do away with the discrepancy between the two services – DG Relex and Secretariat General of the Council – creating an opportunity for establishing a Foreign Policy Commission. A single diplomatic service drawing heavily on seconded officials from the member-states as well as services of the Commission will not only allow to optimise the available resources but will also create the basis for greater unity of ideas and values.
>
> (WG WD 51)

The 'Foreign Policy Chief' would be a facilitator between these two different institutional logics (WG WD 51).

90   Inception of the EEAS

These different positions were not easily reconcilable. An overview of the variety of options discussed at this point (see Table 4.1) illustrates at least five categories of proposals. All of the most favoured options were integrationist to varying degrees. Only individual government representatives were supporting the status quo arrangements between Commission and Council and even fewer attempted to work for a slight repatriation of powers to the national level.

While Table 4.1 shows the variety of options available to Conventioneers, it also clearly illustrates the integrationist leaning even in the institutional arrangements in foreign policy. The status quo, or indeed any renationalisation of roles in foreign policy, was a minority view and did not receive serious consideration during the debates. Nevertheless, this did not pre-define the precise nature of institutional change. The course of debates in working group and plenary highlights in more detail how a specific compromise on institutional change was entered into the overall draft.

A tableau of options

At the end of November, the Secretariat and Group leadership had revised the Draft final report to take into account the evolution of the debate. It did so mainly by incorporating the wide differences in a set of options presented in a structured manner. The revised draft final report subsequently presented an increased number of options, both on the question of the HR and on the question of the administrative support structure (WG WD 21/1). These ranged from (a) simple practical measures to support the separate functions of the HR, (b) a full merger of administrative structures into the Commission, (c) a 'double-hatted' merger with a variety of

Table 4.1 Categories of reform considered during Convention

Integration level/ Org. element	Federalist	Integrationist	Limited integration	Status quo	Status quo 'minus'
Head	Foreign Minister	European External Representative	High Representative	HR and separate Commissioner	HR in Council
Deputy/-ies	Political	Political + Community deputies	–	–	–
Administration	Commission	Commission/ new entity	New entity	Status Quo (SQ)	SQ
Delegations	Integral part of service	Integral part of service	Delegations under COM	SQ	SQ
Staff	Merger of 3	Merger of 3	Additional national diplomats	SQ	SQ

Source: own compilation.

Inception of the EEAS   91

titles, and (d) a double-hatted merger with deputies for CFSP and Community policies, to (e) an EU Foreign Minister under the President of the European Council (WG WD 21/1). With regard to the administrative support, any double-hatted arrangement would include a 'joint service of DG RELEX officials, the Council Secretariat, and seconded staff from national diplomatic service' or keep 'distinct administrations with separate merged service for CFSP with a joint Private Office' (WG WD 21/1). By the end of November 2002, the structure was still disputed but a new merged organisation was on the table of the working group.

There was also a clear link between this option and the double-hat arrangement of having a High Representative also in charge of the Commission portfolio of External Relations. This favouring of a direct link between the double-hat figure at the helm of EU external action and a joint service below was mirrored in an interview with a senior Convention member:

> It was also a concern that we needed a service, and naturally, when we came up with the idea of the double hat with the Commission, immediately the idea of one service for the two functions was raised. So in the discussions, we had also lots of discussions with Patten (…). At the start, he was very near to the position of Solana, but following our discussions he evolved and was very supportive for what the working group had proposed. Solana never accepted completely what we proposed.
>
> (Interview 05, Convention Member, 2011)

The majority of amendments supported a double-hatted arrangement and differed only on the question of whether this should be supported by a single administration or not. The German delegation went into more detail of what a double-hat arrangement would entail in order to convince sceptics (WG WD 53). Only a week after the first revision of the report in November 2002, a second version included a much clearer recommendation: at the head of the external representation of the EU should be the double-hatted 'European External Representative' and this office should be supported by the 'creation of one joint service (European External Action Service) composed of DG RELEX officials, Council Secretariat officials and staff seconded from national diplomatic services' (WG WD 21/2). It was in this revised version of the report that the European External Action Service was named. From here on, it would become one of the standard elements in the discussion of the EU's organisational architecture in foreign policy and external relations. At the same time, its report on the discussions continued to reflect the diversity of proposals that had been presented in the working group.

A third revision of the Draft Final Report in early December 2002 did nothing to fundamentally alter the shape of the recommendations (WG WD 21/3). It did, however, spell out additional details, which included the creation of a 'diplomatic service' and an 'EU diplomatic academy' (WG WD 21/3). The report also specified some decision-making changes, which included the proposal to have

92 Inception of the EEAS

the European External Representative chair the Foreign Affairs Council and allow the post holder to coordinate external relations portfolios inside the European Commission (WG WD 21/3).

A few days after the third revision, on 12 December 2002, another round of proposed changes was brought forward. The Finnish representative asked to insert the long-term goal of integrating the service into the Commission (WG WD 61), while Peter Hain, the UK's government representative, repeated his opposition to the double-hat position as well as the creation of a diplomatic service or EU embassies (WG WD 66). A Swedish representative (WG WD 68) and French government representative (WG WD 72) echoed this criticism of the 'double-hatted post'. More generally, member state representatives from states with strong traditions of independent diplomacy and large member states proved more sceptical about such a merger. Support for the institutional arrangements proposed in the report came from MEPs Elmar Brok, Pervenche Beres and John Cushnahan (WG WD 70, WG WD 71). The German position evolved in the process, embracing the merger approach of bringing together staff from different sources. The first step in adaptation was to maintain DG RELEX but develop

> a consolidated foreign policy unit ('European Foreign Policy Unit'), which should consist of those parts of the Council Secretariat currently responsible for foreign policy (...) and of civil servants seconded for a certain period from the member states and the Commission.
> (European Convention 2002 WG VII, WD 28: p. 3)

The main element of interest next to the double-hat arrangement seems to have been that:

> the person holding the function of HR, [...] it was essential for him/her to have sufficient staff at his/her disposal in Brussels, and underlined the importance of strengthening his/her staff with seconded diplomats and officials of the Commission and the Council Secretariat.
> (Amendment by Hans Martin Bury, 12 December 2002, WD 63, WG VII: p. 20)

The French government's representative Dominique du Villepin inserted amendments introducing into the debate the position of a EU foreign minister, placed organisationally under the President of the European Council, but did not specify organisational arrangements underneath the new post (WD 52, WG VII). In that sense, the French and German positions were largely compatible. On the other side of the debate on the double-hat, the representative of Finland repeatedly deleted reference to the double-hat in various versions of the draft final report (European Convention 2002 WG VII WD 61). From these contributions it becomes clear that even the more basic shape of the new external relations organisation was still in dispute by the end of 2002. Nevertheless, even the more critical voices generally did not question the need for some kind of new

Inception of the EEAS 93

institutional arrangement. An exception to this general trend was the British position, which was expressed by Peter Hain:

> One final point: of course it makes sense to increase contact between Commission, Council Secretariat and Member State diplomats working on EU external policy. But greater coherence is not the same as merger. Why create new institutions such as an EU Diplomatic Service and EU Embassies when we can cooperate much better in more practical ways?
>
> (P. Hain, Intervention 20 December 2002, Verbatim Record, European Convention)

This pragmatic line of keeping two separate organisational entities with separate leadership was, however, not supported by the majority in the group and also not by the chairman of the group. The majority of conventioneers in the working group supported the double-hat arrangement as a 'compromise between inter-governmentalists and integrationists' (Rueger 2011: p. 208). Most strongly expressed support came from representatives of the European Parliament and the German government. It was equally accepted in the process that a joint administrative arrangement would be supporting the new office:

> Someone said, now we've got this single post of High Representative we can't continue to have two separate administrations. We need to bring these administrations together. And in a sense, it looked so obvious at the time, I don't recall anyone seriously challenging that, not necessarily as a bad idea per se, but at least saying well, but how is this going to work? What are the issues that this is going to throw up? I don't think we had that discussion really at all. It was one of those proposals within the Convention that extremely rapidly just became acquis within the Convention. Yes, you know the big issue was the High Representative, there were discussions around that, but once that had been proposed, it seemed to flow quite naturally that following on from that there should be a joint administrative structure for the high representative.
>
> (Interview 16, Secretariat Official, 2012)

The working group in the end settled for a mix of the positions discussed above (see also Appendix 2), with a clear tilt towards the federalist vision of a foreign minister supported by a single organisation, the European External Action Service. It committed itself to creating a new organisation, with staff from the Commission, the Council Secretariat and the member states' diplomatic services. It also agreed on the (at that stage) much less controversial issue of EU delegations. On 16 December 2012, the working group issued its Final Report, which included the 'European External Representative' as single post covering both the tasks of the High Representative and the European Commissioner for External Relations (European Convention 459/02). It also foresaw the 'establishment of one joint service (European External Action Service) composed of DG RELEX

94 *Inception of the EEAS*

officials, Council Secretariat officials and staff seconded from national diplomatic services' (European Convention 459/02). The additional elements added in the second revision, i.e. a diplomatic academy as well as a diplomatic service with EU embassies, were equally retained (European Convention 459/02). A journalist observing the Convention later evaluated the working group report: 'It was a skillfully drafted work that glossed over divisions inside the group' (Norman 2003: p. 112). He observed that

> the report's significance lay in the way it maximized partial agreement in the working group to push an integrationist agenda. Its conclusions were a synthesis between the community and intergovernmental method of running an area of policy where, in the previous ten years, considerations of national sovereignty had meant little movement away from the system agreed at Maastricht.
>
> (Norman 2003: p. 114)

From working group to plenary

The working group's report then made its way back to the plenary of the Convention on 20 December 2002. The contributions to this debate highlight how far the discussions in the group had come to gather support for the structure recommended (see Appendix 1). More than 30 speakers professed varying levels of enthusiasm for the double-hat solution of merging the High Representative's office with the office of Commissioner for External Relations (Verbatim Record, European Convention, 20 December 2002). Criticism of the double-hat arrangement was voiced not only by intergovernmentalists, but also by more federalist-minded members of the Convention. An intervention by Andrew Duff in the December plenary debate illustrates some of the concerns of the Convention members on this point:

> In fact increasingly as the debate proceeds I begin to feel fairly sorry for the European External Representative. There is still a certain clumsiness in the relationship between the Commission and the Council. **It is not impossible to serve two masters, but it is improbable**. I find especially worrying the fact that the person will be a full member of the Commission with a mandate from the Council. He will be able to act without the authority or even the agreement of the Commission. *It is a recipe for a fraught relationship with the President of the Commission, and he could easily be seen to be a Council cuckoo in the Commission's nest.* My own preference is firmly for option two, as summarised in the Dehaene report.
>
> (European Convention Verbatim Record 20 December 2002
> (emphasis added))

Of course, this does not mean that support was unanimous. Several members of the Convention, including the British government representative Hain, Swedish

Inception of the EEAS 95

government representative Hjelm Wallen, Estonian Parliamentarian Tunne Kelam, as well as Peter Skaarup from the Danish Folketing, expressed concerns about this arrangement. Also the Spanish government representative Dastis and Portuguese Parliamentarian Azevedo urged caution and noted that there was a need to study these options in more detail before committing to them (Verbatim Record, European Convention, 20 December 2002). Nevertheless, these opposing, or at least more cautious voices, were vastly outnumbered in the debate.

As the joint service had by this point in the debate become almost a necessary next step from the double-hat position, it received only a few mentions of specific support in this debate. But the question of the service would resurface almost at the very end of the Convention.

Plenary struggles and intergovernmental agreements

Both documentary evidence and interviews show that the final agreement on the institutional structure in external relations was also dependent on the settlement of other, at the time of debate, open institutional questions like the European Council Presidency. One aspect mirrored in the debates of the Convention was the relationship between the permanent President of the European Council and the High Representative/Union Minister for Foreign Affairs. Many members in the WG on External Action were against the creation of such a permanent post at the helm of the EU. Later in the process the chairman of the working group turned this juxtaposition of views into a bargaining tool. In negotiations with the Chairman of the Convention, an ardent supporter of the post of President, an agreement was reached that included both positions in the final text coming out of the Convention (Interview 5, Convention Member, 2011). This also reflected the Franco-German agreement, which was published in early 2003 and included an EU foreign minister together with a more permanent president for the European Council. The Franco-German proposal, at least in terms of symbolism, went a bit further than other proposals with respect to the external service, referring to a 'Europäischer Diplomatischer Dienst' ('European Diplomatic Service'). The organisational structure, however, was the same: DG RELEX with parts of the Council Secretariat and the member states diplomatic services.

When a bilateral understanding on institutional questions had been found between the German and the French delegates, the institutional set-up of the EU according to the Convention began to take a more reliable shape. This included not only the double-hat of an EU's external representative, but also a 'double presidency' with an elected president of the European Council alongside the Commission President. The final version of the institutional arrangement made at the Convention also left a loophole for further institutional consolidation at the helm of the EU: while the President of the European Council was precluded from holding a national office, the Draft Constitutional Treaty remained silent as to whether he may hold another European office to allow for a merger with the position of President of the European Commission (Interview 5, Convention Member, 2011).

96 *Inception of the EEAS*

Nevertheless, the institutional set-up in external action did not naturally find unanimous approval. Commission representatives O'Sullivan and Ponzano repeatedly entered amendments making the Commission the sole representative of the Union for Union matters, leaving the new foreign minister to be responsible for CFSP only (O'Sullivan and Ponzano, am to art. 35). They also introduced amendments aimed at underlining the situation of the delegations within the Commission system, rather than in the new service with an amendment to art 36 of the draft treaty:

> Union delegations, **which are part of the services of the Commission**, shall operate under the authority of the Union's Minister for Foreign Affairs. **These delegations and Member States' missions in third countries shall cooperate closely.**

The purpose of this amendment was to 'clarify that the 128 delegations of the Commission, which will become Union delegations, will continue to be managed administratively by the Commission' (O'Sullivan and Ponzano am to art. 35). While the precise timing of the amendments cannot be ascertained from the archives of the Convention, the thrust of Commission amendments is clear: that since there will not be one centre of gravity inside the Commission, the new service should largely be a CFSP organisation.

The text of the draft treaty including the EEAS struggled to find a fixed place in the drafting of the overall document. It was only specified later in a declaration on the service. Text on the EEAS had not been entered into the Convention draft treaty at the beginning. Only after several amendments tried to rectify this, was the first mention of the service entered into a footnote to article I-27 only in May 2003. By May, institutional discussions had entered plenary in full swing. Despite following a general trend, details like the title of the double-hatted post were still to be ironed out, but the institutional settlement had gained acceptance. Proposed amendments included terms such as 'Secretary of Union' (Duff +5 am. 11); 'European External Representative' (Hain am. 16); 'Foreign Representative' (Huebner am. 21); 'Foreign Minister' ('Aussenminister') (Kaufmann am. 22); 'Minister for Foreign Affairs' (Kelam *et al.* am. 19); 'External Representative of the European Union' (Liepina *et al.* am. 28); 'European Representative for External Relations' (Queiro am. 34); 'Union Minister for Foreign Affairs' (Roche *et al.* am. 34) or 'Member of the Commission' (Helle am. 18). France's representatives also still attempted in vain to subordinate the foreign minister to the new President of the European Council (de Villepin am. 10). Joschka Fischer still added some fine details to the draft, e.g. that the Political and Security Committee be chaired by a representative of the foreign minister (am. 2). Other proposals, such as the creation of at least two deputies for the two policy arenas that the foreign minister will deal with, also failed to gain traction in the Convention (Huebner am. 21, Liepina *et al.* am. 28, Roche *et al.* am. 35).

There were also continued amendments deleting references to a foreign minister and other elements that presented a symbolic advance in integration of

Inception of the EEAS 97

foreign policy, such as creating a permanent chair of the Foreign Affairs Council or independent actions of the Union Minister (Bonde amendments to art 35; Hain amendment, Heathcote-Amory amendment to art 36). Nevertheless, the documentary evidence is overwhelmingly on the side of deeper integration. The settlement found was a double-hatted post with extended competences. Because of the way some amendments have been archived, it is not possible to date them precisely. But since they refer to draft versions of the constitutional treaty, they must have originated in the later stages of the Convention. This highlights the underlying conflicts surrounding some of the compromises coming out of the working groups as well as the drafts on treaty text deriving from them.

At the end of June 2003, Foreign Minister Fischer proposed adding a declaration on the service to the annex of the treaty draft (European Convention 821/03; see also Norman 2003: pp. 295–296). A month later, joint amendments were proposed by Elmar Brok, Andrew Duff and Giuliano Amato to bring the service firmly into the Commission's fold (European Convention 829/03), but failed to secure full support. The political conflict has not completely been settled. Due to the nature of the Convention, nothing was agreed until everything was agreed. But the combined efforts of several different actors showed the need for at least some elaboration of administrative detail on the service. The EEAS was entered into the second draft constitution through a sub-paragraph on the foreign minister, a footnote and a declaration in the annex (European Convention 836/03). Dissatisfied with the current state of play, the Commission representatives Barnier and Vitorino attempted to win approval of an amendment introducing the 'Joint European External Action Service' as a headquarters organisation in the European Commission (European Convention 839/03). This amendment also failed to gain support and the draft remained substantially unchanged.

Another attempt to include the EEAS in the Commission

Towards the end of the Convention, in July 2003, final discussions on the external action package came to a head. Amendments to the drafts presented by the chairman and the Secretariat show the vast differences between members of the Convention, spanning the European divide between integrationist, pragmatist and to a lesser extent eurosceptic positions. Members of the Convention were unhappy at the drafting of the text on the European External Action Service. The debate, which had already been rehearsed half a year earlier, resurfaced quickly. Brok argued again for an explicit inclusion of the service in the European Commission, rather than creating the service 'in a footnote' (Verbatim Record, European Convention, 4 July 2003):

> I think it is not right to create, through a footnote in part III and a declaration, a new external Service, which could be interpreted in a way that it is a third organisation between Commission and Council.
>
> We cannot allow that de facto a new administration exists under the Foreign Minister, that the President of the Commission and the Commission

98   *Inception of the EEAS*

exist only as single market machine and thus create a restriction of the rights of the European Parliament.

> (European Convention Verbatim Record, 4 July 2003
> (Own translation))

A lot of voices re-appeared arguing for the inclusion of the service into the Commission. It was the then German Foreign Minister Fischer who was defending the vague agreement found in the Convention with expressed but lukewarm support from the French government representative (Verbatim Record, European Convention, 4 July 2003). Fischer specified only that the new service would remain governed by the conditions of employment of the Commission:

> There will be a unitary external representation; *with regard to conditions of employment it will remain part of the apparatus of the Commission. It will thus far also be under the budgetary control and the overall political control of the European Parliament.* I could wish for more. This is only to maintain a balance between the double-hat functions, which are attached on the one hand to the Council and on the other to the Commission.
>
> *The control remains in a unitary administration with the Commission; it remains a unitary European administration.* It is controlled, of course, where Parliament has rights of control, as far as it concerns control of the Commission and it will be then a part of a common external service, while naturally the other parts of the Commission also continue to exist.
>
> (European Convention Verbatim Record, 4 July 2003
> (Emphasis added; own translation))

Brok responded directly to FM Fischer's remarks, complaining in particular about the openness to interpretation of the agreement.

> If all of the things that he has said were in the text that he has put forward, I could move in his direction. But since all of that is not there, most interpret the text the way I did. Thus, it is either a bad text, or it has been manipulated on purpose. I ask the praesidium for these reasons to look at it intensively again, so that we can have clarification, because this formula is not even the opinion of Minister Fischer. It is for that reason *necessary to prevent this third bureaucracy, this kind of kingdom in the middle, from being constructed.* European Convention Verbatim Record, 4 July 2003.
>
> (Original in German. Emphasis added; own translation)

Several speakers in the debate argued for a need to be more precise on the service, such as the Italian parliamentarian Dini:

> There must be a clarification of the relationship between the European Union diplomatic service and the Commission. We debated that this morning, with an exchange of views between Mr Fischer and Mr Brok. *We*

Inception of the EEAS 99

believe that we ought to revise the wording to make sure that we do not create a body that is entirely unique, autonomous and independent of the Commission, but one that has some relationship.

(European Convention Verbatim Record, 4 July 2003 (Emphasis added))

Brok and Fischer were left to work on a joint text on the details of the service during the debate (Verbatim Record, European Convention 4 July 2003). Unsurprisingly, considering the differences on the floor and the agreement between governments, the final outcome fell far short of putting forward concrete organisational proposals. The issue of the European diplomatic service and its structure were thus only settled on an abstract level. While it was regretted in the Secretariat that there had not been enough time to 'work out a better plan for the EEAS', it was also acknowledged that further discussions on details 'would have destabilized the agreement' (Interview 3, Convention Secretariat official, 2011). The EEAS was thus left without a clear structure or indication which part(s) of the EU institutions would enter into it. This vagueness would, of course, continue to exert knock-on effects in later stages of the creation of the new service, when exactly these conflicts resurface during the establishment of the EEAS (see Chapters 5 and 6).

A stable compromise: the fate of the draft Constitutional Treaty

The European External Action Service was finally entered into a paragraph in the second chapter of Title V on Common Foreign and Security Policy of the Constitutional Treaty and a declaration as to its composition and creation. This less than prominent positioning had to do with the central focus on the foreign minister role and would come back to be used as evidence of the service's minor institutional role.

The draft Constitutional Treaty was then put forward from the Convention to an Intergovernmental Conference setting, which took place between October 2003 and June 2004. As members of the Convention had guessed, member states found themselves in a bind over the substance of the treaty. A careful balance of compromise had been created at the Convention, which proved difficult to change at the IGC, despite resulting in political upheavals at the time (König and Finke 2012a: pp. 154–169). This stickiness is illustrated by the German government's rather rigid position stating that the result of the Convention 'should not be questioned' and that 'whoever brings up a question also carries the responsibility of finding a new consensus' (Intergovernmental Conference 2003 CIG 14/03). A document of the Italian Presidency highlighted that in particular the position of 'Union Minister of Foreign Affairs' was 'widely considered to be one of the main achievements of the Convention' (Presidency Intergovernmental Conference 2003 CIG 2/03). The Note continues: 'The concept of double-hatted Foreign Minister has not been called into question by any delegation' (Presidency CIG 2/03). This of course is only the precursor to highlight those

100 *Inception of the EEAS*

more specific issues that delegates of the IGC did find troublesome, such as the standing of the foreign minister in the European Commission (Presidency Intergovernmental Conference 2003 CIG 2/03: pp. 1–2).

Despite these discussions, the inability to bring the IGC to a conclusion immediately, and some significant subsequent changes in Treaty text regarding, e.g. the specific rules of resignation of the Union Minister and the post's role in chairing the Foreign Affairs Council, the administrative and organisational characteristics remained stable across the different versions of the Draft Constitutional Treaty. Appendix 4 shows that the IGCs merely moved text from a declaration into the treaty leaving only procedural points on the establishment of the service in the Declaration on the EEAS. Because of the stable nature of the double-hat arrangement and its direct linkage to the EEAS, the service survived the IGCs in 2003/04 and 2007/08 intact. Appendix 4 also shows how diligently the treaty text had been transposed after the rejection of the Constitutional Treaty in the Netherlands and France, highlighting the effect of the choice to make the treaty negotiations with reference to the Constitutional draft treaty (König and Finke 2012a). The wording of the Lisbon Treaty on the service corresponds perfectly to the wording of the earlier IGC text. Despite reducing the symbolic title of 'Union Minister' back to a more limited High Representative, no deviation from the original draft was introduced in the future organisational structure of the EU in external action.

The IGC thus adopted the elements of external action substantially unchanged. This holds equally true for the subsequent rebranding of the draft constitutional treaty into the Lisbon Treaty, again driven also largely by German reform considerations (König and Finke 2012b: pp. 174–175) on overall EU structures. In the end, the Convention consensus narrowed the available policy space considerably, determining that the external relations structure would be run by one individual with two functions and supported by an independent service merged from the European Commission, the Council Secretariat and the member states diplomatic services. Of course, these are only general elements and do not settle precise terms of the creation of the new external service. This was to be negotiated at a later stage between another set of actors (see Chapter 5). At the same time, the basic understanding of the EEAS as a 'tripartite' organisation that was not fully integrated into one of the existing institutions would not be changed in the implementation process.

Conclusion

Tracing the process of decision-making in the Convention on the Future of Europe reveals the origin of the European External Action Service as a political organisation. While its organisational roots may lie with the Council Secretariat's structures and the European Commission's external service, its political roots are in the European Convention. Previous attempts at creating a merged administration linking EU foreign policy with EU external relations had failed (see Chapter 2). The Convention, however, provided an arena that allowed the

Inception of the EEAS 101

institutional rules of treaty change to be stretched, opening up something of a critical juncture for institutional change. Due to the inclusion of various groups, MEPs, national parliamentarians and representatives of candidate states, a wider bargain was found than could have been possible in an intergovernmental conference.

In the case of the EEAS, the driving force in the Convention was the political conflict between integrationists and intergovernmentalists. Both camps naturally contained within themselves a variety of individual opinions. Only in a broad compromise pushed forward by MEPs and the praesidium did the Convention create a double-hatted figure of 'High Representative' or 'Foreign Minister', who would be supported by a new tripartite organisation, the EEAS. The wording with regard to the new organisation was deliberately vague so as to allow for a number of possible interpretations, much to the chagrin of several MEPs. In particular Elmar Brok's hope that the new service ought not to be a third organisation in addition to Commission and Council Secretariat was in vain.

In these negotiations, actors found a compromise, which did not resemble the preferred shape of any particular individual or group, but rather represents an amalgam of interests of the member states, MEPs, national parliamentarians and European institutions. The political conflict that drove the direction of the Convention discussions was between integrationist-federalist Convention members and those that supported more intergovernmental solutions. Because of this political conflict, the Convention set out only the most general rules regarding the new service, avoiding detail where agreement could not be found. As a result, while deciding on the creation of the EEAS and setting the ground rules for the EEAS, it left the duties, functioning and organisation characteristics to be worked out later.

This broadest of possible enacting coalitions was driven by the Praesidium's intention to present a coherent treaty text by the entire Convention rather than presenting a study of a variety of options. It was championed in the Convention by a group of integrationist MEPs in conjunction with the leadership of the Convention, who left a central imprint on the institutional design. In a sub-group of the Convention, the working group on external action, the EEAS was conceived and supported by a majority of the members and the group's influential chairman. The EEAS was nevertheless also contested in plenary by a number of actors, including the European Commission whose representatives first tried to bring it into its structure and later attempted to remove elements from the service. The EEAS only entered the treaty proposal firmly at the end of the drafting period. The service and its very basic structure were entered into this draft treaty through something that resembled a logrolling process: some members of the Convention and Member States accepted each other's demands in exchange for acceptance of their ideas on the new EU external action structure. A Franco-German institutional reform agreement backed up the compromise. It included a double-hatted 'foreign minister', strongly supported by the German government and many MEPs in the Convention – as well as a permanent President of the

102 *Inception of the EEAS*

European Council, which many MEPs had objected to vigorously. The French conception of the European Council President will continue to influence discussions in the latest consolidation stage (see Chapter 7). The shape of this enacting coalition was thus very diverse. Due to the differences between the views of the actors, the institutional compromise remained vague. This had knock-on effects in the subsequent building of an enacting coalition, as illustrated in Chapter 5. But it is clear that it was the political compromise in the Convention that must be considered the moment of inception of the EEAS.

This consensus draft treaty provision on external action was later more or less carried over by intergovernmental conferences, carefully removing titles and language that resemble a state-like structure in external action and elsewhere after the failure of ratification. The fact that most of the substantial agreements, however vague, made it past a complicated set of intergovernmental negotiations (for a detailed description see König and Finke 2012) showed in many ways how surprisingly stable the main compromises were. Member states, despite having veto powers over treaty change, found themselves unable to stop an integrationist move and only managed to enter limited changes. The institutional structure of the Convention in combination with the drive by the Convention leadership to produce treaty text produced a lock-in, which was hard to unpick even when the opportunity arose. This also gives an indication of the importance of path dependency in the process of institutional change, as the outcome of the Convention completely structured the debate in the following implementation of the revised Lisbon Treaty. Not all issues were settled, but member states did not renege on the overall structural design. They and other actors in the Convention would, however, return to contesting the details of the new organisation during its establishment (Chapter 5) and consolidation (Chapters 6 and 7).

References

Allen, David 2004: The Convention and the draft constitutional treaty. In Cameron (Ed.) *The Future of Europe. Integration and Enlargement*, pp. 18–34. Routledge: London.

Deloche-Gaudez, Florence 2004: Le Secretariat de la Convention Européenne: un acteur influent? *Politique europeenne*, vol. 13, pp. 43–67.

Edwards, Geoffrey and Pijpers, Alfred (Eds.) 1997: *The Politics of Treaty Reform. The 1996 Intergovernmental Conference and Beyond.* Pinter: London.

Finke, Daniel, König, Thomas, Proksch, Sven-Oliver, and Tsebelis, George 2012: *Reforming the European Union: Realizing the Impossible.* Princeton University Press: Princeton.

Kleine, Mareike 2007: Leadership in the European Convention. *Journal of European Public Policy*, vol. 14, no. 8, pp. 1227–1248.

König, Thomas and Finke, Daniel 2012a: Principals and Agents: From the Convention's Proposal to the Constitutional Treaty. In Finke, König, Proksch and Tsebelis, *Reforming the European Union. Realizing the Impossible*, Princeton University Press: Princeton, pp. 151–169.

König, Thomas and Finke, Daniel 2012b: In the aftermath of the negative referendums. In Finke, König, Proksch and Tsebelis, *Reforming the European Union. Realizing the Impossible*, Princeton University Press: Princeton, pp. 170–187.

Lindner, Johannes and Rittberger, Berthold 2003: The Creation, Interpretation and Contestation of Institutions – revisiting Historical Institutionalism. *Journal of Common Market Studies*, vol. 41, pp. 445–473.

Magnette, Paul 2005: In the Name of Simplification: Coping with Constitutional Conflicts in the Convention on the Future of Europe. *European Law Journal*, vol. 11 no. 4, pp. 432–451.

Magnette, Paul and Nicolaïdis, Kalypso 2004: The European Convention: Bargaining in the Shadow of Rhetoric. *West European Politics*, vol. 27, no. 3, pp. 381–404.

Norman, Peter 2003: *The accidental constitution: the story of the European Convention.* EuroComment, 2003: Brussels.

Rueger, Carolin 2011: A Position under Construction: Future Prospects of the High Representative after the Treaty of Lisbon. In Mueller-Brandeck-Bocquet and Rueger (Eds.). *The High Representative for the EU Foreign and Security Policy – Review and Prospects*, pp. 201–233. Nomos: Baden-Baden.

Shaw, Jo 2003: Enhancing Cooperation after Nice: will the treaty do the trick? In Adenas, M. and Usher, J (Eds.) *The Treaty of Nice and Beyond. Enlargement and constitutional reform.* Hart: Portland, OR.

Official documents

Treaty of Nice 2001: Declaration (no. 23) on the future of the Union, Treaty of Nice. Official Journal of the European Communities (OJEC). 10.03.2001, n° C 80, p. 85.

European Council

European Council 2001: Presidency Conclusions. European Council meeting in Laeken 14 and 15 December 2001. Brussels.

Intergovernmental Conference

Intergovernmental Conference 2003: Reply by the Federal Republic of Germany to the Questionnaire on the Legislative Function, the Formations of the Council and the Presidency of the Council of Ministers (CIG 9/03).

Presidency Intergovernmental Conference 2003: Presidency note IGC 2003 – The Union Minister for Foreign Affairs: main points. Brussels, 02.10.2003.

European Commission

European Commission 2002c: Communication from the Commission. A Project for the European Union. COM(2002)247final. Brussels, 22.05.2002.

European Commission 2002d: For the European Union. Peace, Freedom, Solidarity. Communication from the Commission on the institutional architecture. COM(2002) 728final/2. Brussels, 11.12.2002.

European Convention

European Convention Verbatim Record 2002–2003. Archived webpage.

104   *Inception of the EEAS*

European Convention Plenary Documents

CONV/252/02: Mandate of the Working Group VII on External Action. 10.09.2002.

CONV 342/02: Working Group VII. Summary of the meeting held on 8 October 2002. 11.10.2002.

CONV 356/02: Working Group VII. Summary of the meeting held on 15 October 2002. 21.10.2002.

CONV/459/02: Final Report of Working Group VII on External Action. 16.12.2002.

CONV 821/03: Reactions to draft text CONV 802/03. 27.06.2003.

CONV 829/03: Letter from Mr Giuliano Amato, on behalf of the Party of European Socialists, Mr Elmar Brok on behalf of the European People's Party and Mr Andrew Duff, on behalf of the European Liberal, Democratic and Reform Party.

CONV 836/03: Draft Constitution Vol. II. 27.06.2003.

CONV 839/03: Contribution by Mr Barnier and Mr Vitorino, members of the Convention: 'Joint External Action Service'. 30.06.2003.

Amendments

Fischer amendment 2; de Villepin amendment 10; Duff amendment 11; Hain amendment 16; Helle amendment 18; Huebner amendment 21; Kaufmann amendment 22; Kelam *et al.* amendment 28; Liepina amendment 28; Queiro amendment 34; Roche *et al.* amendment 34; O'Sullivan and Ponzano amendment to art. 35; Bonde amendment 35; Heathcote-Amory amendment 36.

European Convention Working Group VII (External Action) *Working Documents*

All documents retrieved from http://european-convention.europa.eu) (Archived webpage).

WG WD 2: Copy of a letter sent by Mr Elmar Brok, member of the Convention, to the President of Working Group VII, Mr Jean-Luc Dehaene. 24.09.2002.

WG WD 4: Intervention de M. Louis Michel, membre de la Convention, lors de la réunion du groupe, le 24 septembre 2002. 24.09.2002.

WG WD 8: Address of the Secretary-General/High Representative Mr Javier Solana at the meeting of WG VII on 15 October 2002. 15.10.2002.

WG WD 11: 'Promoting the community method in the External actions of the EU' – Paper by Mr Adrian Severin, alternate member of the Convention. 28.10.2002.

WG WD 16: 'Improving the efficiency and effectiveness of the CFSP' – Paper by Mr Bobby McDonagh, alternate member of the Convention. 05.11.2002.

WG WD 17: Subject: 'Double hat' – Paper by Mr Gunter Pleuger, alternate member of the Convention. 05.11.2002.

WG WD 21: Preliminary draft final report. 08.11.2002.

WG WD 21/1: Revised draft final report. 22.11.2002.

WG WD 21/2: Revised draft final report. 29.11.2002.

WG WD 21/3: Revised draft final report. 09.12.2002.

WG WD 28: The comments by Mr Hans Martin Bury to the preliminary draft final report of Working Group VII on External Action (WD 021 – WG VII). 15.11.2002.

WG WD 30: Amendments to the preliminary draft final report of Working Group VII on External Action (WD 021 – WG VII), supported by Mr Adrian Severin, Mr Elmar Brok, Mr Alain Lamassoure and Mr René van der Linden. 18.11.2002.

Inception of the EEAS   105

WG WD 33: The comments by Mr Jan Kohout to the preliminary draft final report of Working Group VII on External Action (WD 021 – WG VII). 19.11.2002.

WG WD 34: The comments by Mr Ernâni R. Lopes to the preliminary draft final report of Working Group VII on External Action (WD 021 – WG VII). 19.11.2002.

WG WD 36: The comments by Mr Gerhard Tusek to the preliminary draft final report of Working Group VII on External Action (WD 021 – WG VII). 19.11.2002.

WG WD 40: The comments by Mr Peter Hain to the preliminary draft final report of Working Group VII on External Action (WD 021 – WG VII) and to the draft text on principles and objectives of EU external action (WD 007 – WG VII). 19.11.2002.

WG WD 47: The comments by Mr Gijs de Vries to the preliminary draft final report of Working Group VII on External Action (WD 021 – WG VII) and to the draft text on principles and objectives of EU external action (WD 007 – WG VII). 21.11.2002.

WG WD 49: Document de M. Pierre Lequiller, membre de la Convention – 'Comment parvenir à la convergence des politiques étrangères des Etats membres et des actions extérieures de l'Union européenne?'. 21.11.2002.

WG WD 51: The comments by Ms Danuta Hübner to the preliminary draft final report of Working Group VII on External Action (WD 021 – WG VII). 21.11.2002.

WG WD 52: The comments by Mr Dominique de Villepin to the preliminary draft final report of Working Group VII on External Action (WD 021 – WG VII) and to the draft text on principles and objectives of EU external action (WD 007 – WG VII). 22.11.2002.

WG WD 53: 'Some Questions and Answers regarding the "Double Hat" of High-Representative and Commissioner for External Relations' – Paper by Mr Hans Martin Bury, alternate member of the Convention. 25.11.2002.

WG WD 61: The comments by Ms Teija Tiilikainen to the revised draft final report of Working Group VII on External Action (WG VII – WD 21 REV 3). 12.12.2002.

WG WD 63: The comments by Mr Hans Martin Bury to the revised draft final report of Working Group VII on External Action (WG VII – WD 21 REV 3). 12.12.2002.

WG WD 66: The comments by Mr Peter Hain to the revised draft final report of Working Group VII on External Action (WG VII – WD 21 REV 3). 12.12.2002.

WG WD 68 REV: The comments by Ms Lena Hjelm-Wallén to the revised draft final report of Working Group VII on External Action (WG VII – WD 21 REV 3). 12.12.2002.

WG WD 70: The comments by Mr Elmar Brok and Mr John Cushnahan to the revised draft final report of Working Group VII on External Action (WG VII – WD 21 REV 3). 12.12.2002.

WG WD 71: Propositions d'amendements présentés par Mme Pervenche Berès sur le projet révisé de rapport final (WG VII – WD 21 REV 3). 12.12.2002.

WG WD 72: Propositions d'amendements présentés par Mme Pascale Andréani sur le projet révisé de rapport final (WG VII – WD 21 REV 3). 13.12.2002.

Other

European University Institute 2000: A Basic Treaty for the European Union. A Study of the Reorganisation of the Treaties. Report submitted on 15 May 2000 to Romano Prodi, President of the European Commission. EUI: Florence.

Group of Wise Men Report 1999: The Institutional Implications of Enlargement. Report to the European Commission by Jean-Luc Dehaene, Richard von Weizsäcker, Lord David Simon. Brussels, 18.10.1999.

5 Navigating the 'politics of Eurocratic structure'

The establishment of the European External Action Service

Agreeing to create an institution is one step; actually implementing a new bureaucratic or administrative arrangement quite another. The establishment of the EEAS as a new administrative organisation is the subject of this chapter. It focuses on the negotiations inside and across those institutional actors that created the new body. Since agreement on the most general issue of the institution's existence had been reached earlier, this is the story of negotiating the details of an administrative arrangement among a variety of actors with diverging interests and agendas. It will move from the enacting coalition deciding on the EEAS to the executing coalition, i.e. the coalition of actors implementing through legislative acts what the service will look like. As the decision-making shifts from Convention to inter-institutional decision-making at the EU level, the analytical perspective changes. Inter-institutional processes for the establishment of new administrative actors have been approached through an EU-specific adaptation of the 'Politics of Bureaucratic Structure' (Moe 1989) to European regulatory institutions, namely the 'Politics of Eurocratic Structure' (Kelemen 2002; Kelemen and Tarrant 2011). While remaining firmly embedded in the institutionalist approach, it takes account of the specificities of the EU political system and the different preferences of the actors within it. It will be the main approach used to address the questions of how the organisation was created, and more specifically what determined its final administrative or organisational shape.

The politics of Eurocratic structure approach, discussed in more detail in Chapter 3, leads to certain expectations about actors' preferences in the decision-making process. It sees member states in the Council cautious about transferring powers to a new body and seeking avenues to limit the authority of the new organisation and insert monitoring mechanisms. It sees parliament as seeking public oversight processes, while the Commission will be less likely to favour transfers of competences to outside bodies where key competences are concerned (Kelemen 2002). These standard patterns of preferences interact with the institutional structure to produce an organisational form and operation that responds to the interests of the actors involved in the creation and their relative weight in the decision-making process. This is relevant also in the case of a non-regulatory organisation such as the EEAS. As shown below, despite the fact that

Establishment of the EEAS 107

the EEAS decision was to be adopted by the Council with consent of the Commission, the European Parliament created leverage over the outcome by using its powers from shared legislative areas.

From the official record, it is clear that the negotiations within the European Commission started in 2004 and continued in 2005. Member states were particularly involved in discussions in 2005. After the failure of the Treaty through referenda, negotiations halted until 2008 when the Council restarted the debate under the Slovenian Presidency. After several meetings, the preparations had to be abandoned because of the failure to ratify the Lisbon Treaty in Ireland. Only with the imminent ratification of the Lisbon Treaty would the member states' preliminary agreement be revived for concrete preparation of the new service. The outcome of those negotiations would not steer far from this early developing equilibrium of positions of member states, the Commission and the EP (Erkelens and Blockmans 2012; Murdoch 2012; see below). Between 2005 and 2008, negotiations on the salvaging of the substance of the Constitutional Treaty between member states touched upon external relations and the High Representative and EEAS, but did not make substantive changes or further specifications to the structure (Council of the EU 2007). This chapter covers the timeframe of the beginning of administrative preparations in 2004 up to the adoption of the EEAS decision in 2010.

When looking at the organisational set-up, three items stand out for particular political relevance for the actors involved in the negotiation: the *status* of the new service as an EU body, the *scope* of the administration in terms of policy areas and topics included and the *staffing* of the organisation. While there were other areas of political interest, these were the issues most directly concerned with the administrative structure of the EEAS and thus most directly relevant for this research. These core themes will structure the discussion of all three groups of actors in this chapter. The following sections will illustrate how the three core actors, the Council and the member states in it, the European Commission, and finally the European Parliament developed their views on the EEAS and negotiated specific rules of the organisation's set-up. In addition to these three central themes of an administrative organisation such as the EEAS, the sub-sections discuss other central issues specific to each actor. Because of the nature of the politics of Eurocratic structure approach, i.e. its focus on positions and inter-institutional decision-making rules, the importance of the temporal dimension is less pronounced for the outcome of the bargain. The actors' positions and their institutional capacity to enter them into the outcome is the central concern. The analysis will highlight the relative stability of preferences of the main actors involved and how a compromise was reached among them.

All about access: member states and the EEAS negotiation

Because the EEAS was intended to be an organisation in foreign policy, it touched directly on prerogatives of the member states and their administrations, which made it a core concern for all of the EU's member states. An official

108 *Establishment of the EEAS*

described the level of interest in negotiations on the EEAS: 'Everyone was extremely interested in this dossier. Not necessarily in the same things. Everybody was very much involved in this' (Interview 1, Council Secretariat official, 2011). Discussions among the member states about the core areas of setting up the new service started in 2005, and were revived in 2008/2009 when the Treaty implementation became a more concrete task. In 2009 and 2010, the main negotiations on the legal document took place (see Murdoch 2012).

Status

Under the leadership of the Luxembourg Presidency in the first half of 2005 and following the demands of the draft Treaty at the time, first rounds of discussions took place between the Commission and the Council Secretariat (Interview 6, Senior Commission official, 2011). The Presidency undertook bilateral meetings with member states in order to involve them in the preparatory discussion as well as to develop an idea of individual positions. While it has so far been accepted in the literature that the preliminary discussions in 2005 produced very little (Missiroli 2010: p. 434; Murdoch 2013: p. 1015), this section will illustrate how they essentially narrowed the options available during the later rounds of discussions. In a preliminary survey of member states delegations in 2005 by the Luxembourg Presidency, key concepts, such as the 'sui generis' nature of the 'autonomous' new service already appear (Luxembourg Presidency 2005: p. 3.). The option to create the EEAS as an agency was dismissed by the member states, largely because it implied subordination to the Commission (Interview 1, Council official, 2011).

An indication of the sensitive nature of the preparations was the fact that institutional discussions were led by the Committee of Permanent Representatives COREPER II rather than a working group level meeting (Interview 1, Council official, 2011). Additional difficulties arose from the rejection of the treaty in Ireland, which again nearly stopped preparations. Only a procedural trick in the Council made continuing discussions on the implementation of the Lisbon Treaty provisions possible. Because early on in 2008, COREPER II could not discuss informal documents for political reasons, the Council Secretariat rebranded the discussions as 'meetings of Permanent Representatives' instead (Interview 1, Council official, 2011). The elements on the institutionalisation of the EEAS were thus discussed and prepared in the Antici group (Interview 18, Council official, 2012) and then settled in COREPER II meetings (Interviews 1, Council official, 2011, 18; Council official 2012, 16; Senior Council official, 2012). Similar observations regarding the decision-making at the top of the hierarchy are seen in the other institutions' dealings with the EEAS set-up (see below, also Missiroli 2010; Murdoch 2013): the EEAS dossier in the Commission was handled exclusively at cabinet level (Interview 6, Senior Commission official, 2011).

On the question of the institutional status of the new service, agreement could be found only on the expression of 'sui generis' nature (Interview, Senior Commission official, 2011), which was derived from the Issues Paper published

Establishment of the EEAS 109

as an attachment to the Barroso–Solana report of 2005 (Joint Progress Report 2005: p. 4). The Barroso–Solana Report itself was the first step in the stop-and-go negotiations, written after the Convention on the future of Europe and trying to join up thinking on the EEAS between the European Commission and the Council of the EU and its foreign policy apparatus. While the sui generis expression does not say much in terms of concrete legal expectations, it precludes options that have established concepts in EU institutional terminology. The Issues Paper appears to leave the location and status of the service open: 'The question arises as to whether this should be an autonomous service, neither in the Commission nor in the CSG, or whether it should be partly attached to either or both' (Joint Progress Report 2005: p. 9). It is doubtful whether it was an equally open question for member states. A Council official recounts: 'In 2005 and 2008 there was an option of putting it on the same level as an agency of the Commission, but that the member states never agreed to' (Interview 1, Council official, 2011). When the discussions on the EEAS were reactivated in the process of preparing the overall implementation of the Lisbon Treaty, member states returned to the state of discussions of 2005 to continue to work out their positions. A Slovenian Presidency progress report to the European Council in June 2008 directly acknowledged the preparations and discussions undertaken in 2005: 'discussions began on the EEAS, with reference to the very useful work already undertaken in 2005' (Council of the EU 2008: p. 9). Three formal discussions had gone into the report on 10 April, 13 May and 11 June (Council of the EU 2008: Annex). It went on to summarise the most recent discussions: the sui generis status had been accepted but needed additional detailing (Council of the EU 2008: p. 9).

The lack of fit with existing institutional arrangements such as a European agency or Commission service derived precisely from the majority view of the member states that foreign policy could not be transferred too close to the Commission. 'That was a condition for member states accepting that the whole security and defence part in the CSG became part of the service; that there should be autonomy' (Interview 8, Senior diplomat, 2011). In legal and organisational terms, such autonomy could only be achieved by treating the EEAS as a so-called assimilated institution for the staff and financial regulations, while at the same time member states were stopping short of making it one: 'But this [the autonomy on budget and staffing] never meant that the EEAS was meant as an independent institution' (Interview 8, Senior diplomat, 2011). The fine line that needed to be maintained is illustrated well by the amended wording of the draft Council decision on the EEAS from June 2010:

> '~~In order to ensure the budgetary autonomy necessary for the smooth operation of the EEAS,~~ The Financial Regulation should be amended in order to ~~treat the EEAS as an "institution"~~ **include the EEAS** within the meaning of **in Article 1** of the Financial Regulation, with a specific section in the Union budget.'
>
> (Emphasis and corrections in original, Council of the EU 2010a: p. 4)

110   *Establishment of the EEAS*

It was essential not to call the EEAS an *institution*, but to ensure it could behave like one. A look at the German government's position further illustrates the contradictory position the member states found themselves in:

> in the implementation of the Lisbon Treaty, it was particularly important for Germany that the [EEAS] would be independent from member states, Council Secretariat, and Commission and on the other hand would allow for a tight interlocking ['enge Verzahnung'] with the member states. Member states have asserted their position on this point and have been able to create a new sui generis organisation.
>
> (Auswaertiges Amt 2012: p. 2, own translation)

This quote highlights the apparent contradiction that member states saw the need for the EEAS to be independent – not only from other EU institutions, but also from other member states – yet at the same time were working to ensure a close link to the national system. These types of contradictions became a recurring feature in the negotiations on the new organisation and in the first operational phase, which is discussed in Chapter 6.

The subtle agreements on organisational status eventually became more reliable with the Swedish Presidency and its report on the progress on the EEAS (Council of the EU 2009). The report states:

> It [the EEAS] should have autonomy in terms of administrative budget and management of staff. The EEAS should be brought within the scope of Article 1 of the Financial Regulation.
>
> (Council of the EU 2009: p. 6)

An official describes it as a final lock-in of the agreement:

> [the document] was endorsed by the European Council, not adopted – that is not its role – but it had its blessing. You cannot really depart from this report as it had the blessing of the prime ministers and the member states agreed on the principles.
>
> (Interview 1, Council official, 2011)

It also had another knock-on effect for the negotiations:

> On the EEAS decision, the EP was only consulted. We had to have an opinion but we didn't have to listen to it. But in order to make of the EEAS what the member states wanted to make of it, a quasi-institution – what we call an assimilated institution in the sense of article 1 of the financial regulation, the European Parliament had to agree rather than merely being consulted.
>
> (Interview 1, Council official, 2011)

Establishment of the EEAS   111

While the states continued to 'design' the EEAS between 2008 and 2010, the core issues resurfaced. And while member states did reopen the debate anew, they continued from 2008 to clarify the basic understanding of the service they had developed in 2005. The unique status, the 'sui generis' nature of the EEAS, had been agreed on earlier, but needed a clear interpretation of what it actually entailed. Thus, member states were required to develop additional detail in terms of defining the relations with the other institutions, inserting the service into the EU's legal rules on operation and financial processes as well as integrating their staff into the civil service structure of the EU. In fact, member states agreed to treat it as an institution for all functional purposes, without actually using the term. In addition to determining its administrative status, which parts of the existing machinery would enter the service, or the service's scope, was another core concern in the negotiations.

Scope

The scope of the EEAS as an organisation would determine which elements of the existing institutions would be transferred to the new organisation. The agreement found in the Convention had been specific only in naming the three sources: the European Commission, the Council Secretariat and the diplomatic services of the member states (see Chapter 4) without specifying organisational parts. While an equal balance may have been the original intention, it was accepted by all sides that the Council Secretariat, simply in terms of numbers of staff, would not be able to carry one-third of the new organisation.

Already by 2005, the component parts of the new service were seen by most delegations as encompassing the Council Secretariat's DG-E and Policy Unit as well as DG RELEX of the Commission together with relevant geographical desks of other Commission services (Luxembourg Presidency 2005: p. 4). While most delegations agreed already that Trade was considered outside the organisational purpose of the EEAS, 'many argued that development aid ("a major element of EU foreign policy") should be included' (Luxembourg Presidency, 2005: p. 3.). In the Joint Progress Report, support for this position had shrunk to 'a few' delegations (Joint Progress Report 2005). This resembles quite strongly, albeit not perfectly, the final shape of the EEAS set out in more detail five years later by Council Decision of 26 July 2010.

Another Slovenian Presidency progress report to the European Council in June 2008 detailed that some aspects of the organisation's scope should be focused on the policy unit and DG-E (External policies) of the Council Secretariat and DG RELEX of the European Commission (Council of the EU 2008: p. 10). It mirrored the earlier documents cited above by not including development and trade and reported the insistence of 'some delegations that the establishment of the EEAS should aim at budget neutrality' (Council of the EU 2008: p. 10). While upholding the previously discussed positions, it did also foreshadow additional demands, which would come to the centre of negotiations again in 2009–2010. There seem to have been no fundamental surprises in terms

112   *Establishment of the EEAS*

of scope between 2005 and 2010. But this is not to suggest that no disagreements existed on the issue. Negotiators were far from unanimous, and divergences were quite visible. While it was generally accepted that '[o]ne of the principal aims of the EEAS is to remove the duplication of tasks inherent in the current structures by merging the Council Secretariat positions with their counterpart in the Commission' (Foreign and Commonwealth Office 2013: p. 2), which positions would be entered into the merger was not clear.

The German government supported the inclusion in particular of the European Neighbourhood Policy and its funding in the EEAS: 'Neighbourhood Policy remained in the Commission, even though it represented from a German point of view a central element of the EU's external action and should have sensibly been integrated into the EAS' (Auswaertiges Amt 2012: p. 2). The UK government represented a similar position in discussions in Council in 2009, but relating to a different policy area: 'We don't want to continue with the present split between DGs Development and RELEX (with the latter becoming the EAS)' (Foreign and Commonwealth Office 2013: p. 1). But a split between member states in the Council prevented them from finding agreement on including further elements of EU external action in the EEAS. In particular, programming and implementing financial instruments in development policy were contentious:

> [Some said] the purpose of EEAS is to have entire external action in EEAS so it [development] should be too. And in the end you will see it is half-half, the mainline of divergence.
>
> (Interview 1, Council official, 2011)

Since the complete inclusion of development did not materialise, evidence from the UK government highlights the shifting nature of government positions on the fluid matter of the EEAS decision: the UK then focused on a 'strong Development Commissioner' (Foreign and Commonwealth Office 2013: p. 13) together with an 'EEAS role in the strategic allocation of assistance funds' (Foreign and Commonwealth Office 2013: p. 20), two views that are not from the outset fully compatible. At least the last point would become an essential element of the consolidation phase of the EEAS (see Chapter 6). Partially contradictory demands like these appeared repeatedly in the negotiations of governments, which have to represent multiple domestic audiences and interests and react to changing majorities in Council.

One major difficulty in the determination of the EEAS's scope was the refusal of the French government to let military and defence structures, which had developed over time in the Council Secretariat, be transferred to the new service (Interview 4, EEAS official, 2011).

> There was disagreement. It was solved at the stage of the report in October. About the military structure, the military staff, planning of operations, you have a chapter in the report about this. All the structures that deal with

ESDP, CSDP; there was a divergence of views. There was not a divergence of views like half-half, everybody was more or less OK that these structures should be in EEAS, as the EEAS is about CSFP including ESDP, only the French had difficulties with this. They agreed in the end, provided structures are under direct authority of the HR. That's why you see some strange formulations in the decision. Again, it is mainly about structures and administrative arrangements rather than about substance.

> (Interview 1, Council official, 2011, similar Interview 4, EEAS official, 2011)

These comments by a Council official highlight how in this setting administrative structures are actually substantial and substantive policy choices and governments consider what precedents agreements to institutional structures may create. French fears over the inclusion of military matters in the EEAS were thus only alleviated once it had been made clear that these structures would remain under the direct authority of the High Representative rather than being fully integrated into the service's wider organisational structure. With these general organisational principles on the table, another element was to become the main concern in all member states: the question of access of member states' staff to the EEAS and its senior positions.

Staffing

Member states' concern with staffing of the EEAS surfaced first in the preparatory rounds of 2004/2005. The Joint Progress Report stated:

> As its staff will be drawn from three sources (Council Secretariat, Commission and Member States), Member States underlined the importance for them of having a sufficient number of national diplomats in the EEAS and in a range of positions at all levels.

> (Joint Progress Report 2005: p. 6)

Far from being just another point of discussion among many, this developed into a core demand of the member states vis-à-vis the Commission and the High Representative. Directly linked to this demand was the position of member states that diplomatic personnel sent to the EEAS should be 'temporary agents rather than seconded national experts to ensure that all staff in the EEAS had the same status and conditions of employment' (Joint Progress Report 2005: p. 6). From this early mention in the 2004/05 discussions, the staffing question gains centrality like no other individual issue area for the member states. The 'importance of ensuring an adequate number of diplomats from the Member States participating in the Service at all levels' is equally repeated in the 2008 Presidency Report (Council of the EU 2008: p. 10) and remained the central point of contention for member states throughout the setting up of the service. The questions were to return repeatedly in the negotiations, but these basic positions of direct and deep

114 *Establishment of the EEAS*

access to the EEAS and the status of member states' staff were not revised after 2005. These demands, however, created the need to adapt EU legislation on the civil service to take into account the new staff. This meant the revision of financial and staffing regulations to include the EEAS and its staff from three different sources. And while vague agreement on a principle like 'sui generis' could be found, the negotiations about detail were more complex than simple amendments to existing legislation.

Managing the financial and staff regulation through the Council was described as 'very painful', as it 'touched directly upon member states' (Interview 18, Senior Council official, 2011). Member states realised that because of their nature as specialised administrations in Brussels, both the European Commission and the Council Secretariat would be 'in first, which triggered the mistrust' (Interview 18, Senior Council official, 2011). Staffing thus became a major element for member states to keep a close eye on the new organisation and in many ways anticipated issues of control that were to resurface in the operation phase discussed in Chapter 6. Despite disagreements over other issues, this staffing dilemma proved to be at the core of the negotiations for member states:

> The member states also didn't negotiate very well, by the way, because their attention was disproportionately on numbers, again: how do we get in? At what level, with how many people? They were putting in second order the structure and the functioning. They [the member states] were not worried about the Council Secretariat, they were worried how they could get into the system.
>
> (Interview 2, Council official, 2011)

This emphasis on a narrow issue had a negative impact on the strength of the member states' negotiation position in addition to the challenges that the Council's negotiated position presented vis-à-vis the European Commission's centralised decision-making (Murdoch 2012). The focus on personnel numbers and hierarchy levels relegated other important elements of the decision to a less essential status. It did, however, present an issue in which member states were not divided in their negotiations. Even in the final rounds of negotiations in 2010, small coalitions of member states addressed the need to create entry points for national staff. A joint letter from the British and Swedish Foreign Ministers Miliband and Bildt to Catherine Ashton from 3 March 2010 states: 'There must be a <u>concerted effort to bring temporary agents at all levels, including delegations, into the EAS</u> at the beginning' (Miliband and Bildt 2010: p. 2, emphasis in original). They also express the worry described by an official above that the EU institutions would use the interim period to fill interesting, and open, posts in the absence of an agreement on the EEAS:

> We are concerned with the fact that both the Council Secretariat and the Commission continue to fill such appointments in the interim period, or that in some cases they are being moved outside of the scope of the EAS altogether; this is not the way it should be.
>
> (Miliband and Bildt 2010: p. 3)

The UK government also continued to press for setting up a new recruitment system to the EEAS after a short transitional period with the Commission system (Foreign and Commonwealth Office 2013: pp. 2, 7, 42). Other concerns in the UK documents relate to the speed with which member states are notified of open positions (Foreign and Commonwealth Office 2013: p. 7) and EU-typical language requirements (Foreign and Commonwealth Office 2013: p. 7), favouring officials from the institutions. Member states perceived getting into the EEAS as a major challenge, despite the fact that their diplomatic services were supposed to supply one-third of EEAS staff.

A relevant sub-element of this discussion in Council is the status of national diplomats as temporary agents, which was also reflected in the German position on the matter. The German Foreign Office, or Auswaertiges Amt, stressed that it

> insisted during the negotiations that they [national diplomats] would be treated equally to EU civil servants and can fill any function in the service (as temporary agents) and are not limited to desk officer jobs like seconded national experts.
>
> (Auswaertiges Amt 2012: p. 2)

The document continues to highlight the need for diplomatic expertise and that only national diplomats would be able to guarantee 'a tight interlocking with national capitals' which should create 'ownership' in the member states (Auswaertiges Amt 2012: p. 2, own translation). These are indications that member states realised that the organisation could become more independent than the name 'service' implies and that having control of staffing in the service may be the most effective way of influencing it once operational. This concern for operational control played out even more directly in the next phase of institutional creation, discussed in Chapter 6.

Other topics of negotiations: when policy meets institutional design

While the scope, structure and staffing of the EEAS were the core themes of negotiations, they were not the only points of contention in the negotiation. Various quasi-institutional arrangements, such as the chairing of the different Council preparatory bodies, were of some concern to the member states as well. Member states in Council also started to dissect the chairing arrangement, clearly being hesitant to hand over chairmanship of all Council preparatory bodies to a permanent EEAS chair (Council of the EU 2008: p. 11). From the documentary evidence from the UK and Germany, it is also clear that at least some of the issues discussed in the form of an institutional choice were of a substantive foreign policy nature. The UK, for example, looked beyond the creation of the EEAS to restructure the EU's administration in relation to the importance of certain regions and countries: 'Building up capacity in EU delegations'; 'targeted reinforcement in places like Beijing and Washington'; plugging geographical gaps in the EEAS: e.g. need for a 'proper Turkey desk' (Foreign and Commonwealth Office 2013: p. 31). It also started

116　*Establishment of the EEAS*

interrogating potential issues that would arise after the Council decision, such as the capacity of the EEAS to work on external effects of internal policies, the handling of crisis management in EEAS senior management and 'the relationship between the very top team' (Foreign and Commonwealth Office 2013: p. 30). These notes highlight the fact that institutional choices with regard to the EEAS were seen as policy choices and that negotiators were consciously discussing on that basis. A particular institutional settlement – the non-inclusion of a policy area under the HR, for example – would mean a policy run differently and thus with potentially different outcomes or attention. Equally, the creation of an additional layer of hierarchy enabled immediate insertion of member states' diplomats, something that may have been made slower and more difficult by retaining the original hierarchical layers without managing directors.

As member states were so directly concerned and very interested, their preferences played a major role in the negotiations. An important element of structural politics at the EU level is that while mechanisms exist to find internal agreement, factors external to each of the EU institutions are brought in during the internal negotiations. In this case, member states could not settle on a final opinion before having to take into account the opinions of the other actors. As the Treaty changes required an agreement from the European Commission, the Commission was from the outset an essential element in the negotiation.

Protecting prerogatives: the European Commission

In the negotiations on the EEAS, the European Commission was always positioned as a central actor. Both the original mandate of the Constitutional Treaty and the mandate of the Lisbon Treaty demanded the agreement of the Commission for the decision establishing the EEAS by mandating that the Council needs to 'obtain the consent of the Commission' (Council of the EU 2009). This veto power made any agreement dependent on how the European Commission envisaged the new service as well. The Commission was thus always a party to the negotiations, both for practical reasons due to its role in EU external relations and because of the procedural requirements of the legal text. The Commission had also been party to the discussion that created the EEAS in the European Convention, as highlighted in Chapter 4, and continued to develop a strategy on what type of administrative organisation to build to further its own interests.

Status

In the early preparations, even before the publication of the Solana Barroso Progress Report, the Commission was already developing its position on the scope of the EEAS. For the Commission this was perhaps the most essential part of the negotiations as it would determine which parts of the institution were to be transferred to the new service. These early discussions between the Commission and the Secretariat around that time were characterised 'not only by the negative fearful attitude of my side, the Commission, but by the way in which, in the

Establishment of the EEAS 117

Council Secretariat also, this was seen very much as a struggle for power' (Interview 6, Senior official, DG RELEX, 2011; similar in Interviews 2 and 16, Senior Council officials, 2011, 2012). 'The Commission was notably absent from this inter-institutional dispute and never for one moment supported the Parliament' in positioning the service in the Commission (Interview 6, Senior official, DG RELEX, 2011; Interview 16, Council Secretariat official 2012; Interview 23, Senior EEAS official, 2012; Interview 24, EP Assistant 2012). The reason for this was at the time seen in the upcoming renomination of Barroso as Commission President (Interview, Senior Commission official, 2011). Despite appearing a surprise, the position is consistent with some of the positions taken by members of the Commission during the Convention, as demonstrated in Chapter 4. Already in the Convention, the Commission stressed the need for a single institutional source, but it did move away from the position that the 'centre of gravity for policy initiative and for ensuring coherent action should therefore lie within the Commission' (European Commission 2002c: p. 13) to a weaker position where it should 'benefit[ing] from the administrative infrastructure of the Commission' (European Commission 2002d: p. 13).

From the very start in 2004/5, member states discussions and inter-institutional discussions were strongly linked. The European Commission started a slow process of internal preparation, which played an important role in the institution's positioning vis-à-vis the new service. After the member states had found agreement on the final text of the Constitutional Treaty in 2004, the preparation of the new service began on a small scale and lasted until May 2005 (Juncos and Whitman 2010: p. 34). Within the European Commission, an inter-service group encompassing representatives from the Secretariat General, the Legal Service, and the various external relations services discussed options (Interview, Senior Commission official, 2011). In a draft document circulated in the European Commission at the time, the process and options facing the EU institutions with the expected ratification of the Constitutional Treaty were spelled out (European Commission 2004). Some parts of this document later became an annex to the first Joint Progress Report by the Commission and the High Representative on the EEAS in 2005 (Joint Progress Report 2005). This highlights the difficulties of starting preparations because the Treaty had not been ratified and the new European Commission had not taken office officially. From the point of view of the Commission, this ruled out any formal preparatory discussions with the Council Secretariat. At the same time, the draft document does consider that strategically the first step of preparations should be 'Council Secretariat and Commission should dialogue and, if possible, develop common ideas, before engaging in discussions with member states' (European Commission 2004b: p. 6.).

Scope

The Commission services clearly saw the potential range of organisational options still available to them based on either a restrictive or expansive reading of the Treaty text. In a narrow reading, the service could be construed as only

118 *Establishment of the EEAS*

serving the second pillar, or questions of Common Foreign and Security Policy. This option was seen as best suited to 'protect and preserve the Commission's autonomy' (European Commission 2004b: p. 8), while at the same time not providing any improvement on the EU's ability to act coherently abroad. The EEAS, under this arrangement, would be little more than fulfilling the role of Council Secretariat 'but under another name' (European Commission 2004b: p. 8).

A wider interpretation would include all first and second pillar elements of the EU's external action and bring with it an opportunity to improve the EU's coherence and visibility in external action. At the same time, the draft discussion document warned of the 'risk of interference of the intergovernmental method' (European Commission 2004b: p. 8). It was also seen as reducing the 'Commission's independence in the field of external affairs' (European Commission 2004b: p. 8). The resulting conclusion is that the Commission's interest would be for 'the EEAS to have an administrative status as close as possible to a service of the Commission' (European Commission 2004b: p. 10). The question of which Commission departments would be joining the service would depend on the role of the service.

Under a limited second pillar understanding this would be only the CFSP parts of the Commission and would exclude other services and even the delegations (Interview 6, Senior Commission official, 2011). This 'total resistance' argument retreated one step further, as the official noted:

> it doesn't say in the Treaty that it (the system of EU delegations) would be in the EEAS, so it's not in the EEAS and it should be separate structure coming under the HR.
>
> (Interview 6, Senior Commission official, 2011)

On the contrary, under a wide interpretation of the provisions, also presented in the options paper, the Commission could foresee the inclusion of all geographic and thematic Commission services including Trade and Development joining the EEAS. But this wide approach did not gain the support of the Commission either.

A paper circulated jointly by Barroso and Solana in March 2005 argued that the insertion of a new legal basis in the Treaty meant that the creation of a 'new integrated service' was required, albeit leaving open the question of whether it should be autonomous or attached to either or both parent institutions (Joint Progress Report 2005). On the structure of the new service, it included, as previously thought, almost all of the CSG external relations services, leaving in doubt only the Situation Centre. With regard to the Commission, it accepted the integration of geographical desks from DG RELEX. It excluded most parts of the Directorates-General Trade, Development and Enlargement from being integrated into the service.

> From the maximalist vision of having everything [in the service], but that is exactly the Commission vision, they did not want a very strong EEAS. Yes, strong, but within boundaries. No question of putting development, enlargement or humanitarian money in it. When I say the Commission,

Establishment of the EEAS 119

I don't mean the Commission departments that ended up in the EEAS, I mean the Commission as an institution. That's the vision we have now in the EEAS; it's a limited EEAS.

(Interview 2, Council Secretariat official, 2011)

In the short period between November 2004 and spring 2005, the Commission had considered a range of options and was already preparing to withdraw thematic elements from the reach of the EEAS. Divisions between member states over which elements to include enabled a narrower conception of the service (Joint Progress Report 2005: p. 4). Because the internal process in the Commission was highly political and decision-making was led by cabinets, and in particular the cabinet of the President of the European Commission (Interview 6, Senior Commission official, 2011; 16, Council Secretariat official, 2012, Interview 18, Council official, 2012), documentary evidence for its position is hard to come by. This is balanced by both the literature which has to date focused on the negotiations, and by interviews with observers and participants in the process. The Commission equally did not entertain revising its position later in the process. The growing literature on the negotiations of the service appears to concur that the Commission in the 2009–10 negotiations 'sought to ensure a strong influence [of the Commission] over the new service' (Lefebvre and Hillion 2010: p. 3). This strategic behaviour on the part of the Commission is illustrated by what Erkelens and Blockmans called 'bureaucratic manoeuvres' (2012: p. 6).

This manoeuvring included making the head of the Barroso cabinet the director general for external relations in the Commission, and subsequently promoting him to the desirable posting in Washington, DC. This move seems to have fuelled the distrust that had developed between the negotiating parties. Barroso also removed parts of DG External Relations dealing with climate change and an energy task force, to maintain full control over Community areas (Erkelens and Blockmans 2012: p. 6): 'The Commission continues to insist that it should manage the EU's delegations abroad and wants to limit the scope of the EEAS, reserving policy areas for itself' (European Voice 2010a). The Commission's position had thus remained unchanged from its contributions to the Convention on the Future of Europe (see Chapter 4). And even in 2010, the Commission had not given up on the network of delegations. Finally, Barroso also decided that the head of the EEAS, the High Representative and Vice-President could not stand in for him because of the HR's particular mandate (Erkelens and Blockmans 2012: p. 6). These moves of 2010 are consistent with the position of 2004–2005 that the service was essentially seen as an actor that needed to be contained, by restructuring its constituent parts inside the Commission and at the same time maintaining control over relevant policy areas and budgetary expenditure.

Staffing

For the Commission, staffing questions were directly linked to the question of scope, as the scope of the new service determined how many Commission

120 *Establishment of the EEAS*

officials and sections would be transferred to the EEAS. Because of the nature of delegations, which would include officials from Commission departments in greater numbers than staff of the EEAS, staffing in the EEAS, in particular with regard to Heads of Delegation, was of direct concern to the Commission. While in early preparation there had been, at least for argument's sake, a position within the Commission that stated the delegations for the EEAS would be separate from those of the Commission,

> it never said in the Treaty that the delegations would be part of the EEAS. You know it says there will be EU delegations, it doesn't say that they would replace the Commission delegation, so it took about a year or so to, in the Commission for people of common sense […] to get it accepted that point 1: the union delegations would be formed out of the Commission delegations. There were actually people saying: 'oh, there are going to be two networks, isn't that the best solution for the Commission'.
>
> (Interview 6, Senior Commission official, 2011)

This was at least to a degree a reflection of the positions in the 2005 Issues Paper (Joint Progress Report 2005: p. 11), where it states that

> the question arises as to whether in view of the various responsibilities in terms of external representation of the EU as described in the treaty (see Articles 22, 26 and 296 in particular), the delegations should form part of the EEAS or not.

This again reflected the Commission's view during the Convention, when its representatives attempted to carve out the delegations from the EEAS structure (see Chapter 4). Although in the final outcome it did not achieve anything nearly as complete as carving out the delegations from the new service, the Commission maintained a say on the staff nominations. The Council decision itself remains rather general on this question, merely stating that 'Representatives of the Member States, the General Secretariat of the Council and of the Commission shall be involved in the recruitment procedure for vacant posts in the EEAS' (Council of the EU 2010b: p. 35). On the basis of this general principle, the EEAS and the other actors would set up specific procedures during the consolidation phase (see Chapter 6).

Other elements: lines of command and operational expenditure

In addition to scope and staffing, the Commission's specific relation to the EEAS and delegations meant that it was concerned about the nature and path of directives given by the EEAS to the delegations and their staff, as well as the budgetary management of Commission-run funds. Decentralisation efforts in the external relations field had by the early 2000s created a system whereby a larger number of decisions about project implementation were being run by delegations in the country rather than by headquarters in Brussels.

On budgetary matters, the Commission was aiming at '[p]reserving and protecting its prerogatives' (Interview 6, Senior Commission official, 2011) under the Community way of policy-making. The EEAS as an entity with non-Commission staff could not carry the ultimate responsibility on 'all operational expenditures' (Erkelens and Blockmans 2012: p. 22). Erkelens and Blockmans found that 'as a result from the quadrilogue the budgetary connection between the Commission and those departments it had "lost" to the EEAS was to a large extent restored' (2012: p. 23). These financial and budgetary management obligations would also have organisational repercussions by creating the most unusual institutional arrangement between the EEAS and the European Commission. Elements of the Commission dealing with the implementation of financial programmes including CFSP instruments remain part of the Commission but are directly linked by hierarchy to the High Representative (Interview 21, Commission official, 2012). This Foreign Policy Instruments Service (FPI) is legally an integral part of the Commission and its staff are Commission staff, while at the same time being included in the EEAS organogram and occupying part of the EEAS building. Despite being a small service, it represents an interesting organisational expression of the EEAS–Commission divisions and linkages. It also illustrates the double-hatted nature of the HR as not only head of the EEAS, but also VP of the Commission.

From cheerleader to controller and back again?
The European Parliament creates leverage

Several authors have highlighted how the European Parliament used its leverage as a legislator over the staff and financial regulations to gain concessions from Council (Murdoch 2012; Raube 2012), but much less detail is known about the origin of the EP's position and its evolution over the course of the negotiations. The EP's move from the sidelines to the negotiating table shows the strong institutional and supranational elements in the setting up of the EEAS. Much as the Council had done, in 2009 the EP reiterated and expanded on the positions it had already expressed in 2005.

From a simple legal perspective, the European Parliament was an outsider in the negotiations on the European External Action Service. Nevertheless, it played a major role in the discussion on the structure of the service and entered a new form of negotiations, the quadrilogue between the High Representative, the Council, the Commission and the EP, thought up for the purpose of setting up the EEAS. As parliaments would normally be suspected to be less coherent than governments, one surprising element of the EP's negotiating position is the stability of its views from the Convention to the EEAS decision. Just like the Council and the Commission, the EP needed to find an internal compromise first in order to enter into the concrete negotiations. To achieve this internal coherence, the EP had set up an ad hoc format, formally led by the EP President. It included the rapporteurs from different relevant committees in the EP and reflected the EP's make-up in terms of party groups. The main work of

122 *Establishment of the EEAS*

negotiation rested, however, on the team of three rapporteurs for the EEAS, conservative Elmar Brok, liberal Guy Verhofstadt and socialist Roberto Gualtieri. A green MEP, Franziska Brantner, acted as a liaison between the rapporteurs and the green MEPs. The following substantive analysis of the European Parliament's views on the setting up of the EEAS will follow the structure established above as the issues of status of the service, its scope and staffing were central also from the EP's point of view, even if not necessarily from the same angle.

Status

The European Parliament engaged early on with the developing discussion on the EEAS and its set-up in 2005. This engagement is not surprising, considering the active role that members of the European Parliament had played during the inception of the EEAS at the Convention on the Future of Europe (see Chapter 4). It adopted a 'European Parliament resolution on the institutional aspects of the European External Action Service' on 26 May 2005, tabled by Jo Leinen from the Constitutional Affairs Committee (European Parliament 2005). The EP reiterated its main institutional point, which set it apart from the majority in Council and even from the Commission: the EP stated explicitly that 'the EEAS should be incorporated, in organisational and budgetary terms, in the European Commission's staff structure' (European Parliament 2005: p. 1). The EP maintained the position that its member of the European Convention had repeatedly voiced: that the EEAS should be part of the Commission and function under the control of Council only in CFSP and specific intergovernmental parts of EU's foreign policy. And while the EP declaration acknowledged the need for the 'Foreign Minister' to follow Council processes in the case of foreign policy, it equally insisted that she follow majority decisions of the College of Commissioners in external relations (European Parliament 2005: p. 2). In this general resolution, the EP underlined that 'a decision to set-up the EEAS cannot be taken without Parliament's agreement' (European Parliament 2005: p. 1) although the legal mandate refers to a mere consultation of the EP (Council of the EU 2009). This foreshadows the shrewd use of its legislative role in negotiating with the Council and the Commission later in 2008–10 (Dinan 2011: pp. 112–113). The establishment of the EEAS necessitated amending the staff and financial regulations for which the EP acted as a co-legislator. Through this legislative role, the EP leveraged itself into a seat at the negotiation table for the establishment of the EEAS, the format of which was commonly referred to as a 'quadrilogue', consisting of the Council, the Commission, the High Representative and the European Parliament.

These positions on the status of the EEAS from 2005 were reactivated upon the ratification process of the Treaty of Lisbon in 2009. Very much like the Council, the EP re-opened the case on the EEAS after the treaty reanimations of 2008/09. In a detailed 'European Parliament resolution of 22 October 2009 on

Establishment of the EEAS 123

the institutional aspects of setting up the European External Action Service', the EP repeated its central demands and added considerable detail to its original position (European Parliament 2009b). It also made a political call on the Commission to 'put its full weight as an institution behind the objective of preserving and further developing the Community model in the Union's external relations' (European Parliament 2009b: p. 2).

The EP reaffirmed its position that 'as a service that is sui generis from an organisational and budgetary point of view, the EEAS must be incorporated into the Commission's administrative structure' (European Parliament 2009b: p. 3). The EP apparently did not consider the notion 'sui generis' to necessarily mean that the EEAS needed to be situated outside of the Commission. It further specified that it would see the EEAS's budget as part of the budget of the Commission's administrative expenditure (European Parliament 2009b: p. 3). This arrangement would have resulted in a complete administrative integration of the EEAS into the Commission, but would still have left decisions taken on foreign policy and defence under separate procedures.

In this EP resolution in 2009, the EP made the formal connection between the revision of the financial and staff regulation and the EP's involvement in the setting up of the EEAS (similar also Interviews 1, 2, 4, 8, 18, 24, 2011–13):

> [The European Parliament] recalls the need to find an agreement with the Parliament on the future Commission proposals amending the Financial Regulation and the Staff Regulations; reiterates its determination to exercise its budgetary powers to the full in connection with the institutional innovations; emphasises that all aspects of funding arrangements for the EEAS must remain under the supervision of the budgetary authority in accordance with the Treaties.
>
> (European Parliament 2009b: p. 4)

The fact that the EP repeated its request to the Commission to pull its weight in the negotiations nevertheless shows that MEPs were aware that they needed cooperation from the Commission to achieve changes on the EEAS structure (European Parliament 2009b: p. 2). This support was found lacking, as one staffer reveals: 'The EP saw itself as an ally of the Commission and that may have been a mistake' (Interview 24, EP assistant, 2012). The Commission had not cooperated well with the EP during the negotiations (Interview 6, Senior Commission official, 2011; Interview 24, EP assistant, 2012).

The more detailed preparation for the negotiation with the Council and Commission in the quadrilogue dampened expectations. In a 'non-paper' written by two of the three rapporteurs in early 2010, i.e. Elmar Brok and Guy Verhofstadt, the EP position was limited to arguing that the EEAS should be autonomous and 'in administrative, organisational and budgetary terms linked to the Commission' (Brok and Verhofstadt 2010: p. 2). Between the first official stance of the EP on the institutional structure of the EEAS in October 2009 and the actual negotiation preparation in March 2010, some demands were muted considerably.

124   *Establishment of the EEAS*

Nevertheless, the EP delegation to the EEAS negotiations, or quadrilogue, held on to its positions for a long time. As late as June 2010, the Conference of Presidents, an internal political steering organ of the EP, stated:

> However, there is so far no agreement on the nature of the EEAS. The Parliament believes that the Service should be more communitarian than intergovernmental in character, and this is why the Parliament insists that it is attached to the Commission.
>
> (European Parliament 2010a)

In particular, Verhofstadt was considered to have held on to the EP 'line' the longest (Interview 24, EP Assistant, 2012). In the end, the EP had to concede that the EEAS would be sui generis in a stronger sense, i.e. that it was not going to be an integral part of the Commission. The final Council decision did, however, include full budgetary control over operational expenditure for the European Commission. This in turn gave the European Parliament the budgetary control it sought to maintain.

Scope

The EP's position on status may have been crystal clear, but its view of the scope of the new organisation was less so. With the uncertainty over the negotiating outcomes and high levels of concern for the 'Community model in the Union's external relations' (European Parliament 2009b: p. 2), the EP apparently did not want to dismantle all of the Commission's external relations departments: 'it is not, however necessary to strip the Commission Directorates-General of all their external relations responsibilities, particularly in fields where the Commission has executive powers' (European Parliament 2009b: p. 3). Its more specific points demanded that external relations units 'in the stricter sense' and senior delegation officials should be integrated into the EEAS (European Parliament 2009b: p. 3), but the EP indicates flexibility when it comes to which subset of Commission departments is finally integrated into the service (European Parliament 2009b: p. 3).

At first, the EP remained cautious about areas in which the Commission retained strong powers. This is unsurprising, given that the EP saw the EEAS as 'a logical extension of the acquis communautaire in the sphere of the Union's external relations' (European Parliament 2009b). It wanted the EEAS to bring Community control into areas of foreign policy, rather than allow member states to regain control over established supranational policy areas. Nevertheless, the Brok–Verhofstadt (2010) working paper was maximalist rather than anything else in terms of the EEAS's scope: it foresaw the inclusion not only of geographical desks and multilateral action, but also development, human rights and democracy promotion, and international environmental policy. In particular development policy is an interesting inclusion, as it was also on the organisational wish list of several member states (Foreign and Commonwealth Office

2013; Interview 3, Convention official, 2011; see also above in this chapter) but was not retained in the final outcome.

As in the case of the Council, positions of the Parliament shifted in response to the process of negotiations and submitting their demands to the scrutiny of the other negotiating partners. One participant in the negotiations recalled:

> I think that Brok became convinced during the process that there was no possibility of the Parliament getting what they were asking for and actually gave higher priority to what he called the political accountability of the HR than to issues like its attachment to the Commission.
>
> (Interview 8, Senior diplomat, 2012)

Linking the EEAS closely to the Commission was only ever one concern among several, and the EP held on to its position until a relatively late stage with a view to achieving other goals as well. As one official noted: 'sometimes the EP has very militant immediate requests but the effects are difficult to evaluate, even for them' and the EP 'plays in the medium term, like the Commission' (Interview 2, Council official, 2011). The EP may have settled for change in areas that appear of limited importance today, in order to create precedents for future changes. One element where this negotiating behaviour has become apparent is the question of staffing in the EEAS.

Staffing

Like the member states, the EP had in 2005 addressed staffing concerns, albeit of a different nature. The EP wanted 'balanced and appropriate proportions of officials' originating from the three different sources (European Parliament 2005: p. 2). In particular the dominance in terms of numbers of European officials vis-à-vis national diplomats was a central point of concern in the European Parliament (Interview 1, Council official, 2011, Interview 20, Senior EEAS official, 2012, Interview 24, EP assistant, 2012). The EP also insisted repeatedly since the Brok–Verhofstadt working paper that EP officials should equally be able to join the EEAS (Brok and Verhofstadt 2010: p. 7; Interview 18, Council official, 2012; Interview 24, EP assistant, 2012). The EP secured both a minimum of 60% European officials in the service and the opening of the EEAS posts for EP staff from 2013.

The EP's demands on staffing were driven by a wish for fair geographical representation, especially from those member states less well represented in the Commission and Council. In April 2010, Brok and Verhofstadt still recommended the use of a system similar to the hirings into the Commission after enlargement:

> The legitimacy of the service, building on the sense of ownership by all, strongly depends upon an adequate geographical representativity of its staff of all grades and posts. For that purpose, national indicative recruitment

126 *Establishment of the EEAS*

targets should be established for all nationals. The principle of temporary provisions as applied in the Council Regulation 401/2004 shall be laid down for under-represented Member States.

(Brok and Verhofstadt 2010: p. 8)

In particular, Polish MEP Saryusz-Wolski was a regular campaigner for increased access of new member states' personnel, but failed to secure quotas or stricter rules for enforcing so-called geographical balance (European Voice 2010a). Another element that developed into a contentious point for the European Parliament in the negotiations was the nomination of EU ambassadors to the EEAS delegations. The Brok–Verhofstadt working paper clearly staked out the demand:

Appointees to senior EEAS posts and strategically important political decisions on the ground (Heads of Delegations, EUSRs) are to be heard by the relevant parliamentary committee, before taking up their duties, so as to provide them with sufficient political legitimacy and authority.

(Brok and Verhofstadt 2010: p. 5)

Other elements: political accountability

In addition to demanding a say in the personnel policy of the EEAS, this demand was one element of the drive towards political accountability, which characterised the negotiation of the EP delegation. The outcome did not result in US-style hearings in the EP, but rather a European compromise. A parliamentary Committee behind closed doors would exchange views with heads of delegations after they had been nominated but before they took up their post (Interviews 2, Council official, 2011; Interview 20, Senior EEAS official, 2012; Interview 24, EP assistant, 2012). The original proposal by the HR in conjunction with the member states had only foreseen an 'informal exchange of views with [heads of delegations to] strategic partner countries' (Interview 20, Senior EEAS official, 2012). The EEAS underlined the fact that these were 'non-hearings', while the EP stressed that it had achieved the right to a hearing of heads of delegation (Interview 20, Senior EEAS official, 2012). While the EP clearly did not get what it wanted out of these negotiations, neither did the other side. Where the initial proposal planned on informal meetings for a limited and clearly defined number of posts, the EP received formal meetings for those posts the EP deemed strategic or relevant (Interview 20, Senior EEAS official, 2012). Some perceived this as a placebo, or a 'smokescreen', for the European Parliament (Murdoch 2012: p. 1018). In the medium term, a different interpretation of the outcome may yet emerge, as a senior EEAS official speculated: 'if a member state has a good diplomat who has been through the whole system, assessment centre, shortlist, appointment by HR; if that person is then dumped by EP, it will create real problems' (Interview 20, Senior EEAS official, 2012).

Like the exchanges of view with heads of delegations, other elements of the EP position were retained in the negotiation but not in the Council decision, instead ending up in a declaration on political accountability. While the exchange of views clearly relates to nomination and influence on staff and their priority, some other features belong in a separate category: political accountability. The special declaration on accountability (DPA) by the HR linked directly to the Council decision on setting up the EEAS was the European Parliament's consolation prize (Helwig 2013: p. 244). The parliament's delegation had focused on it when major other demands outlined above seemed unlikely to materialise. The DPA codified the concessions made to the EP on exchanges of view of nominated ambassadors, including specific agreements on information exchange with CFSP and CSDP missions, and the requirement of a politically accountable representative to appear in parliament (High Representative 2011a).

Towards the 2010 decision

In between the inter-institutional triangle above, the negotiations on the setting up of the EEAS are distinct in one specific way. Institutionalist theory expects the institutional landscape to change with the creation of a new organisation. Moe has put it most concisely: 'Once an agency is created, the political world becomes a different place' (Moe 1989: p. 282). The EEAS was only created at the end of these negotiations, of course, but there was a new element in the negotiations. The High Representative of the Union for Foreign Affairs and Security Policy was appointed in November 2009 and was party to the 'quadrilogue' negotiations, in particular since the HR was required to propose the decision on the setting up of the EEAS (Council of the EU 2009: p. 3). As High Representative, Catherine Ashton had been tasked to draft the decision to set up the EEAS and implement it. Of course, without an administration of her own (Erkelens and Blockmans 2012: p. 14) the HR had to resort to a number of administrative stopgap measures to make up for the missing institutional back office usually in charge of such a task.

The Swedish Presidency had foreseen a preparatory group to assist Ashton in her task, but Ashton chose to follow a different approach (Interview 8, Senior diplomat, 2011). In early 2010, she set up a 'steering committee' (Murdoch 2012: p. 1017) or 'high level group' (Erkelens and Blockmans 2012: p. 15), which included a strong representation of the Commission and the Council and representatives of the rotating Council presidencies tasked to deal with the EEAS set-up (EUobserver 2010; European Voice 2010a). While one might think that this strong buy-in of the two main parties needed for agreement should be conducive to finding a compromise, it was not. Murdoch reports the 'collapse' of this format after only a few meetings (2012: p. 1017). A senior official summed up the result as follows: 'That group started to work, but frankly without much success' (Interview 8, Senior diplomat, 2011). This is a recurring theme in the relevant interviews, sometimes described in even more negative terms: 'It was a dark period [...]; the atmosphere was very bad. Nothing had happened in this

128   *Establishment of the EEAS*

group she had set up' (Interview 8, Senior diplomat, 2011). While this is not corroborated in Erkelens and Blockmans (2012), the gist of the argument – that substantial progress on a draft decision was only made upon appointing a senior Danish diplomat, Poul Skytte Christoffersen as special advisor – is consistently presented in the literature (Murdoch 2012: p. 1017) and in interviews (Interview 1, Council official, 2011; Interview 8, Senior diplomat, 2011). From then on, a small informal team started to do the work of the steering committee, albeit with less guidance: the group had 'no specific mandate, no specific task'; they were 'not even paid' (Interview 8, Senior diplomat, 2011). Seconded national diplomats, the Council and the Commission, rather than EEAS own staff, thus did the first round of drafting on behalf of Ashton. It was also observed that the work that had been done before was 'really based on a very narrow concept of the EEAS. Sort of an administrative unit for CFSP and [it] did not at all correspond to the broad approach, which was I think the consensus among member states' (Interview 8, Senior diplomat, 2011). This appears to reflect an approach by parts of the Commission towards the EEAS (see above).

The new group representing the EEAS in at least an informal way built its work on the Swedish Presidency report and the earlier discussions in COREPER (Interview 8, Senior diplomat, 2011). HR Ashton was particularly involved in elements of the ensuing negotiation with the Commission, which is unsurprising given her previous post as Trade Commissioner and the fact that she had a cabinet with those direct links to the Commission. These negotiations of course concerned staff numbers, divisions of development policy and the EEAS as well as the nominations of heads of delegation (Interview 8, Senior diplomat, 2011). At the same time, Ashton's cabinet seem to have kept more distance from the other parts of the negotiations (Interview 8, Senior diplomat, 2011). Despite this approach towards the Commission, pressure does not appear to have eased the during negotiations:

> Ashton in the compromise [...] had been quite forthcoming towards the Commission. And actually agreed solutions [...] went further than most member states actually thought was wise in pleasing the Commission. But I would say that we didn't have a positive response or benefit from that by having a more flexible approach to the Commission.
>
> (Interview 8, Senior diplomat, 2011)

In addition to being 'framed' by the European Council from before taking office (Erkelens and Blockmans 2012: p. 10), the HR/VP had to contend with a very demanding European Commission.

The decision

The final outcome of the four-party negotiations, i.e. the 'Council decision of 26 July 2010 establishing the organisation and functioning of the European External Action Service' (Council of the EU 2010b) had taken several steps to mature,

Establishment of the EEAS   129

including the Swedish, Spanish and Belgian Presidency. After several rounds of talks, the 'last and decisive round of quadrilogues took place in Madrid on 21 June 2010' (Erkelens and Blockmans 2012: p. 20). Despite a hiccup in the negotiations (Murdoch 2012: p. 1017), the final set-up of the EEAS has remained in the framework set out in earlier documents. Its official status was determined to be a 'functionally autonomous body of the European Union separate from General Secretariat of the Council and from the Commission with the legal capacity necessary to perform its tasks' (Council of the EU 2010b: art. 1). This channelled the 2004–05 terminology of 'sui generis' by not defining any known type of EU institution, agency or office as a legal template. It answers the question raised in the 2005 Joint Report 'as to whether this should be an autonomous service, neither in the Commission nor in the CSG, or whether it should be partly attached to either or both' (Joint Progress Report 2005), with the answer already given during member states discussions in 2005 (Luxembourg Presidency 2005) and fixed into the text of the Swedish Presidency Report of 2009: 'the EEAS should be a service of a sui generis nature separate from the Commission and the Council Secretariat' (Council of the EU 2009: p. 6). A legal commentary noted that '[t]his suggests that the EEAS cannot be regarded as a service of the Commission and must therefore be separate from it' (Blockmans *et al.* 2013: p. 7) – an observation thrown into some doubt by administrative practice, as detailed in Chapter 6. The decision nevertheless almost explicitly returned to an equidistant formula between the Commission and the Council, highlighting that not much had shifted between 2004 and 2010. Despite this vague conception, the decision did refer to the fact that the EEAS received a quasi-institutional status in decisions regarding its staff, budget and its organisation through the amended staff and financial regulations (Council of the EU 2010b: recitals 8, 14). This reflected in many ways the intra-Council compromise among member states.

The scope of the EEAS was equally determined in the decision's annex. It was in many ways an expanded version of the early discussions in 2005 and 2009. While in 2005 the member states' view were still widely dispersed, their middle ground was the inclusion of the external policies part of the General Secretariat as well as DG RELEX. The inclusion of the military parts of the CSG as well as the Situation Centre were also still in doubt. By 2009, these parts had been agreed in principle as part of the new structure (Council of the EU 2009: p. 3). Other policy areas and DGs were excluded and remained excluded in the final decision. Together with any functions relating to expenditure of the general EU budget, the Commission retained these parts with the support of the EP. In particular in terms of budget, the decision developed more detailed rules in articles 8 and 9 in order to both ensure cooperation with the Commission in programming and safeguard the Commission's powers (Council of the EU 2010b).

Staffing had been identified as a special issue since the inception of the EEAS. Bringing in officials from three distinct sources was seen as one of the major innovations in organisational design aimed at providing the ability to bridge the institutional divides of earlier days. But staffing also concerned the central institutional self-interest of the administrative actors involved, as well as

130 *Establishment of the EEAS*

the member states. The decision also specifies that one third of staff need to be from the EU member states' diplomatic service, while at the same time at least 60% of staff must be permanent civil servants of the EU (Council of the EU 2010: art. 6.9). This was a variation of the original language of three equal sources, which had been seen as impossible to maintain given the divergence in numbers between the Council Secretariat and the Commission. It also represented both the interest of member states to have a minimum share of staff, while ensuring a majority of supranational civil servants as demanded by the EP. The EP and some member states' demands for geographical and gender balance have also been included in the staffing rules of the decision (Council of the EU 2010: art. 6.8). Based on the argument that EU budgetary rules required the Commission to be in charge of the budget's execution, all staff working on budgetary management had been retained by the Commission.

The decision, which also entailed a declaration on political accountability by the HR, thus addressing concerns voiced by the EP, was a more detailed version of the general compromises found in earlier rounds of discussions between the actors in the setting up of the EEAS. This entailed the level of information the EP were to receive from the HR/VP on her and on the EEAS's activities, as well as who could represent the HR/VP politically before the EP. It was agreed that depending on the legal nature of the topic, either a Commissioner or a representative of the Rotating Presidency would replace the HR in the EP. Ashton also agreed to increased dialogue with the EP and made some concessions on confidential information in foreign policy (Erkelens and Blockmans 2012: p. 28). The EP as a recent addition to the fold has received some assurances but mostly outside of the legal text of the Council decision.

Conclusion

The establishment of the EEAS during the inter-institutional settlement shows how the EU institutions and member states involved pushed for their institutional preferences to be included in the legal set-up of the EEAS. The politics of Eurocratic structure approach would have expected member states to be cautious in relation to the transfer of powers to an EU body. It would also expect the Commission to attempt to integrate any new tasks into its own organisational structure if they were concerned with the Commission's core mission. The EP was seen as supporting any structure that would increase its influence in the policy area.

By looking at the contested elements of the EEAS with a specific focus on status, scope and staffing in the new service from 2004 until the final negotiations in summer 2010, the EEAS appears as an illustrative case of Eurocratic politics. The politics of Eurocratic structure clearly accounts for the cautious transfer of powers from the side of the member states and their attempts at securing entrance into the new structure via staff. Sovereignty concerns by the member states also determined the negotiation of the status of the EEAS, which member states sought to keep distant from the European Commission. Member

Establishment of the EEAS 131

states struggled with finding an agreement on the organisation's status, scope and staffing. They wanted the EEAS to be independent to prevent Commission interference, but not so independent that it could challenge the member states themselves. When they agreed on the general position to make the EEAS an *assimilated* institution, it not only locked in the nature of the EEAS, it also locked in the change of negotiating format. Instead of being only reliant on the Commission for agreement, changes to legislative instruments brought in the EP as a potential roadblock.

The European Commission and the European Parliament counterbalanced this pressure to a relevant degree by creating strong procedural links between the EEAS and the Commission in budgetary procedures. Despite the fact that the EEAS concerns core Commission business, the position of the member states prohibited the Commission from integrating the service completely into its fold. As a consequence, the Commission as early as 2005 sought a different strategy: it aimed to minimise the impact of the new organisation on the Commission's authority, thus working towards a reduced institutional status and scope as well as strong control over staffing und the budget. The Commission pushed for a close link and strong safeguards of Commission policy areas and responsibilities.

The European Parliament was seeking incorporation of the EEAS into the Commission in order to increase its oversight over the new body and EU foreign policy, despite its limited formal powers in the policy area. This activist position is in line with expectations of Eurocratic politics, but remains only partially satisfied by acts of the High Representative in relation to information flow to the EP and to budgetary control, as well as hearing-like discussions with future heads of delegations. The European Parliament continued to demand EEAS integration into the Commission as a bargaining chip and only surrendered it late in the negotiations.

In this executing coalition of four actors, preferences held in the inception phase of the EEAS reappeared in the negotiation, linking the political conflict about the exact establishment of the service to the political conflicts that shaped the original decision to create it. While the legal link to the previous stage was tenuous, the actors entered the negotiations with long held and long expressed beliefs about how this new organisation should be shaped, and deviated very little from agreements made early on. Path dependency in this second stage seems largely to have been determined by stable preferences over the institutional outcomes and unwillingness to renegotiate an agreed text. More detail was added to already agreed elements of the organisation's design. Changes to the institutional rules under which decisions take place, in this case the need for the EP's approval, added additional layers onto the decision. Considering that some of the actors remained the same individuals, for example in the parliamentary delegation, the outcome was arguably shaped by the negotiation format as much as by the weight of earlier political disagreements. The HR as a new actor on the scene wielded modest but increasing influence over time.

As with the inception phase, the establishment of the service provided the EEAS with a legal base and more detailed structure and operating requirements,

132   *Establishment of the EEAS*

but left many of the details of the day-to-day running of the organisation and the management of relations to other organisations at the EU level to be developed later. The following chapter will look more closely at how the new organisation started to operate, how it took its place in the Brussels administrative concert. In the process, it will show how bureaucracy theories and bureaucratic politics are helpful in understanding the new organisation's behaviour and environment in a phase of consolidation.

References

Blockmans, Steven; Hillion, Christophe; Cremona, Marise; Curtin, Deirdre; De Baere, Geert; Duke, Simon; Eckes, Christina; Van Vooren, Bart; Wessel, Ramses A. and Wouters, Jan, *EEAS 2.0 2013: A Legal Commentary on Council Decision 2010/427/ EU Establishing the Organisation and Functioning of the European External Action Service* (7 February 2013). CEPS Paperbacks, Brussels.

Dinan, Desmond 2011: Governance and Institution: Implementing the Lisbon Treaty in the Shadow of the Euro Crisis. *Journal of Common Market Studies Annual Review*, vol. 49, pp. 103–121.

Erkelens, Leendert and Blockmans, Steven 2012: Setting up the European External Action Service: An institutional act of balance. *CLEER working paper* 2012/1. CLEER: Den Haag.

EUobserver 2010: EU mandarins drafting blueprint for diplomatic corps. Brussels, 22.01.2010.

European Voice 2010a: Turf wars continue over EU's diplomatic corps. Brussels, 10.03.2010.

Helwig, Niklas 2013: EU Foreign Policy and the High Representative's Capabilities-Expectations Gap. *European Foreign Affairs Review*, vol. 18, no. 2, pp. 235–254.

Kelemen, R. Daniel 2002: The Politics of 'Eurocratic' Structure and the new European agencies. *West European Politics*, vol. 25, no. 4, pp. 93–118.

Kelemen, R. Daniel and Tarrant, Andrew 2011: The political foundations of the Eurocracy. *West European Politics*, vol. 34, no. 5, pp. 922–947.

Lefebvre, Maxime and Hillion, Christophe 2010: The European External Action Service: towards a common diplomacy? *SIEPS EPA* no. 6.

Missiroli, Antonio 2010: The New EU Foreign Policy System after Lisbon: A Work in Progress. *European Foreign Affairs Review*, vol. 15, pp. 427–452.

Moe, Terry 1989: The Politics of Bureaucracy. In Chubb and Peterson (Eds.): *Can the Government Govern?* Brookings: Washington, DC.

Murdoch, Zuzana 2012: Negotiating the European External Action Service (EEAS): Analyzing the External Effects of Internal (Dis)Agreement, *Journal of Common Market Studies*, vol. 50, no. 6, pp. 1011–1027.

Juncos, Ana E. and Whitman, Richard 2010: The Lisbon Treaty and the Foreign Security and Defense Policy: Reforms, Implementation and the Consequences of (non)-Ratification. *European Foreign Affairs Review*, vol. 14, pp. 25–46.

Raube, Kolja 2012: The European External Action Service and the European Parliament. *The Hague Journal of Diplomacy*, vol. 7, no. 1, pp. 65–80.

Establishment of the EEAS 133

Official documents

Auswärtiges Amt [German Foreign Office]

Auswärtiges Amt 2010: Ortez vom 27.09.2010. Errichtung des Europäischen Auswärtigen Dienstes: praktische Auswirkungen auf die Arbeiten unserer Auslandsvertretungen. [Establishment of the European External Action Service: practical implications for the work of our foreign representations.]

Auswärtiges Amt 2012: Brief betr. Anfrage vom 16.11.2012. Europäischer Auswärtiger Dienst: Deutsche Positionen. Berlin, 20.12.2012. [European External Action Service: German positions.]

Council of the EU

Council of the EU 2007: General Secretariat of the Council of the European Union Note to Delegations. IGC 2007 Mandate. 11218/07. Brussels, 26.06.2007.

Council of the EU 2008: Progress report from the Presidency to the European Council. Preparatory work in view of the entry into force of the Lisbon Treaty. 10650/08. Brussels, 13.06.2008.

Council of the EU 2009: Presidency report to the European Council on the European External Action Service. 14930/09.

Council of the EU 2010b: Decision of 26 July 2010 establishing the Organisation and Functioning of the European External Action Service 2010/427/EU.

Joint Progress Report by the Secretary General/High Representative and the European Commission (Joint Progress Report) 2005: Joint Progress Report on the European External Action Service. 9956/05. Council of the EU: Brussels.

Luxembourg Presidency 2005: European External Action Service. Report on Discussion with Member States. 01.05.2005.

European Commission

European Commission 2002c: Communication from the Commission. A Project for the European Union. COM(2002)247final. Brussels, 22.05.2002.

European Commission 2002d: For the European Union. Peace, Freedom, Solidarity. Communication from the Commission on the institutional architecture. COM(2002)728 final/2. Brussels, 11.12.2002.

European Commission 2004b: Draft options paper circulated in the Commission Services. 4.11.2004.

European Parliament

Brok, Elmar and Verhofstadt, Guy 2010: Proposal for the establishment of the EEAS. Working Document by Elmar Brok (AFET) and Guy Verhofstadt (AFCO), rapporteurs on EEAS.

European Parliament 2005: European Parliament resolution on the institutional aspects of the European External Action Service on 26 May 2005.

European Parliament 2009b: Report on the institutional aspects of setting up the European External Action Service. Own Initiative Report (Brok Report) INI 2009/2133. Brussels.

European Parliament 2010a: Conference of Presidents Report on the EEAS. Brussels.

134   *Establishment of the EEAS*

Foreign and Commonwealth Office

Foreign and Commonwealth Office 2013: Response to Freedom of Information request FOI 1256–12. London, 27.03.2013.

High Representative

High Representative 2011a: Declaration of Political Accountability. High Representative of the Union for Foreign Affairs and Security Policy (HR) 2011.

High Representative 2011b: Report by the High Representative to the European Parliament, the Council and the European Commission. Brussels, 22.12.2011.

Other

Miliband, David and Bildt, Carl 2010: Letter to the Right Honourable Baroness Ashton, High Representative of the Union for Foreign Affairs and Security Policy, Vice-President of the Commission. London/Stockholm, 03.03.2010.

6 Bureaucracy, competition and control

The consolidation of the European External Action Service

With the block transfer of staff from the European Commission and the Council Secretariat on 1 January 2011 (EEAS 2010), the EEAS finally appeared as a full organisation on the Brussels institutional scene. While an inter-institutional agreement on the EEAS had been reached already by July 2010 and senior management had been subsequently nominated in December 2010, it was in 2011 that a full organisation including rank and file was put into place. So short was the notice of the final transfer that a European weekly concluded 'Muddle and delay blight start of diplomatic corps' (European Voice 2010b).

In order to explain how the new organisation operated in the early years of its existence, this chapter analyses the consolidation of the EEAS as a functioning organisation from 2011 to 2013 from a bureaucratic theory perspective. It addresses the consolidation of the EEAS as a new organisation in the EU bureaucratic environment and seeks to explore how the EEAS operates within it. Whereas previous chapters have focused on the EEAS as an object of political contestation between external actors during the European Convention and in the run-up to the EEAS decision, this chapter begins by looking at the EEAS's internal operation. As the EEAS is first and foremost a bureaucratic organisation, bureaucracy theory is used to explore the early development of the new organisation. Bureaucratic politics informs the analysis where inter-relations between organisations or parts of organisations are concerned.

Any new organisation will at first be concerned with establishing its own hierarchical structure, operational processes and boundaries. Bureaucracy theory offers a number of tools to approach the internal factors of organisation. It predicts that the EEAS, and indeed any new administrative body, has an interest in expanding its budget, sphere of competence and autonomy of action (see Chapter 3) as set out in the EEAS decision and its institutional environment. As bureaucratic politics is mainly concerned with interactions between organisations, it adds to the analysis by explaining the impact that external contestation has on the EEAS organisational structure. A plausibility probe of the main bureaucratic processes, i.e. budget maximisation, bureau shaping and bureaucratic politics (see Chapter 3), shows the EEAS to be a useful case for this type of analysis.

Earlier phases of institutional creation highlighted attempts by other organisations to influence the shape and organisation of the EEAS, and these processes

136　*Consolidation of the EEAS*

are unlikely to have subsided. The focus of the chapter thus shifts to the organisation's environment and considers relations between pre-existing actors in EU external relations and foreign policy and the EEAS. Guided by a bureaucratic politics approach, it explores how far the EEAS as an organisation has been shaped by control exercised from other EU actors and competition between them. Inter-relations between administrative and political actors, conceptualised here as bureaucratic politics and operationalised as instruments of control, were inserted at the stage of setting up the new organisation and further specified in its aftermath. In analysing the relations of the EEAS through the many forms of control experienced by the organisation, this chapter allows for an insight into the contested environment of the new service. Several mechanisms of control, such as oversight mechanisms, staffing and organisation, budget, and administrative procedures, are scrutinised with regard to the relations of the EEAS with other EU bodies. After looking in turn at control of the EEAS by the European Commission, by the member states and the Council Secretariat as well as by the European Parliament, it concludes by highlighting the patterns of control, each distinctive to the relevant institution, exercised over the service through a variety of mechanisms.

In order to explore these two phenomena of internal functioning and the competitive inter-relations with other institutions and organisations, this chapter relies on similar sources as the previous chapters, i.e. semi-structured qualitative interviews and documentary analysis. To capture effects on the level of the individual official, it brings in additional evidence from a small-scale standardised survey of EEAS officials.

The EEAS as an emerging bureau: maximising budgets, shaping the service or bureaucratic politics?

The EEAS had to reconstruct an organisational structure and build a foreign policy and external relations bureaucracy in the first two years of its existence from different elements taken out of other organisations. How this administrative structure can be analysed and whether the evidence supports the insights of bureaucracy theory is the first central question addressed by this chapter. This section focuses on the internal mechanisms of a newly created bureaucracy. Bureaucracies are largely defined in theoretical terms by internal characteristics and processes, perhaps most famously by Downs (1967). Whereas the EEAS has begun to be conceptualised as an administration and as part of the European administrative space (Henökl 2014; for other conceptualisations see Bátora 2013), public choice bureaucracy theory is a novel approach to this line of inquiry. It aims to capture general trends of organisational behaviour that are the driving force behind the organisation's functioning. But does the EEAS follow the main principles of bureaucratic behaviour as set out by bureaucratic theory?

The following analysis of qualitative evidence derived from interviews, archival sources and survey responses will shed light on the operational

Consolidation of the EEAS 137

principles at work in the EEAS and how well they fit with standard assumptions on bureaucratic behaviour (Downs 1967; Dunleavy 1991; Niskanen 1971; Tullock 1965). It will look at budget maximisation, bureau shaping and bureaucratic politics as drivers for EEAS behaviour. It will also analyse whether expected bureaucratic processes such as over-formalisation occur within the EEAS. It will build on the notion that the EEAS is driven by organisational self-interest and then by competing actors' preferences, or bureaucratic politics, as explored by Michael E. Smith (2013).

Budget maximisation

The central objective of any bureaucratic organisation according to bureaucracy theory as established in Chapter 3 is the drive towards extending the organisation's own budget. Despite later arguments that the autonomous choice of tasks is more relevant than mere money supply (Dunleavy 1991; see below 'Bureau shaping'), a new organisation should be concerned about expanding its resource base. This should be visible in several ways. First, we should observe political statements of necessary budgetary increase; and second, less directly, an organisational focus on those tasks delivering a service to the budgetary authority. Finally, budget maximisation should manifest itself in budget increases, even if not all budget increases may be due to an organisational drive to obtain them.

Budget maximisation for the EEAS took a distinct note, given the role that budgetary questions had already played in the establishment of the EEAS (see Chapter 5). It was strongly influenced by a difficult economic climate and general opposition of many member states to increase spending at the EU level. At the same time, the general budget proposals of the European Commission included an increase, and the European Parliament demanded increases in each of the years of the EEAS's early existence (European Voice 2011b; European Voice 2012). The EEAS itself argued in statements to the EP, which acted as a budgetary authority in 2012, that its budget was insufficient as it was based on 'pro-rata transfers from the previously drafted budget of the Commission and the GSC'. 'This resulted', the EEAS budgetary report continued, 'at times in appropriations on certain lines being inadequate to deal with the actual expenditure on those lines' (EEAS 2012: p. 2).

Table 6.1 EEAS budget 2011–2016

Budget (million €)/Year	EEAS HQ	EEAS DEL	Total (% increase on previous year)
2011	188	276.1	464
2012	184.1	304.5	488.6 (+5.3%)
2013	195.81	312.95	508.76 (+ 4.1%)
2014	212.9	305.7	518.6 (+1.9%)
2015	218.9	383.9	602.8 (+16.2% – incl. COM transfers)
2016 (draft)	222.6	411	633.6 (+5.1%)

138 *Consolidation of the EEAS*

Political opposition from some member states, in particular on the part of the UK, was public and strong (EUobserver 2011). In the second budgetary report, the EEAS noted that it had proposed another 5.7% increase, which had been adjusted down to 4.1% by the budgetary authority, i.e. the Council and the European Parliament (EEAS 2013b: p. 5). Despite the fact that the EEAS has a record of noticeable budgetary increases, the organisation maintained its position that increases were 'limited' (EEAS 2013b: p. 5), indicating that the EEAS is at least rhetorically responding to the demands for economies by the member states. Nevertheless, there is a clear record of real budgetary increases in the first years, as Table 6.1 illustrates.

It remains unclear whether this level of growth can be sustained beyond the first years of operation, but here it is mainly of importance that the organisation has tried to obtain it and succeeded against the explicit wishes of some stakeholders. In order to gain the support of part of the budgetary authority, bureaucratic theory would foresee a reorganisation to deliver services to the budgetary authority, the Council and the European Parliament. As the establishment plan of the EEAS is not public and could not be obtained, interview evidence does not provide a clear picture. On the one hand officials are aware of the importance of positive relations with the European Parliament in particular:

> That's why what [we are] with the EP is very important, because it's the budgetary authority with Council, and if we can convince the EP that we're doing a good job and that the EEAS is added value, what we do in Brussels and in our delegations, the role of the delegations is extremely important. [...] This may pay off as regards the budget, that is why we are investing a lot in the parliament.
>
> (Interview 20, Senior EEAS official, 2012)

This importance of the EP for the new service is also partially reflected in the study by Henökl and Trondal, who find that 'an interesting observation concerns the relative importance that is given to the EP' when it comes to taking political signals into account (Henökl and Trondal 2013: p. 21). But while this appears a clear orientation, the official also did not report an increase in staff dealing with the budgetary authority and reported a rather mixed staffing effect due to the administrative merger, with some officials transferring out of the units to be merged before the creation of the service (Interview 20, Senior EEAS official, 2012).

Bureau shaping

A further refinement in bureaucracy theory as noted in Chapter 3 hypothesised that what is more in the organisation's interest than mere budget size is control over the type of tasks undertaken by the organisation. This concept of *bureau shaping* (Dunleavy 1991) would mean that there is a visible self-interest in the service to acquire desirable tasks and shed undesirable ones. While this

Consolidation of the EEAS   139

appears simple, an empirical manifestation of this effect is not particularly easy to identify. In the EU political system, the substance of tasks is largely derived from the treaty mandate and can hardly be changed by the administrative organisation. In an organisation responsible for external relations, events in the outside world play a large role in setting the policy agenda. Nevertheless, internal organisational processes will not completely come to a halt except in the most extraordinary circumstances. Some observations of these processes should thus be possible.

The clearest instance where the EEAS was organisationally shaped by substantive interest of the leadership, i.e. the High Representative, was the top structure of the EEAS and in second order the case of crisis management structures. A diplomat recalled that

> [they] made a first organogram, which was consulted with Ashton and she approved that. But then she sort of disowned it later on. [The] organogram was clearly a Secretary-General and two Deputy Secretaries General, while at a certain stage [Ashton] wanted in reality some sort of collective leadership where the Director and the Deputies should be more or less at the same level.
>
> (Interview 8, Member State Diplomat, 2011)

This collective leadership, which solidified into the corporate board on the organogram, shows some impact of the HR's structural preferences on the organisation. The HR had developed and expressed preferences in terms of the person and approach to be taken and an organisation role was found (Interview 4, EEAS official, 2011).

Additional evidence of bureau shaping could be found in the early transition period and the first establishment of an organogram as well as frequent adaptations to it in the first years of operation. Despite its many variations, none of the adaptations touches the leadership structure designed as a collective 'board', the level of managing directors and the overall basis of the organogram on largely existing structures of the Commission. If bureau shaping was taking place, it was occurring on a more narrow and subtle level as illustrated below.

The appointment of Agostino Miozzo as a Managing Director for crisis response had organisational implications as he created a 'quasi-institutionalised inter-service' coordination platform (Oxfam 2012: pp. 21–22). Tercovich argues that the appointment and subsequent restructuring were Ashton's way 'to fill what she perceived to be a fundamental gap in the EU's crisis management structures' (Tercovich 2014: p. 3). Tercovich also links this institutional substructure to a specific type of policy response to crises, the EU's comprehensive approach (Tercovich 2014: pp. 3–4), highlighting the link between policy preferences and institutional structure inside the EEAS. Both outside pressures from the member states as well as internal preferences combined to shape the organisation: 'outside pressure, Ashton having special ideas and preferences in this part [...] meant that the top became rather top heavy' (Interview 8, Member

140   *Consolidation of the EEAS*

State diplomat, 2011). In the EEAS review in 2013, the EEAS addressed this issue by suggesting a reduction in Managing Directors (EEAS 2013a: p. 4). Since a reduction of these senior posts would negatively affect the ability of member states to influence the staffing of the organisation, it was not a likely to be an immediate outcome of reorganisation. As these examples indicate, internal processes of consolidation are not neatly separable from external effects and have an impact on internal processes.

Bureaucratic politics: internal effects of external contestation

Bureaucratic politics are processes most likely observed at senior levels of the administration, where negotiations about resources and rules and interaction strategies with other organisations are discussed. Nevertheless, if bureaucratic politics persist, they should also have effects on the administrator level. Both the corporate and the individual desk level will be considered here in turn.

At the corporate level, the way rules about interactions with other organisations were set gives telling insights into the early phase of relations between the Commission and the EEAS. Several interviews from the earliest days of existence of the service illustrate that although the service had taken over a host of administrative processes from the Commission, internal formal procedures needed to be established:

> We are working on formal channels, but at the moment we don't have them in all areas. There are still fundamental questions that need answering.
>
> (Interview 4, EEAS official, 2011)

The result was not seen as an exercise in streamlining procedures:

> In each and every case, one has chosen complicated solutions. Only because of this mistrust created by this outsourcing, merger, divestiture, take-over, whatever you want to call it, which has happened, everybody tried to feather their own nest.
>
> (Interview 14, Senior EEAS official, 2012)

This work was done in parallel with negotiating the procedural links to other organisations, further complicating the matter. It was also done while the organisation was not only building internal processes, but also building internal structures to deal with these types of corporate processes. A comparison of an early version of the organogram with a later one illustrates that the corporate side of the EEAS consolidated considerably from 2010 to 2012, moving from a structurally semi-attached grouping of units to the level of managing directorate.

Due to the difficult nature of the early days of cooperation, relations with the Commission needed spelling out in ever-greater detail. Commission staff

Consolidation of the EEAS 141

involved in writing the 'Vademecum on Working Relations with the European External Action Service' (European Commission 2011a, b) described the evolution of the document:

> The focus of that document is therefore rather bureaucratic, and naturally left a lot of questions open – either because answers still needed to be worked out in practice, over time, or because some questions hadn't even been imagined at that moment in time.
>
> (Interview 23, Commission official, 2012)

As a result, a revision followed with an increase in technicality that is also visible in the vademecum's length, which grew from 26 to 40 pages (European Commission 2011a, 2011b). The latter version was then revised and restructured in the 'Working Arrangements between Commission Services and the European External Action Service (EEAS) in relation to External Relations Issues' (European Commission 2012a) but has stabilised at a similar level of detail.

But also at the more political level of the administration, the HR's cabinet appears to have acted largely as a barrier, as interlocuters of the EEAS perceived it: 'I had to have links to the cabinet and to her, to the extent that it was possible, which was very difficult' (Interview 8, Member State diplomat, 2011) or 'Nobody replies to our mails, nobody returns our phone calls' (Interview 2, Senior Council Secretariat official, 2011). While this was largely a feature of the earliest operation of the new organisation and has since improved, it did appear to shape the perception of the EEAS's external collaborators. It also indicates the direct links that exist between the internal functioning of the EEAS and its relations to the institutional environment it operates in. At the EU level, no organisation is an island.

This fraught relationship at the corporate relations level between the EEAS and the Commission also has repercussions at the desk level for each individual official. Here, two indicators are used to explore how officials in the EEAS view the other actors at the EU level. The first asked them to rank the reliability of an actor for providing reliable information, the second asked the respondents to rank institutional actors according to whether they are supportive of the EEAS or not. If bureaucratic politics persist, distrust towards other bureaucratic actors, especially the Commission, would be high. Similarly, actors which do not have bureaucratic links to the EEAS should be seen as more supportive than those that do. The evidence derived from the small-scale standardised survey of EEAS officials will be the best guide to the type of perceptions of other organisations present at level of desk officer.

As a first indicator for bureaucratic politics in action at the desk level, the survey contained a question on the reliability of an actor as an information source. The item 'For additional information on a policy, the European Commission services/Council Secretariat/Permanent representations are a reliable source' tried to capture whether between the three sources of the new service, trust has been damaged in the process of operation. For the European Commission, 14

142 *Consolidation of the EEAS*

respondents either agreed or strongly agreed that the Commission is a reliable source, which represents more than 90% of respondents. For the Council Secretariat, 46%, or seven respondents, agree it is a reliable source, while five are undecided. Two respondents disagree that the Council Secretariat is a reliable source of information, with one strongly disagreeing. With regard to member states' permanent representations, the answers appear even less positive. While six respondents, agree that the permanent representations are a reliable source, an equal number are undecided, and the remaining 20% disagree. This seems to indicate less of a bureaucratic politics contestation between the EU-level actors and rather a higher level of distrust towards the member states and their agents in Brussels. Respondents who joined the EEAS from the European Commission exhibit distrust for the Council Secretariat. Those officials who joined the EEAS from the Commission exhibit distrust towards the member states' representations.

This touches on the concept of institutional loyalties and their impact on the behaviour of individual officials, an established research area in the study of EU bureaucratic structures (see for example Egeberg and Trondal 2011; Trondal and Veggeland 2003). This research has shown a layered picture of loyalties, in which national and supranational loyalties are not completely contradictory. The EEAS has already provided scholars of officials' orientation with a fertile field (Juncos and Pomorska 2013; Henökl 2015; Henökl and Trondal 2015). Henökl identifies different orientations in the objectives of officials from different backgrounds (2015). Juncos and Pomorska underline the positive attitudes to the newly created EEAS of its staff and the prevalent strong levels of identification with the EU more generally (Juncos and Pomorska 2013). These observations on loyalties are relevant for the operation of the service, in particular in the long run. As the focus in this last consolidation phase shifts to a bureaucratic perspective, individual bureaucrats' loyalties are a second-order measure. Simple measures of levels of trust in other institutions are used, not to determine the loyalties of individuals and impact on their actions, but rather to gauge whether institutional conflicts are reflected in attitudes at the desk level. The focus is thus less on the loyalty towards one institution than on the mistrust towards another.

When the question 'At the European level, which organisation should be driving European foreign policy?' was asked, expected divisions appeared more sharply. Respondents from the national diplomatic services indicated that the Council and European Council should be the driving force, while Commission officials and others largely saw the EEAS in the driving seat. Similarly, when it came to the answers on what the central roles for the EEAS ought to be, respondents displayed slightly varied role preferences for the EEAS depending on whether they had undergone a long-term diplomatic training programme or not. Those who had not gone through diplomatic training were less likely to consider the role of the EEAS as a platform for collaboration for member states. But this should not be overstated; the majority of respondents still saw this as an important or very important function of the EEAS.

Consolidation of the EEAS 143

In another item on bureaucratic politics, respondents were asked to judge which actor is most supportive of the EEAS, to gauge whether there was also a positive perception of which actors in Brussels were engaging positively with the EEAS. When combining the ranking of most supportive and supportive of the EEAS, the President of the European Council came out on top, just one response ahead of the European Parliament. The member states ranking was very divided: despite a high number of responses ranking them as supportive and very' supportive, they also received rankings as less supportive and least supportive. In this ensemble of institutional actors the European Commission was seen by eight respondents as less or least supportive, which is the most negative ranking among the choices presented.

The rankings that the Commission received for being supportive are, interestingly, not from those respondents who joined the EEAS from the Commission, but from respondents who joined the EEAS from the member states' diplomatic services and from outside of the EU and national institutions. This strengthens the observation made earlier that many Commission officials did not feel their institutional allegiance was rewarded when the EEAS was created and still see the Commission as not acting in the new service's interests. The effects of the turf war between Commission and EEAS were clearly still felt at the level of the individual administrator.

In sum, the first indicator for bureaucratic politics as shown in Table 6.2 focused on reliability of information emanating from an organisation. While it does not present a complete view of bureaucratic politics, it does highlight the distrust towards the Commission as the main bureaucratic competitor. This finding is supported by the second indicator, which asked about which organisation was most supportive of the EEAS. Former Commission officials also maintain high levels of trust towards the member states. Staff originating from the Commission in particular mistrust the Commission as an institution, while staff from the Secretariat and the member states are not less likely to trust their institutions of origin. It is noteworthy that staff joining from outside of the Brussels institutional circle are less likely to mistrust the Commission, which could indicate a shift in perception of the Commission in future when fewer staff will have had direct experience of the formative conflict.

If one links this evidence to the struggles about prominence and role in interactions between the EEAS and the Commission presented in the first part

Table 6.2 Perception of support by other EU bodies

Rank/Actors	Most supportive	Supportive	Less supportive	Least supportive
European Commission	–	6	4	4
European Parliament	2	8	3	–
President of EUCO	1	11	2	–
Member States	4	6	3	2

Source: own survey.

144 *Consolidation of the EEAS*

of this chapter, bureaucratic politics and the self-interest of organisations to act autonomously in their respective field can explain the rocky development of working relations between the new service and the existing EU institutions. The Commission needed to reassert its authority by blocking EEAS documents where it felt its mandate had been overstepped (Interview 23, Commission official, 2012). From before the actual creation of the EEAS until long into its early operational phase, interviewees referred to turf wars and inter-institutional battles between the EEAS, the Commission and the Council Secretariat (Interview 10, Senior EEAS official, 2011; Interview 19, Senior EEAS official, 2012; Interview 20, Senior EEAS official, 2012; Interview 28, Senior Commission official, 2013). At the same time, the survey points to the importance of experience in maintaining bureaucratic politics, which may mean that with increasing exchange of staff between member states' national diplomatic services and between delegations and headquarters, conflicts could lose intensity in the medium to long term. As the inter-organisational rules have been settled, the conflicts have subsided (Interview 23, Commission official, 2012).

While there is ample evidence for bureaucratic processes at work in the early operation phase of the EEAS, from interview, survey and other sources, there is also a clear indication that these processes are not independent from the previous contestation by outside actors. Some organisational parts, such as the managing directors, were clearly reflecting the interests of the member states in a stake in the running of the EEAS. This was even spelled out in a 2014 European Court of Auditors report on the setting up of the EEAS:

> As most of the management posts transferred to the EEAS were already occupied by permanent officials, the EEAS created a top-heavy structure, allowing a significant number of top posts to be occupied by Member State diplomats.
>
> (European Court of Auditors 2014: pp. 12–13)

The report went on to detail the increased levels of hierarchy used to accommodate the different stakeholders of the EEAS via senior management posts (European Court of Auditors 2014), a striking piece of evidence for the importance of external drivers for the internal organisation of the EEAS: analysed in more detail in the second part of this chapter.

Several internal processes, e.g. staff selection, were borrowed from Commission processes, indicating a strong link on the administrative level. An analysis of the early operation of the EEAS must thus also take into account the environmental conditions and how the actors that were involved in shaping the organisation early on continue to make their presence felt throughout this phase of consolidation (see also Chapter 3).

Building on quicksand? The EEAS and its institutional environment

The contestations about the EEAS have previously been traced through the treaty reform ideas of the European Convention and the legislative process leading to the EEAS decision in 2010. But even on the basis of treaty and decision, disagreements on the role and structure of the EEAS did not disappear with the organisation's birth. Rather, they have shifted towards focusing on controlling the EEAS's agenda and competing for competences, where they are not clearly prescribed through the legal text. These are familiar processes in institutional politics at the administrative level, and are often referred to as 'bureaucratic politics'. It is this bureaucratic politics that will inform the analysis of inter-administration collaboration and competition, especially between the Council Secretariat General and the European Commission. For more political institutions, such as the Council and European Parliament, the EEAS is not an administrative partner, but an administrative tool available to them. Here the element of controlling what the EEAS does may be of more concern. This struggle over control of the EEAS during its phase of consolidation by the organisations involved in its inception and establishment is the second central aspect of this chapter.

Any exercise of control will need to take into account the resources of the EEAS in terms of institutional status. The Council Decision establishing the organisation and functioning of the EEAS defines the *status of the EEAS* as:

> [a] functionally autonomous body of the European Union, separate from the General Secretariat of the Council and from the Commission with the legal capacity necessary to perform its tasks and attain its objectives.
>
> (Council of the EU 2010b)

As an outcome of the negotiations leading to the EEAS's establishment in Chapter 5, the EEAS is treated 'as an institution for the purposes of the financial and staff regulations' (Regulations 1080/2010 and 1081/2010). While the first description of the EEAS as an autonomous body is more concerned with establishing the distance of the organisation to other actors, the second legal description provides it with de facto institutional powers in at least its internal organisation.

While much has been made of the fact that it is not a legal institution, the EEAS possesses all the characteristics of a political and bureaucratic one. This ambiguity, which had its roots in the inception of the organisation during the European Convention, allows different interpretations of the organisation's autonomy to be played out in a continued game of 'structural politics' (Moe 1989). This of course is relevant in an inverse relationship to the level to which the EEAS is controlled by other organisations. This 'game' plays out differently in the relations with different actors, because the core actors in the EEAS's institutional environment have different tools at their disposal to seek influence on the

146 *Consolidation of the EEAS*

organisation. These differences become apparent by looking at each relevant actor, or indeed groups of actors: the European Commission, the Council and the member states, and the European Parliament.

The many faces of control: European Commission

The European Commission is still the main actor in the EU external relations field per se, as it retains important policy areas such as development and trade under its control, and is also tied to the EEAS in procedural matters. 'Procedural requirements affect the institutional environment in which agencies make decisions and thereby limit an agency's range of feasible policy actions' (McCubbins, Noll and Weingast 1987: p. 244) by inserting requirements into the decision-making process of an agency, such as notification of activities, rights of participation and others (McCubbins *et al.* 1987: pp. 257–258).

Administrative procedures

The EEAS as a foreign policy service presents a challenging environment for administrative procedures as it does not take regulatory or redistributive decisions. Its tasks are information gathering, strategy development, preparation of the decision-making process and programming, i.e. tasks that do not normally concern traditional administrative provisions. Most procedural requirements will thus be in the area of programming and financial implementation. The evolution of cooperation and competition between the EEAS and the Commission has peculiar beginnings, already introduced above.

The administrative negotiations started partly in parallel to the political discussions on the Council EEAS decision. All parties saw it as an extremely arduous task (Interview 4, EEAS official, 2011; Interview 15, Senior EEAS official, 2012; Interview 18, Council official, 2012; Interview 23, Commission official, 2012). An EEAS official involved in the negotiations described the situation: 'It was a bit schizophrenic [...] you were negotiating with the Commission, being part of the Commission yourself' (Interview 10, EEAS official, 2011). The administrative separation from the Commission started at least partially in an administrative void. Staff involved in the early negotiations on the administrative set-up of the EEAS recall the ambiguous situation: '[...] was running the show within the institutional limits [...] in the sense that [...] didn't have a mandate to be running the show' (Interview 10, EEAS official, 2011).

In addition to the difficult and ambiguous framework within which negotiations had to be conducted, the negotiations themselves were marred by a lack of mutual purpose. Instead of negotiations being simplified because both sides were Commission staff or had until recently been Commission staff, the negotiations left the EEAS negotiating side disillusioned with their former colleagues (Interview 10, EEAS official, 2011; Interview 14, Senior EEAS official, 2012; Interview 17, EEAS official, 2012). Finding an agreement with the Commission and the Council Secretariat, specifically on which members of staff were to join the

Consolidation of the EEAS   147

EEAS, was seen as a 'very, very complicated exercise' (Interview 10, EEAS official, 2011). For the staff to be transferred to the EEAS, the Commission's stance on their transfer was perceived very negatively: 'The Commission strategy was realistically not to try to incorporate the EEAS; we need to admit it's outside, but we will strangle it' (Interview 14, Senior EEAS official, 2012). The lack of trust in negotiations is a recurring theme in the administrative negotiations, but is also reflected among staff attitudes in the recent literature (Juncos and Pomorska 2013).

On the side of the Commission, the conclusion about the multitude of difficulties of this establishment process was that 'we had to do surgery, cut off one limb and in a way that it would work afterwards. The lesson we learned from this is to never ever do it again' (Interview 23, Commission official, 2012). The perception was that 'the corporate part of DG RELEX then had to reconstruct itself as EEAS' (Interview 23, Commission official, 2012). But there was also the acknowledgement that 'Things are not ideal, we need to have a reflex to coordinate. Some still have that first reflex to coordinate and then are told not to' (Interview 23, Commission official, 2012). Of course, the coordination reflex had always been an objective of EU foreign policy cooperation among the member states. The necessity to coordinate now includes the European Commission through a variety of new administrative processes. While the will to coordinate may still return, control and competition are still relevant mechanisms of relations between the two organisations: 'EEAS tries to write [documents, which are not in their mandate], they get caught' (Interview 23, Commission official, 2012).

Despite taking over the majority of administrative systems from the Commission, the newly created administration did not simply 'hum along' (Interview 10, EEAS official, 2011). This was due to the small numbers of administrative and support staff available to the service, which had not been foreseen in the negotiations with Council and Commission (Interview 10, EEAS official, 2011). As a consequence, the EEAS needed a number of 'service-level agreements' (Interview 10, EEAS official, 2011; European Commission 2010a, 2011c). The administrative agreements were perceived at least at first as one-sided: 'none of them were written inside the EEAS, they were written in the Commission. They were written from a Commission perspective and we had no other choice but to say, it's sink or swim, we'll take it' (Interview 14, Senior EEAS official, 2012). This unilateral stance by the Commission shows its invariably stronger negotiating position vis-à-vis the EEAS. The Commission's exercise of control thus started before the organisation had officially taken off. At the same time, it is clear from these documents that they prescribe obligations not only on the part of the EEAS, but also on the part of the Commission for services to be delivered to the EEAS (European Commission 2010a). Nevertheless, the feeling of 'betrayal' experienced by former DG RELEX staff has been documented elsewhere, too (Juncos and Pomorska 2013: p. 6).

The administrative after-effect of the 'surgery' was a vademecum for the staff of the Commission on how to deal with the EEAS (European Commission

148   *Consolidation of the EEAS*

2011a, b). Its first version was an internal guidance (European Commission 2011a; Interview 10, Commission official, 2011; Interview 28, Senior Commission official, 2013), i.e. a unilateral script by the European Commission on relations with the EEAS. The revision of the guidance already required a negotiated document with the EEAS (Interview 23, Commission official, 2012; European Commission 2011b; European Commission 2012), acknowledging the new role of the EEAS in co-determining the organisation of relations between the two organisations. An involved Commission official recalls the atmosphere as conflictual, but with a positive endnote: 'all needed to make their point and get it out of the system. It's much better now' (Interview 23, Commission official, 2012). But hierarchical elements were never out of sight: 'The EEAS is not an institution but a service, so cannot be named at the same level as the Commission' (Interview 23, Commission official, 2012). The Commission's supremacy in matters where the Treaties assign it independent powers had been successfully safeguarded throughout the establishment of the new organisation. Not incidentally, this 'protection of Commission prerogatives' had been an objective floated in the Commission as early as the inception phase of the EEAS (see Chapter 4).

Administrative procedures for the EEAS tied it deeply into Commission processes (European Commission 2011a, 2011b, 2012), at the end of which may then still lie a decision-making process involving the Council or the Council and EP. These procedures, however, also tied the Commission, making the picture more complex than simply one of control by the Commission. The EEAS is enmeshed in a network of agreements and procedures with its administrative collaborator, the European Commission. The EEAS is thus subordinate to its procedures, with the exception of Common Foreign and Security Policy where the Commission's involvement is still limited. This type of deep interwoven process that has been established between the Commission and the EEAS fits the pattern of 'administrative procedures as instruments of political control', or in this case bureaucratic control, identified by McCubbins *et al.* (1987).

Staffing and organisation

In addition to administrative procedure and service provision, the Commission retained in the decision on the EEAS a central role on senior staff selection, as the discussion of EEAS nomination procedures of heads of delegation illustrates. For senior civil servants in the EEAS, which includes the large number of heads of delegation, the procedure is complex. A Consultative Committee on Appointments (CCA), which was established in 2011, takes major preparatory steps for appointments in the service (High Representative 2011b: no. 27). Murdoch *et al.* illustrate how much these processes had been shaped by Commission procedure (Murdoch *et al.* 2013: p. 4; Murdoch *et al.* 2014), mirroring the acceptance of established Commission administrative practice for the majority of administrative processes discussed above. The CCA determines the selection panel for senior appointments and draws up the shortlist of candidates for appointment (Council of the EU 2010b: p. 3). The CCA consists of representatives of the member states (two), the Commission (one) and the Council Secretariat (one), and of course the EEAS (two). The Commission's leverage here has two layers. First, the shortlist of candidates itself needs agreement by the Commission, in particular where it concerns heads of delegations (European Commission 2012b). Second, the Commission is also still represented in the committee with a seat, which is significant if one remembers that Commission portfolios are more technical in nature and may provide opportunities to address difficult questions to future heads of delegation.

These nomination procedures indicate that both member states and the Commission have strong influence on nominations to the service, even if the final decision lies with the HR herself. First evidence in the literature suggests attempts by the EEAS to use its informational advantage in order to create greater autonomy in staffing (Murdoch *et al.* 2013: pp. 5–6). Murdoch, Trondal and Gänzle argue that due to reliance on pre-existing patterns of selection processes and a direct route to applications, the EEAS has remained 'largely independent of member states' influence' (Murdoch *et al.* 2014: p. 83). This finding sits somewhat uneasily with the fact that many heads of delegations have been nominated from the member states' diplomatic services:

> And this [the delegations] has at the same been the main gateway for member states, because they believed it was necessary to quickly arrive at one third of ambassadors from the member states and I think now after two years we are already at 31%, which is considerable. Since 2010 we have nominated 55–60 new ambassadors, which is almost half, and of these only four or five came from former DG RELEX.
>
> (Interview 14, Senior EEAS official, 2012)

It also does not consider the dependence of the EEAS on the European Commission through these procedures, which for this study is of equal relevance.

Beyond mere nominations of staff, early disagreements about process illustrate how deeply the Commission still reached into the organisation of the EEAS. Minutes of the College of Commissioners from December 2012 hint at the concern about unilateral action by the EEAS on reorganising delegations:

> any decision connected with the decisions referred to above [delegation business] and concerning the adoption of new organisation charts or amendments to existing ones, and any decision to (re)deploy Commission resources, would have to be taken in accordance with the cooperation procedures put in place by the Commission and the High Representative and in accordance with internal Commission procedures.
>
> (European Commission 2012c: p. 11)

Even before nomination procedures are enacted, the Commission retains involvement in deciding the organisation structures, such as delegations to which staff are later nominated. As has been shown above regarding administrative

150 *Consolidation of the EEAS*

procedures, EEAS autonomy over its own organisational structure is thus far from unlimited and external processes reach deep into the organisation. Another instance of these limits to autonomy can be found with regard to the EU delegations. Already in the EEAS decision, the need for Council and Commission to approve proposals to open or close delegations was written into the legislative text (Council of the EU 2010). The minutes of the 2028th meeting of the Commission record the 'Commission agreement on the opening of a European Union delegation in the United Arab Emirates, a full delegation in Myanmar and the closure of the delegation in Suriname' (European Commission 2012c: p. 10). The Commission's need to underline the importance of its role in this area of decision-making shows the need to reaffirm its veto power over the organisation of the delegation network. But the European Commission is not the only limit on the EEAS's organisational autonomy, as the role of the Council in the same case illustrates below.

Budget

Another central requirement of a modern bureau, besides its organisational structure, is the financial management of resources at its disposal as shown above. The budget was discussed there as a resource desired by the new organisation. In this section, the budget is more relevant as a path to influencing the organisation's behaviour through providing or denying resources to act. The Commission plays an essential role in the budgetary process for the EEAS in two distinct ways. First, it proposes the budget that is negotiated between the budgetary authorities Council and EP. Second, it dispenses EU funds abroad and is central to the programming of financial instruments. It is the Commission that 'sub-delegates' the authority to manage budgets to the Head of Delegation from the EEAS (Regulation 1081/2010: art. 51; European Commission 2012a). It remains the Commission that reports and controls other aspects of financial management, which is seen as its treaty-based prerogative (Interview 23, Commission official, 2012).

The EEAS acts in the budgetary process like other parts of the Commission. It gives 'coordinated' input for the annual budget draft to DG Budget as well as for the multiannual financial framework. The EEAS prepares country allocations, strategy papers and indicative programmes for some of the funding instruments, with the requirement to be in agreement with DG Development and Cooperation (European Commission 2012a). Because the EEAS acts like a Commission service in the formal inter-service consultation process, and is treated like one (Interview 23, Commission official, 2012), the Secretariat-General acts as arbiter of conflicts between the services. The Commission has retained considerable leverage over what the final output is (Interview 23, Commission official, 2012). Since the Secretariat-General is also directly linked to the Commission President, the power balance between the two actors is clear: it is skewed strongly in favour of the Commission.

The Commission's leverage over the new service is considerably higher than the original 'equidistant' formula (Interview 6, Senior Commission official,

Consolidation of the EEAS 151

2011) between Council and Commission would suggest. There are two reasons for this: first, the role of the HR as a member of the Commission subjects many decisions to Commission collegiate decision-making and the Commission process. Second, in the negotiations about the establishment of the EEAS, the EP attempted on various occasions to integrate the service into the Commission, as illustrated in Chapter 5. When this did not materialise, their position shifted to keeping most of the financial management under Commission control (Interview 24, EP assistant, 2012). These provisions give the European Commission a 'real-time' ability to control many (but certainly not all) activities of the EEAS: 'As an internal joke spells it out; if the EEAS needs to buy a newspaper, it needs to ask the Commission' (Interview 2, Senior Council official, 2011; similar Interview 20, Senior EEAS official, 2012; Interview 21, Commission official, 2012). Information and communication budgets in delegations had been historically in the operational budget under DG RELEX and were retained in the Commission's Service for Foreign Policy Instruments, or FPI (Interview 21, Commission official, 2012, see also European Commission 2013: pp. 36–37). This is an example of how the EEAS's control of funds is curtailed.

The provisions are also detailed procedural requirements for the EEAS about when to consult with which parts of the Commission. These financial requirements are also one of the elements that dramatically increased the complexity of the EEAS's operational environment, as two independent financial 'circuits' are used for the EU to operate its network of delegations, EEAS and Commission funds flowing through its own channels. In that way, the financial structure echoes the structure of political communications, with the Commission still having a direct line to the Commission staff in EU delegations. The financial prerogatives that were safeguarded by the Commission also had a direct organisational effect. Because the Commission retained control of the operational budget, the Foreign Policy Instrument Service was created to execute specific foreign policy budget lines (Interview 21, Commission official, 2012). The FPI is likely the most unusual administrative arrangement in the environment of the EEAS, as noted in Chapter 5. It consists of Commission staff and is legally part of the Commission, but at the same time is directly responsible to the High Representative and co-located with the EEAS (Council of the EU 2010b). While the EEAS has control of the administrative budget, the operational budget remains the responsibility of the FPI (Interview 21, Commission official, 2012). 'If the EEAS had been given more executive powers with regard to the budget, [the FPI] would have most likely been merged with a Directorate there' (Interview 21, Commission official, 2012). The FPI also hired some staff from the EEAS, as there is an overlap in staff profiles between both organisations (Interview 21, Commission official, 2012).

From these varied formal inter-bureaucratic relations, it is clear that the Commission is both the central collaborator with the EEAS as well as its central competitor. The Commission's role vis-à-vis the EEAS is also not fully captured by these two labels. It also exercises large amounts of control over the EEAS, for example through administrative procedures, staff selection and financial management. The power balance in this relationship clearly favours the

152 *Consolidation of the EEAS*

European Commission. At the same time, the Commission was always just one of the two parent organisations and one of three sources of staffing. The EEAS's relations with the Council Secretariat and the member states are the other immediate inter-bureaucratic linkages for the new service.

The many faces of control: the Council Secretariat, the President of the European Council and the member states

Despite the fact that the Council Secretariat is one of the parent organisations of the EEAS, it is not the only linkage between member states and the EEAS. It is therefore necessary to look at the relations not only of the Council Secretariat as an administrative actor, but also at the Member States in Council as they retain high stakes in EU foreign policy and its administration. Both elements of the Council display different mechanisms and different interests in their relations with the EEAS, adding to the complexity of the institutional environment.

Negotiations on administrative process with the Council Secretariat (CSG) started on a similar footing to those with the Commission. Although considerably smaller numbers were involved than had been the case with the Commission, the CSG also contained military elements of EU foreign policy, which were not smoothly integrated into the civil administration of the EEAS. Just as with the Commission, the operation of the EEAS depended on the continuation of services and service-level agreements.

Oversight

The member states' ambiguous interest, keenly guarding competences while complaining about ineffectiveness, was further illustrated a year into the EEAS's existence by the 'Non-paper on the European External Action Service' of December 2011 (Non-paper 2011). In it, the foreign ministers of 12 member states voiced their evaluation of the EEAS performance as a new body. It critically reviewed the internal organisation of the EEAS, as well as its coordination with the European Commission (Non-paper 2011: pp. 1–2). The signatories also underlined the importance of their own involvement in the EEAS:

> To avoid the setting up of a new structure disconnected from the Member States, there should be a close interaction between the EEAS and the Member States. In this regard, an important prerequisite for EEAS effectiveness is the close involvement of Member State personnel.
>
> (Non-paper 2011: p. 3)

Two years on from the initial negotiations on the service's functioning in 2009, the participation of member states' diplomatic personnel in the service was still a major point of contention. While those voicing their objectives were representing only a particular subset of member states, the similarities in their expression of concern compared to earlier phases detailed in Chapter 5 of this book are striking.

Consolidation of the EEAS 153

Another non-paper on the 'Strengthening of the European External Action Service' was prepared two years later by a group of member states including Austria, Belgium, Denmark, Estonia, Finland, Germany, Italy, Latvia, Luxembourg, the Netherlands, Poland, Slovakia, Spain and Sweden (Non-paper 2013). It expressed wider concerns about the organisational structure, including the need to review 'the processes and structure at senior management level [...] with a view to ensuring clear reporting lines and division of tasks' (Non-paper 2013: p. 2). Also in relations with member states, the internal processes of the EEAS are up for debate. Staffing concerns were somewhat downgraded, but still featured in this non-paper. The paper also stressed that the one-third requirement of national diplomats should be interpreted as 'a minimum level and not an upper ceiling' (Non-paper 2013: p. 3), opening the potential for an increase in the number of member states' diplomat numbers in the service and thus a potential increase of member states' control.

The main concern for the operation of the service, however, shifted for this group of member states towards the relations between the EEAS and the European Commission, which were seen as an impediment to an effective EEAS. In terms of both programming and financial management, the group pushed for a stronger role of the EEAS and more independence from the Commission's procedures (Non-paper 2013: p. 2). The internal organisation of the EEAS was equally not perceived as functioning at an optimal level (Non-paper 2013: pp. 2–3), which had both internal and external causes (see above). Of course, over the course of the first two years, not all member states subscribed to this stronger prospective role for the EEAS. As with the Commission before, the role of the Council in the restructuring of the delegation network is noteworthy. It has been shown above that the Commission's consent is required for opening or closing a delegation in a third country. The same holds true for the Council of the EU. In the case of the opening of delegations in the United Arab Emirates and Myanmar, as well as the closure of the Suriname delegation, the Council's approval was also required and given in a written procedure (COREU 645/12; COREU 664/12). As in the case of the Commission, the Council did not raise a veto but underlined that its consent was needed.

Administrative procedures

As far as the Council Secretariat was concerned, it was seen that it would continue to provide services to various policy fields including foreign affairs and that the chairing of meetings continued to require the expertise of the Secretariat (Interview 1, Council official, 2011; Interview 4, EEAS official, 2011; Interview 10, EEAS official, 2011). This was a position that had been opposed by the staff to be transferred to the EEAS:

> For the Secretariat General it was simply obvious that the Secretariat would have to continue to do its Secretariat functions. For people destined to go to

154 *Consolidation of the EEAS*

the EEAS this was an inconceivable duplication of functions; the EEAS could perfectly do the Secretariat functions as well.

(Interview 2, Senior Council official, 2011)

The corporate side of the Secretariat General insisted on this maintenance of tasks and the member states grudgingly accepted (Interview 1, Council Secretariat official, 2011; Interview 2, Council Secretariat official, 2011). An interlocutor from the external relations side of the Council predicted in 2011:

They [i.e. the remaining external relations sections of the Council Secretariat] are not a Directorate General on its own terms. This will change, it is because the thing was very controversial, so it was thought better not to make it too visible. But this will change.

(Interview 2, Council Secretariat official, 2011)

After having been loosely attached to the Secretary-General, the retained posts had by 2014 been restructured into a Directorate-General C for Foreign Affairs, Enlargement and Civil Protection. While this may not be the 'mini-foreign service' that EEAS staff had feared might be constructed in the Council Secretariat (Interview 10, EEAS official, 2011), it does show the struggle to determine the roles of the EEAS in relation to its second parent organisation, the Council Secretariat.

While implementing the arrangements for the EEAS, member states also worked hard to ensure that their role in the form of the Presidency of Council meetings would not be entirely erased. Vanhoonacker and Pomorska outline the different approaches of the Presidency to the EEAS and how far the member states were willing to relinquish their role (2013: p. 10). Helwig, Ivan and Kostanyan attempted to capture the practical application two years after the EEAS's creation, and present the detailed rules of chairing in a policy report (Helwig *et al.* 2013). The increase in complexity is largely a result of an attempt by both Council Secretariat and member states to retain their respective roles. An experienced former DG RELEX official recalls arguing about the role of the member states and the secretariat during the transitional period when the EEAS came into existence:

We pleaded for an immediate takeover of the Presidency tasks; in fact they were taken over by delegations one year before the administrative set-up at headquarters [...]. We argued very strongly at the time, saying if we didn't seize the day there was a danger that the old Presidency system would somehow persist into the new structures, which in a way it has to a surprising degree.

(Interview 19, Senior EEAS official, 2012)

Administrative procedures provided both the Council Secretariat and the member states with avenues to safeguard their own role. For the Council Secretariat this meant a supporting role at the negotiating table in Council, while for member states this translated into regaining some control over Presidency tasks, which elsewhere have been transferred to the High Representative, and by extension, to the EEAS.

In another instance of member states' control of EEAS activities, delegations played a central role. For example, from the beginning of the EEAS's operations, the new UK government used the change in organisational structure and legal foundation to challenge the established practice relating to joint representation of the EU in international organisations. Its diplomats were urged to look out for and stop the process of 'competence creep' by the EEAS (Burke 2014: p. 15). As early as a few months into the EEAS's existence, the British foreign minister was quoted as issuing a warning to the new organisation 'We will always guard against mission creep. We are very clear about what is the UK's responsibility, and what is the EEAS responsibility. I am certainly giving a pre-emptive warning' (Telegraph 2011a). For diplomats on the spot in international organisations, this proved a difficult scenario to manage. During the establishment process of the EEAS, depending on which country ran the presidency, they could either speak for the EU or not (Interview 13, Commission official, 2012). Member state diplomats were very cautious and let a new set of standard procedures accepted by the member states evolve only slowly (Interview 13, Commission official, 2012).

Staffing and organisation

Staffing was a major concern during the initial inception and setting up of the service. Despite the compromise of three sources found during the Convention and its further institutionalisation through the EEAS Decision, conflicts over who is present where in the EEAS never completely subsided.

While the Council Secretariat continued the delivery of administrative service arrangements, it rendered the relationship between the Council administrative structures and the EEAS fraught with conflicts resembling those with the European Commission. These conflicts arose in various administrative processes, such as the management of information systems. The EEAS was responsible for managing information systems, but as the management was not carried out by external relations staff in the Council Secretariat, the staff involved were not transferred and had not been considered in the Council decision's annex (Interview 10, EEAS official, 2011). In some ways, the Secretariat outdid the Commission in the conflicts over post transfers, in one instance transferring empty posts (Morgenstern 2011: p. 19): 'They gave us empty posts rather than persons. They created new posts for persons and then gave us the empty posts' (Interview 10, EEAS official, 2011). The EEAS raised this with the EP as budgetary authority in 2012: 'This transfer of budgetary resources was not always accompanied by the corresponding support staff' (EEAS 2012: p. 1). In a similar instance, administrative posts were handed over, in order for the Council Secretariat to retain a number of foreign policy and external relations staff in return (Interview 4, EEAS official, 2011).

156 Consolidation of the EEAS

The Council Secretariat staff assigned to move to the EEAS appeared to have had a less than smooth integration process, coming from an organisation with a different working environment and structure than the Commission. With smaller overall numbers and without strong backing from the corporate Council Secretariat, Council officials had to find a place in the new structure:

> [The officials] that worked in the CSG – they are basically applying for posts within this structure. But it was not supposed to be this way. It should have been a merger. Now they are going to be selected or not selected by the Commission hierarchy.
>
> (Interview 2, Senior Council official, 2011)

In exceptional individual cases, this may have proven a positive career development, but structurally, the interviewee perceived that the Council Secretariat's foreign policy parts had nearly disappeared (Interview 2, Senior Council official, 2011). How officials who performed similar tasks dealt with the new tasks depended largely on the circumstances and arrangements between the people involved (Interview 13, Commission official, 2011). For the corporate part of the CSG, staffing and organisation concerns were mainly about safeguarding its own role and minimising other types of administrative links to the EEAS.

For the member states, staffing concerns were so central an element in the race for influence on the new service, that it was largely dealt with through the formal oversight channels built into the EEAS decision (see above 'Oversight'; also Chapter 5). The EEAS decision contains several specific requirements for member states' staff overall and a balanced geographical distribution across member states (Council of the EU 2010b: art. 6(6), art. 13). From early in the negotiations, the member states' staffing quota was an essential 'deliverable' for the EEAS:

> When the EEAS has reached its full capacity, staff from Member States, as referred to in the first subparagraph of paragraph 2, should represent at least one third of all EEAS staff at AD level.
>
> (Council of the EU 2010b: art. 6 (9))

Equal treatment of member states' diplomats is also enshrined in the EEAS decision (Council of the EU 2010b: art. 6(7)), highlighting that member states were keenly aware of potential advantages of EU personnel in manoeuvring selection processes. Fearing the use of procedures to keep out member states' staff, German representatives refused to support recruitment to the EEAS via the general selection system, or concours, on the basis that national diplomats already passed such a selection (Interview 4, EEAS official, 2011).

At ambassadorial level, the target for member state staff was nearly achieved within the first two years of operation (see above 'Staffing and organisation'). With progress assured in this area, however, the focus of member states shifted to other organisational and procedural matters, as illustrated above.

Budget

The Council Secretariat had, like the Commission, continued to provide services to the EEAS in the framework of service-level agreements. In contrast with the Commission, however, the CSG expressed its desire to end this service provision. The EEAS review of 2013 states that 'the Council Secretariat has made clear they wish to end the SLA in place' (EEAS 2013: p. 10). The experience of difficult collaboration and struggles to take over unfunded tasks at the beginning of the operational phase shine through in the following sentence: 'It is important that where the Council Secretariat decides to end an SLA that the EEAS receives the corresponding resources to take on the responsibility seamlessly' (EEAS 2013: p. 10). The EEAS had clearly learnt about the need for resources in its first two years. As with staffing and organisation, the Council Secretariat appears to aim mainly towards severing what from its perspective seemed like unnecessary links to the service. The inter-linkages of staffing and organisation become apparent in this context. As described above, the CSG had at least on one occasion transferred budgeted posts rather than actual staff. While kept analytically separate here, the exercise of organisational power through the mechanisms of budget, staffing, organisation and administrative procedures can fit less neatly into those categories in reality.

In addition to this inter-bureaucratic rivalry between the Council Secretariat and the EEAS, the relationship with member states represented in Council is arguably the most important link as member states still dominate EU foreign policy. The first three years of operation illustrate that Commission and Council Secretariat play a central role in relations with the EEAS. While bureaucratic contestations by the parent organisations are unsurprising, the member states themselves also shaped the interaction with the EEAS. The close scrutiny by member states was already established in the negotiations surrounding the setting up of the EEAS by inserting distinct review items into the Decision of 2010 (Council of the EU 2010b). The member states' collective role in the Council also gives them a direct say on the budgetary resources available to the EEAS. As one element of the budgetary authority of the EU, the Council's preferences and willingness to provide resources for external policies as well as the organisational structure underpinning it are an essential element of the budgetary process. The position of the member states had been largely dominated by concerns such as the budget neutrality of the new service, and the added value of its operation. Nevertheless, despite some strong views in favour of a reduced budget in Council, the member states needed to find agreement with the European Parliament, and had thus agreed to increases in the EU's and the EEAS's budgets.

Council structures have another link with the EEAS based on the new institutional architecture of the EU after the Lisbon Treaty. In addition to Secretariat and member states in Council, the EEAS is also assigned a role in support of the President of the European Council. Herman von Rompuy occupied this post of semi-permanent chair of the European Council from 2009 to 2014. The President of the European Council (PEC) has at his disposal an extended cabinet, housed

158 *Consolidation of the EEAS*

by the Council Secretariat, a part of which is exclusively charged with supporting the PEC in the field of External Relations. The relationship of the EEAS with the PEC is, mirroring its work for the President of the Commission, largely related to briefings on external relations and foreign policy. Despite early hiccups in finding a reliable communication pattern, the collaboration with the EEAS was regarded very positively in the cabinet (Interview 22, Cabinet member, 2012). Even the working relations with Ashton's cabinet, often derided as closed and unhelpful, were seen as 'very positive' (Interview 22, Cabinet member, 2012). Despite the positive evaluation, the interviewee did not fail to notice the 'institutional sandbox fighting' which characterised many other actors' interactions with the EEAS (Interview 22, Cabinet member, 2012).

But these attempts by member states to shape the functioning of the EEAS are not the only political interventions regarding the new service. A third core actor in the Brussels inter-institutional environment was the European Parliament, which had long championed a common diplomatic service for the EU and was seeking to influence it from its inception and establishment phases (See Chapters 2, 4, 5).

The many faces of control: European Parliament

Another actor with direct political links to the EEAS and an equally deep interest in its organisation and functioning is the European Parliament, where some of the designers of the service hold influential positions. As the EP is not mainly a bureaucratic actor, relations between the EEAS and the Parliament can be expected to differ from those with both the Commission and the Council. Formally, the European Parliament did not have any leverage over the Council decision that established the EEAS. Despite this, it did use its co-decision powers for the necessary revision of the staff and financial regulations and created a package negotiation in order to shape the decision (Erkelens and Blockmans 2012: p. 15; see also Chapter 5). As one part of the EP's agreement with the deal, the HR had to give a 'Declaration on Political Accountability' annexed to the decision setting out basic principles of consultation and information procedures to the EP (High Representative 2011a; see also Chapter 5). The Declaration largely codifies the continuation of previous practice or extends previous practice to other particular areas. It also creates an obligation to send a politically accountable person as opposed to an official to the EP should the need arise.

Oversight

Major review procedures were written directly into final provisions of the Council Decision establishing the EAAS (Council of the EU 2010b: art. 13). As noted above, these requirements included the need for a report to EP, Council and Commission by the end of 2011 focusing on the role of delegations and progress in coordinating instruments. This report was issued in early 2012, but had little observable impact on the functioning of the service. Amid persistent

Consolidation of the EEAS 159

criticism by member states and the media, the EP was thought to have eased up on the criticism of the EEAS in order to give the organisation some respite (Interview 24, EP Assistant, 2012). At least in this instance, the control mechanism was not used as such. In its last oversight task in the period under observation, the EP developed the '2013 Review of the organisation and functioning of the EEAS' (European Parliament 2013b). It included a long list of suggested improvements from the political goals to be achieved to detailed wishes on the organisational hierarchy of the EEAS such as the merger of the office of Chief Operating Officer and Managing Director for Administration (European Parliament 2013b: p. 5). It also tasked the EEAS with 'carry[ing] out a systematic and in-depth audit in order to unify the external policy-related structures put in place by the Commission and the Council Secretariat' (European Parliament 2013b: p. 5), i.e. the EP developed new forms of oversight for future time periods. It also used the opportunity to identify a few mechanisms in staffing and financial management in which the EEAS ought to be strengthened vis-à-vis the European Commission (European Parliament 2013b: pp. 6–7). The EP sought to push back member states' interference with EEAS recruitment (European Parliament 2013b: pp. 9–10). While conveniently overlooking possible interference by the Commission, the EP does not hesitate to fight its own officials' corner by reminding the EEAS of equal access to posts for EP officials (European Parliament 2013b: p. 10).

Staffing and organisation

The EP's role in nominations is comparatively weaker than the Commission's or the member states', but still has potential for some element of control in the future. The EP negotiated for US-style hearings of future ambassadors, and only partially succeeded. The EP now holds a hearing of selected heads of delegation before they take up their post, but after they have been appointed (Interview 20, Senior EEAS official, 2012; High Representative 2011b: No. 7; see also Chapter 5). It has become regular parliamentary practice, as an 'exchange of views with the newly appointed Head of EU Delegation to Saudi Arabia (in compliance with the Declaration on Political Accountability of the HR/VP)' illustrates (European Parliament 2012: p. 3). Legally, this appears to preclude parliamentary control of the nomination, but the EP may express strong opposition to individual candidates. This would certainly undermine their credibility as ambassadors and it is questionable whether such a statement could be ignored (Interview 20, Senior EEAS official, 2012). The EP has in the past assiduously asserted its political powers. In that sense the EP made at least a step towards classical oversight mechanisms with regard to ambassadorial appointments. The EP also surprised the EEAS by writing a letter to the HR with a recommendation after the heads of delegation 'hearings', or exchanges of view (Interview 20, Senior EEAS official, 2012). This procedure, adapted from the hearings of Commissioners before the EP, is an informal way for the EP to tilt the process towards the ambassadorial hearing it desired.

160 *Consolidation of the EEAS*

Surprisingly, the EP as a political body also noted in its 2013 review that:

> to consider in particular, in view of the European Parliament's special role with regard to the definition of objectives and basic choices of the Common Foreign and Security Policy, Parliament's competences as a budgetary authority, its role in democratic scrutiny of foreign policy as well as its practice of parliamentary foreign relations, the possibility for officials from the European Parliament to be able to apply for posts in the EEAS on an equal footing with those from the Council and the Commission from 1 July 2013.
>
> (European Parliament 2013b: p. 10)

Despite the EP's limited administrative base as a political body, the EP had recognised the value of inserting staff into the organisation as a means to influence its operation in the run-up to the 2010 decision, and it repeated its stance in 2013.

Budget

According to the Lisbon Treaty, both the Council and Parliament have equal budgetary rights. Any budgetary revision must therefore be carried not only by member states, but also by a majority in the EP. In addition, the EP has received an affirmation by the HR on specific budgetary information feedback in foreign policy (High Representative 2011a: no. 1). It was also the EP that insisted on maintaining the dominant role of the Commission in operational expenditure matters (Blockmans *et al.* 2013: p. 46), resulting in 'control over what the EEAS can do in the operational sphere' (Blockmans *et al.* 2013: p. 48). This has had direct effects for the EEAS and constrained its ability to, for example, use information and communication budgets. More specific budgetary procedures in Development and European Neighbourhood Policy also tie the EEAS into the Commission (Blockmans *et al.* 2013: p. 47). This strengthens the role of the EP as budgetary authority (Blockmans *et al.* 2013: p. 48), but also limits the financial flexibility of the EEAS. The specific budgetary rules in the operational field created a disconnect in the delegations. While the Head of Delegation can receive sub-delegation for operational expenditure, she can only further subdelegate to Commission staff in the delegations (European Commission 2012a; Blockmans *et al.* 2013: pp. 50–51).

Conclusion

The early operational period of the EEAS, from late 2010 until the review in 2013, was not an easy time for the service. The EEAS had to establish itself as an autonomous hierarchical organisation in an environment replete with actors. In a plausibility probe on the EEAS's structure and internal organisation, factors linked to the bureaucratic consolidation of the EEAS emerged as relevant in explaining the organisation's operation. The EEAS did engage in budget

Consolidation of the EEAS 161

maximisation, receiving declining budgetary increases in each year of operation between 2010 and 2013. The fact that budget increases are declining over time appears to speak for an additional argument made about the processes of consolidating bureaucratic organisations. Dunleavy notes that the pursuit of budgetary increases is very costly politically to administrative leadership and provides relatively few benefits (Dunleavy 1991: p. 174). Considering the political focus of member states in particular on added value and budget neutrality of the new organisation (see Chapters 5 and 6), the political cost of asking for further budget increases could be considered too high for the HR.

Shaping the organisation according to the leadership wishes, or bureau shaping, ought to be a less politically costly endeavour. There is indeed some evidence of bureau shaping by the EEAS leadership, in particular when it comes to the collective board structure around the High Representative and organisational structures dealing with crisis management. The evidence suggests furthermore that at the desk level, individual officials' conception of their own organisational interests shapes the perception of the other actors in the policymaking process. It is one of the ironies of the merger process that officials hired from the member states tended to judge the Commission as a trustworthy source of information to a greater extent than did former Commission staff. Competition about bureaucratic boundaries and resources thus occurs not only at the corporate level of an organisation, but also has distinct repercussions at the level of officials. Nevertheless, some of these observations from within the administrative structure may well be artefacts of the relative youth of the organisation and may disappear over time.

The EEAS did not consolidate its organisation in a political or organisational vacuum. Its relations to political bodies as well as administrative organisations at the EU level were largely determined by bureaucratic politics through attempts to exercise control over the service. The evidence showed that control procedures exist and that it is not only the two political masters of the service, the Council and the Parliament, that exercise control. Its close collaborator, the European Commission, equally exercises strong control through administrative procedures, nominations of heads of delegations, and programming and budgeting mechanisms. Because of this prominence in administrative procedure mechanisms of control, the Commission was able to exercise control in the day-to-day operations of the consolidation phase.

The evidence also demonstrates low levels of trust, in particular among former Commission staff towards the Commission, but also among the member states. Conflicts about the right to preside and speak for the EU, and provide input into administrative processes, as well as conflicts over autonomy in financial management, bear witness to the strong bureaucratic politics that grounded the EEAS. The process has since calmed considerably, indicating that by the end of the early operating phase, turf wars had succumbed to standard operating procedures.

The EEAS set-up includes strong control elements for three actors: the member states have strong influence on staffing and, via the Council, on

Table 6.3 Control mechanisms for the EEAS by actors

Actors/Control mechanisms	Council/MS	EP	Commission
Nominations	HR appointment, Consultative Committee on Appointments (CCA)	'Soft' hearings (before posting, after nomination)	Shortlist approval, Consultative Committee on Appointments (CCA)
Staffing and Organisation	(Staff transfer), consent to open/close delegations	n/a	(Staff transfer), consent to open/close delegations
Administrative Procedures	MS: Decision-making (Presidency tasks) CSG: SLAs, Presidency support	n/a	Programming, budgeting, SLAs
Oversight	HR chair, participation in Council	Hearings, Information requests	n/a
Reporting	Full review	Full review	n/a
Budget	Strong budgetary control	Strong budgetary control	Budget proposal, financial management
Control structures	Council services for foreign affairs	n/a	Secretariat-General

Source: own compilation.

Consolidation of the EEAS 163

the budgetary process. The Commission is deeply tied into the EEAS administrative process and retains control over the operational budget. The EP as a political body has at least the weight of political oversight mechanisms, in addition to its role in the budgetary process. As Table 6.3 shows, the Council and the member states retain the largest number of control mechanisms with access to all levels of control from staffing and nominations, to hearings and reporting and finally the setting of the budget. The EP's strongest mechanism is its budgetary control, and in addition, it has some oversight mechanisms at its disposal.

The European Commission has strong influence over staffing and nominations, but its strongest mechanism is the deep link the EEAS is forced to retain with the Commission in terms of administrative procedures and budgeting processes. It is this deep link that has led some observers to suggest that: '[…] that is exactly the Commission vision, they did not want a strong EEAS. Strong yes, but within boundaries' (Interview 2, Senior Council official, 2011). While collaboration is enforced through the rules of the EEAS decision and the treaties, competition and collaboration are mixed in the inter-bureaucratic relations. The European Commission has retained strong influence on staffing, on financial management as well as all on procedural aspects of external relations. Its relations with the EEAS were settled first unilaterally on the basis of a Commission script, and only later revised in a conflictual negotiation with the EEAS itself. By the end of the first operational phase, the EEAS had a considerably more established corporate part, something akin in function to the Commission's Secretariat-General. The organisation has thus in subtle ways, such as staffing and inter-organisational relations, worked to gain more autonomy than its competitors planned for (Murdoch 2013). Future settlements with the Commission will thus be more balanced than early agreements, but for the early operation period the Commission must be considered the strongest player in the game.

Considering the organisational control structures of other actors is not straightforward either. The European Parliament as a political body would not be likely to deploy high levels of administrative staff in order to fulfil control functions. In the Commission, this is largely done via the Secretariat-General, which already represents a strong organisational element in the Commission and would not likely exhibit an immediate increase in resources specifically in response to the EEAS. In the case of the Council Secretariat, however, the claw-back of a number of external relations staff (Interview 4, EEAS official, 2011; Interview 10, EEAS official, 2011; Interview 18, Council official, 2012) can be seen as a move to safeguard the ability of the Secretariat to monitor the EEAS's activities. From the view of the Secretariat-General itself, this is seen as a more benign delivery of services to the EEAS that the Secretariat would also have provided to the Presidency administration (Interview 1, Council official, 2011; Interview 2, Senior Council official, 2011; Interview 16, Senior Council official, 2012). When weighing the likely impact of abstract and high-cost control facilities such as a full review of the EEAS's functioning together with a narrow focus of specific control items, specifically staffing, the evidence on the exercise of control suggests that the level of control by political actors such as the Council and the

164 *Consolidation of the EEAS*

EP is high but will be reduced over the medium term as the determination to use these mechanisms wanes.

The European Parliament retained limited political influence on nominations and remains of course one of the budgetary authorities of the EU, with resulting influence on the EEAS. Nevertheless, the EP appears to have taken a benevolent view of the service, possibly in recognition of the EP's role in the creation of the service and as a response to the difficult early days of the service. This may also be a reflection of the EEAS's decided focus on being in good standing with the EP as a budgetary authority (see above). The overall evidence from relations with other actors indicates that those actors with less administrative interest, i.e. with little administrative structure themselves, in this case the European Parliament and the office of the President of the European Council, were largely positive towards the service. The first EP report on the EEAS seems to have fallen prey to shifting political approaches to the EEAS. After the service's performance had been discussed at a parliamentary meeting, observers in the EP were surprised at the lenient approach taken by the participants in this small-scale review (Interview 24, EP Assistant, 2012). As studies in the past have shown that the existence of control instruments does not guarantee that they are used (Weingast and Moran 1983: p. 767; Miller 2005: p. 209), something similar appears to have happened in the case of EP–EEAS relations.

The analysis of the EEAS's institutional environment reveals strong contestation from all sides during the operation, but in particular highlights how strongly the European Commission is able to exercise control over the EEAS. Member states have become vocal critics, but they did so outside the control arrangements in place and outside of Council structures. The EP has become a much more supportive actor than previously assumed. Through a conceptualisation of principal agent mechanisms relating to control and autonomy, the struggle for influence over the EEAS between the European Commission and the member states has become apparent. In many ways the supranational Commission and the intergovernmental Council defended existing prerogatives and attempted to curtail EEAS autonomy in the period of consolidation. The EP, on the other hand, after initial criticism developed a more benign relationship with the service.

References

Bátora, Jozef 2013: The 'Mitrailleuse Effect': The EEAS as an Interstitial Organization and the Dynamics of Innovation in Diplomacy. *Journal of Common Market Studies*, vol. 51, no. 4, pp. 598–613.

Blockmans, Steven; Hillion, Christophe; Cremona, Marise; Curtin, Deirdre; De Baere, Geert; Duke, Simon; Eckes, Christina; Van Vooren, Bart; Wessel, Ramses A. and Wouters, Jan, *EEAS 2.0: A Legal Commentary on Council Decision 2010/427/EU Establishing the Organisation and Functioning of the European External Action Service (February 7, 2013)*. CEPS Paperbacks 2013.

Burke, Edward 2014: Deliberate 'spoiler' or misunderstood pragmatist? Britain and the European External Action Service. In Reviewing member state commitment to the EEAS, *EPIN Working Paper*, no. 34, pp. 14–18.

Consolidation of the EEAS 165

Downs, Anthony 1967: *Inside Bureaucracy.* Little, Brown: Boston.

Dunleavy, Patrick 1991: *Democracy, Bureaucracy and Public Choice. Economic Explanations in Political Science.* Harvester: New York.

Egeberg, Morten and Trondal, Jarle 2011: EU-level agencies: new executive centre formation or vehicles for national control? *Journal of European Public Policy,* vol. 18, no. 6, pp. 868–887.

Erkelens, Leendert and Blockmans, Steven 2012: Setting up the European External Action Service: An institutional act of balance. *CLEER working paper* 2012/1. CLEER: Den Haag.

EUobserver 2011: UK attacks Ashton over 'ludicrous' budget proposal. Brussels, 24.05.2011.

European Voice 2010b: Muddle and delay blight start of diplomatic corps. Brussels, 16.12.2010.

European Voice 2011b: MEPs to endorse 5.2% budget increase. Brussels, 20.10.2011.

European Voice 2012: Deal on 2013 budget goes to Parliament's political groups. Brussels, 30.11.2012.

Helwig, Niklas, Ivan, Paul and Kostanyan, Hrant 2013: *The New EU Foreign Policy Architecture. Reviewing the first two years of the EEAS.* CEPS: Brussels.

Henökl, Thomas 2014: Conceptualizing the European Diplomatic Space: A Framework for Analysis of the European External Action Service. *Journal of European Integration,* vol. 36, no. 5, pp. 453–471.

Henökl, Thomas 2015: How do EU Foreign Policy-Makers Decide? Institutional Orientations within the European External Action Service, *West European Politics,* vol. 38, no. 3, pp. 679–708.

Henökl, Thomas and Trondal, Jarle 2013: Bureaucratic structure, geographical location and the autonomy of administrative systems. Evidence from the European External Action Service. *ISL Working Paper* 2013, no. 7.

Henökl, Thomas and Trondal, Jarle 2015: Unveiling the anatomy of autonomy: dissecting actor-level independence in the European External Action Service. *Journal of European Public Policy,* vol. 22, no. 10, pp. 1426–1447.

Juncos, Ana E. and Pomorska, Karolina 2013: 'In the face of adversity': explaining the attitudes of EEAS officials vis-à-vis the new service. *Journal of European Public Policy,* vol. 20, no. 9, pp. 1332–1349.

McCubbins, Mathew D.; Noll, Roger; and Weingast, Barry 1987: Administrative Procedures as Instruments of Political Control. *Journal of Law, Economics and Organization,* vol. 3, no. 2, pp. 243–277.

Miller, Gary 2000: Rational Choice and Dysfunctional Institutions. *Governance,* vol. 13, no. 4, pp. 535–547.

Moe, Terry 1989: The Politics of Bureaucracy. In Chubb and Peterson (Eds.): *Can the Government Govern?* Brookings: Washington, DC.

Morgenstern, Jost-Henrik 2011: Teething Problems of the European External Action Service. *EUSA Review,* Spring 2011, pp. 18–20.

Murdoch, Zuzana; Gaenzle, Stefan; and Trondal, Jarle 2013: 'Making the Grade, Keeping the Gate:' The Recruitment of Member-States Diplomats to the European External Action Service (EEAS). *DSEU Policy Paper* 13.

Murdoch, Zuzana; Gaenzle, Stefan; and Trondal, Jarle 2014: Building Foreign Affairs Capacity in the EU: Recruitment of Member State officials to the European External Action Service. *Public Administration,* vol. 92, no. 1, pp. 71–86.

166   *Consolidation of the EEAS*

Niskanen, William A. 1971: *Bureaucracy and Representative Government*. Atherton: Chicago.

Oxfam 2012: Fit for Purpose? The European External Action Service One Year On. *Oxfam Briefing Paper* 159.

Smith, Michael E. 2013: The European External Action Service and the security–development nexus: organizing for effectiveness or incoherence? *Journal of European Public Policy*, vol. 20, no. 9, pp. 1299–1315.

Telegraph 2011a: Europe's new diplomatic service under fire. 28.05.2011. London.

Tercovich, Giulia 2014: Towards a Comprehensive Approach: The EEAS Crisis Response System. *Journal of Contingencies and Crisis Management*, vol. 22, no. 3, pp. 150–157.

Trondal, Jarle and Veggeland, Frode 2003: Access, voice and loyalty: the representation of domestic civil servants in EU committees. *Journal of European Public Policy*, vol. 10, no. 1, pp. 59–77.

Tullock, Gordon 1965: *The Politics of Bureaucracy*. Public Affairs Press: Washington, DC.

Vanhoonacker, Sophie and Pomorska, Karolina 2013: The European External Action Service and agenda-setting in European foreign policy. *Journal of European Public Policy*, vol. 20, no. 9, pp. 1316–1331.

Weingast, Barry and Moran, Mark J. 1983: Bureaucratic Discretion of Congressional Control? Regulatory Policy-Making by the Federal Trade Commission. *Journal of Political Economy*, vol. 91, no. 5, pp. 765–800.

Wright, Nicholas 2013: Co-operation, Co-optation, Competition? Understanding how Britain and Germany interact with the EU's Common Foreign and Security Policy, and why they employ the strategies they do. University of East Anglia, PhD thesis.

Official documents

Council of the European Union

Council of the EU 2010a: Revised draft of 21 June 2010 Consolidated Version with latest amendments post quadrilogue of 21 June 2010. Proposal for a COUNCIL DECISION of (date) establishing the organisation and functioning of the European External Action Service (25 March 2010).

Council of the EU 2010b: Decision of 26 July 2010 establishing the Organisation and Functioning of the European External Action Service 2010/427/EU.

COREU

COREU CFSP/SEC/645/12: Simplified Written Procedure Regarding the Agreement by the Council on the Opening of EU Delegations to the United Arab Emirates in 2012 and in Myanmar in the next future and the closure of EU Delegations to the Republic of Suriname and in New Caledonia. 25.09.2012.

COREU CFSP/SEC/664/12: Simplified Written Procedure Regarding the Agreement by the Council on the Opening of EU Delegations to the United Arab Emirates in 2012 and in Myanmar in the next future and the closure of EU Delegations to the Republic of Suriname and in New Caledonia. 25.09.2012.

European Commission

European Commission 2011a: Vademecum on Working Relations with the European External Action Service. (Ares 2011)25273. Brussels, 01.01.2011.

European Commission 2011b: Vademecum on Working Relations with the European External Action Service. SEC(2011)1636.

European Commission 2012a: Working arrangements between the Commission services and the European External Action Service (EEAS) in relation to External Relation issues. SEC(2012)48.

European Commission 2012b: Minutes of the 1998th meeting of the European Commission PV(2012)1998final, p. 19.

European Commission 2012c: Minutes of the 2028th meeting of the European Commission, 19 December 2012'. PV(2012)2028 final. Brussels, 15.01.2012.

European Court of Auditors

European Court of Auditors 2014: Special Report No. 11: The Establishment of the European External Action Service. ECA, Luxembourg.

European External Action Service

European External Action Service 2010: A new step in the setting-up of the EEAS: Transfer of staff on 1 January 2011. Press release IP 10/1769. Brussels, 21.12.2010.

European External Action Service 2012: Report on Budgetary and Financial Management 2012. EEAS: Brussels.

European External Action Service 2013a: EEAS Review 2013. EEAS: Brussels.

European External Action Service 2013b: Annual Activity Report. EEAS: Brussels.

European Parliament

European Parliament 2012: Draft agenda Meeting 19–20 September 2012. Committee on Foreign Affairs (AFET)2012/0919_1.

European Parliament 2013b: European Parliament recommendation to the High Representative of the Union for Foreign Affairs and Security Policy and Vice President of the Commission, to the Council and to the Commission of 13 June 2013 on the 2013 review of the of the organization and functioning of the EEAS.

High Representative

High Representative 2011a: Declaration of Political Accountability. High Representative of the Union for Foreign Affairs and Security Policy (HR) 2011.

High Representative 2011b: Report by the High Representative to the European Parliament, the Council and the European Commission. Brussels, 22.12.2011.

EU Legislation

Regulation (EU, Euratom) No 1080/2010 of the European Parliament and of the Council of 24 November 2010 amending the Staff Regulations of Officials of the European Communities and the Conditions of Employment of Other Servants of those Communities.

168 *Consolidation of the EEAS*

Regulation (EU, Euratom) No 1081/2010 of the European Parliament and of the Council of 24 November 2010 amending Council Regulation (EC, Euratom) No 1605/2002 on the Financial Regulation applicable to the general budget of the European Communities, as regards the European External Action Service.

Other

Non-Paper 2011: Foreign Ministers of Belgium, Estonia, Finland, France, Germany, Italy, Latvia, Lithuania, Luxembourg, the Netherlands, Poland and Sweden 'Non-Paper on the EEAS', 08.12.2011.

7 Sailing on a second wind?

Trajectories of consolidation for the European External Action Service

At one point in the movie *The Italian Job*, the main character portrayed by Michael Caine says: 'It's a very difficult job and the only way to get through it is we all work together as a team. And that means you do everything I say.' This particular type of collaboration seems to ring true of EU institutional leaders as well. As a new EU leadership was set to be installed with European Council president, Commission president and new High Representative/Vice-President in 2014, the 'game of structural politics' (Moe 1989) was bound to resume: both between the EEAS and the Commission as well as between the member states and the EEAS. The EEAS 'self'-review in 2013 had partially confirmed most of the critical assessments put forward by the media, think tanks, politicians and academics (EEAS 2013a). Nevertheless, no major changes ensued immediately as the leadership change was already on the horizon. In 2014, in line with EU office term limits and elections, a new High Representative and Vice-President was nominated after some protracted negotiations. The job went to Italian Foreign Minister Federica Mogherini, who was appointed by the European Council on 30 August 2014 (European Council 2014). She was then confirmed as part of the Juncker Commission in October 2014, playing both roles in full as of 1 November 2014.

With new leadership in the EU as a whole, and of the EEAS in particular, the bureaucratic institutionalist model would expect a new rebalancing as part of the ongoing politics of bureaucratic structure in the EU. This chapter discusses the impact of the new leadership on the organisation and its functioning. It analyses first how this rebalancing played out at the beginning of Mogherini's term of office and what this says about how entrenched or volatile the institutional settlements around the EEAS are in the second term. The chapter then briefly investigates the EEAS links to Commission, Council and European Council and European Parliament to assess changes in the level of control and interdependence in inter-institutional relations. It concludes with trajectories of consolidation for the EEAS beyond the Mogherini term of office.

Developments inside the EEAS

The 2013 review already proposed a number of administrative and procedural changes as well as changes to the internal organisational structure of the EEAS

170 *Trajectories of consolidation for the EEAS*

both for the short term and the medium term (EEAS 2013a). Nevertheless, the review does not enter into detailed discussions of a potential revision of the EEAS Decision of 2010, explicitly postponing implementation to the new leadership:

> At this stage, the review deliberately concentrates on policy issues and possible improvements without addressing what these would require in terms of internal organisational changes, modifications in legal texts or other wider issues to be considered as part of the institutional transition in 2014.
>
> (EEAS 2013a: p. 15)

A rationalisation of administrative hierarchy as suggested in the review was always going to be difficult as it was exactly the managerial redundancy that was needed in order to assuage member states' concerns over access to senior levels of the service (see Chapters 5, 6; European Court of Auditors 2014). The audit carried out in 2014 by the European Court of Auditors had delivered additional scathing criticism of the EEAS's top-heavy hierarchy, administrative duplication and lack of mission (European Court of Auditors 2014). While this book has found similar evidence, ascribing these shortcomings to the lack of a strategy by the Court (European Court of Auditors 2014: pp. 8, 11) ignores the structural politics of the EEAS: it is precisely the disagreements over fundamental organisational principles and demands placed on the organisation that are responsible for the administrative shortcomings.

Nonetheless, the implementation of the EEAS Review's recommendation finally proceeded in 2015. In terms of in-service hierarchy, the Executive Secretary-General and Chief Operating Officer roles were merged into the Secretary-General position, and the first appointee to this post was a French diplomat, Alain Le Roy. He has since been succeeded by Helga Schmid, one of the Deputy Secretaries-General under Catherine Ashton. Instead of two, the EEAS now has three Deputy Secretary-General positions, covering CSDP and crisis response, political affairs, and economic and global issues (EEAS 2017; EUISS 2016: p. 37). In the same fashion, the rest of the senior management was structured into a set of eight positions at managing director level – not quite the reduction proposed in the EEAS review (EEAS 2013a: p. 4). In an additional attempt at streamlining, managing directors were deputised, 'effectively cutting out one layer in the hierarchy' (HR 2015: p. 3; Interview 34, EEAS desk officer, 2017). Whether this is a real hierarchical reduction depends largely on whether the positions reflect merely a renamed version of the posts of directors present in the hierarchy before. These structural reforms also purposefully removed the more collective decision-making bodies that had been set up by Ashton, the Corporate Board being among most notable victims (HR 2015: p. 3). Staff in the EEAS nevertheless did note an improvement in the internal decision-making processes, even if it remained a 'steep ladder' (Interview 34, EEAS desk officer, 2017).

The EEAS also returned to a structured consideration of delegation planning with the creation of a 'Working Group on the Network of Delegations in order to

Trajectories of consolidation for the EEAS 171

develop a more strategic EEAS policy on human resources allocations in delegations and identify needs for adjustment to the delegations' network in the medium to long term (two to five years)' (EEAS 2017: p. 9). This process looked very similar to exercises run in the past by the then DG RELEX of the Commission and have been undertaken in the Commission DGs with a presence in the delegations such as Development Cooperation (Interview 38, EEAS official, 2017). The Commission was partially involved in this process due to the policy instrument management and staff in delegations run by the Commission (EEAS 2017: p. 9). Since 2015 the EEAS has received the funds associated with the management of delegation staff, resulting in a significant increase in budget. These administrative funds, while contributing to the budget, are not likely to do much in enabling the EEAS's financial autonomy. The EEAS also was far from independent in designing its own network of delegations, with the Commission being strongly represented at institutional level and at the level of directorates-general in the respective steering committee. Another significant process is the cut in establishment posts required of all EU institutions and equally applied to the EEAS. In the case of the EEAS, this amounted to the reduction of eight administrator posts and nine assistant posts being deleted from the establishment plan, exclusively at headquarters (EEAS 2017). Staffing at headquarters and delegations remained a contested issue for the EEAS, with member states strongly favouring prestigious Heads of Delegation posts and putting forward highly experienced diplomats, as discussed in Chapter 6. In turn, this has resulted in a vast overrepresentation of member states in this staff category and the EEAS has started an attempt to reverse this trend. The 'golden age for member states' has passed (Interview 38, EEAS official, 2017). The European Parliament has also repeatedly raised this staffing issue in the budget negotiations, highlighting that the controversy across stakeholders on staffing issues for the EEAS has remained an active component of contestation (Committee on Budgetary Control 2017).

In her progress report to the Council on the implementation of the EEAS review, Mogherini explicitly did not issue recommendations to adapt the legal instruments around the EEAS, i.e. the Council Decision and the staff and financial regulation: 'There is no immediate need for the High Representative/Vice-President to propose changes [...]' (HR 2015: p. 2). But she did leave a door open to return with proposals at a later time, linking them potentially to the Global Strategy and changes in CSDP and crisis management (HR 2015: p. 2). A backdoor to more significant legal changes regarding the EEAS and the rules of its operation remains ajar.

EEAS and the Juncker Commission: Spitzenkandidat meets European Council nominee

Former Luxembourg Prime Minister Jean-Claude Juncker approached his role as Commission President with an innovative approach to managing the Commissioners, in line with the 'presidentialisation' of Commission policy control (Becker *et al.* 2016). For his new members of the Commission, he discussed

172 Trajectories of consolidation for the EEAS

their role and tasks as well as the structure of the Commission in so-called 'Mission Letters', setting out the conclusions of the discussions and negotiations with member states. On the one hand, the letter contains general statements of intent on the part of the Juncker Commission demonstrating an intent to 'cooperat[e] across portfolios to produce integrated, well-grounded and well-explained initiatives that lead to clear results' (Juncker 2014). On the other hand, it contains more specific objectives for the HR/VP and her role in the new Commission. Juncker stressed the role of Vice-Presidents as coordinators of policy areas, acting as his 'delegates' in implementing the 'Political Guidelines' of the Juncker Commission (Juncker 2014). While this in some ways elevated the role of the Vice-Presidents of the Commission to a steering position rather than a mere coordinating one, the mission letter was ambivalent on the HR/VP position. While it ensured that the HR/VP has pre-eminence in the external relations portfolio, or, as Juncker put it: 'As Vice-President of the European Commission, you will be responsible for steering and coordinating the work of all Commissioners with regard to external relations' (Juncker 2014). It also means a subordination to the Commission President and that, to a lesser degree, the first Vice-President is stronger than in past Commissions – a move that sits uneasily with a post that does not derive its legitimacy exclusively from the Commission. One expression of this subtle rebalancing is the move of HR/VP Mogherini to the Berlaymont Commission building, which Juncker stressed was done at the suggestion of Mogherini (Juncker 2014). Her cabinet was to be of 'appropriate size' and 'about half of [them] will be Commission officials' (Juncker 2014). Compared to Ashton's cabinet, this implied a significant shift towards integrating the work of the HR/VP cabinet into the Commission. It also fits well with staffing as an element of control in the first consolidation phase as discussed in Chapter 6; this time exercised also by the Commission. Juncker also stated the importance of the Secretariat-General of the Commission in the working relations with the EEAS, which had previously been a strong element of Commission control over the new organisation (see Chapter 6). As reported in the interviews, staff noted 'considerable changes in working method' within the Commission and an increase in workload for the Secretariat-General as a result (Interviews 35, 36, Commission officials, 2017).

Commission services and the EEAS

The EEAS clearly is the 'odd one out', acting like a Commission service in some instances, and as a fully autonomous organisation in others. Nevertheless, the Secretariat-General of the Commission has consistently maintained that the EEAS was akin to a service of the Commission and treated it accordingly when it acted in external relations throughout the period of establishment and consolidation (see e.g. Chapters 5 and 6). While the Secretariat-General of the Commission acknowledged that this was not the case in areas of foreign and security policy, this position nevertheless subordinated the EEAS to the oversight of the Commission for a large part of its operations. Conflicts arose from this struggle for control, but subsided over the first period of consolidation as routine operating procedures were established and accepted by the Commission and the EEAS. In this time, policy responses to international crises increased in salience as bureaucratic questions partially declined. The EEAS had developed an opposite number to the Secretariat-General in the Commission in order to build these procedural settings. Although not at first seen as an equivalent, the 2017 organogram of the EEAS contained a general affairs directorate under the Secretary-General of the EEAS with functions resembling a Secretariat-General in EU institutions (EEAS 2017). An institutionalisation, or bureaucratisation, of procedural and relational links to the rest of the EU environment has taken place inside the EEAS in the consolidation phase. This has resulted in a continued reduction of open conflict as the settlement of relations is accepted, although it has not necessarily changed the underlying dynamic of conflict yet.

Commission staff highlighted issues with the (intentionally) high turnover of member states' diplomats in the EEAS, which makes certain procedural questions like which proposals require coordination a recurring issue (Interviews 35, 36, Commission officials, 2017). But here, a settlement has occurred as the EEAS has recently given up its opposition to receiving training on procedural matters from the Secretariat-General of the Commission (Interview 35, Commission official, 2017). In addition to the updating of the procedural documents setting out the working relationships between the EEAS and the Commission, this should reduce the propensity for open procedural conflict even further. In later interviews, Commission officials still acknowledge some fundamental underlying perception that 'the EEAS is not an institution, but it appears as such. But the EEAS has to launch inter-service consultation like all other services [of the Commission]' (Interview 36, Commission official, 2017).

Within the EEAS, officials report a very clear political positioning by the new HR/VP Mogherini on cooperative behaviour with the Commission, in line with Juncker's conception of the new Commission: 'clear marching order that [HR/VP] does not want EEAS and Commission to come out against each other in a working group' (Interview 34, EEAS desk officer, 2017). Inter-service processes to produce joint work had intensified under Mogherini. And while the increased role of the Commission Secretariat General and the mirror EEAS services meant that cooperation was running more smoothly, this development was seen as both 'good and bad for us [EEAS]' (Interview 34, EEAS desk officer, 2017). The role of the Secretariat General of the Commission was perceived as coming largely at the expense of the EEAS by strengthening centralised functions in the Commission Secretariat General that should be the tasks of the EEAS. The official with long experience in foreign policy making also noted that the difference between foreign policy making and decision making wasn't always appreciated on the other side (Interview 34, EEAS desk officer, 2017). In the same vein, the consultation processes and clearing happening inside the Commission were 'alien to the traditional foreign policy world' (Interview 34, EEAS desk officer, 2017).

The remnants of an uneasy relationship in other areas of EEAS competence could be observed throughout the process leading to the adoption of the EEAS

174 *Trajectories of consolidation for the EEAS*

signature policy in 2016. The EU Global Strategy, or to reference its full title: 'Shared Vision, Common Action: A Stronger Europe. A Global Strategy for the European Union's Foreign and Security Policy' (HR 2016), was a document produced to develop a set of strategic objectives that could tie together the many threads of EU's foreign and security policy as well as external action (Tocci 2016; Davis Cross 2016). From the Commission's perspective, the process was 'unorthodox' (Interview 36, Commission official, 2017). And while stressing the amount of input provided by Commission services, a Commission staff member stated 'it was always clear it was a High Representative document' and the EEAS had been very clear that it wasn't to be considered 'co-drafting' (Interview 36, Commission official, 2017). This contributed to uncertainty about substance and terminology that played an important role in the Commission's external relations portfolio, especially in areas like resilience where Commission services had been active in before (Interview 35, Commission official, 2017). The evidence from the process (Tocci 2016) and its evaluation (Davis Cross 2016; Dijkstra 2016a) together showed that while the strategy is a long-awaited tool for EU foreign policy making, and 'an exercise of strategic diplomacy' in itself (Davis Cross 2016: p. 404), it has not bridged the divide between the underlying principles of EU external action. This was witnessed in operation by an official in the EEAS who perceived a lack of 'a holistic view of how the EEAS functions as an entity' and that it tended to 'swing like a pendulum' between Commission way of doing things and foreign policy making (Interview 34, EEAS desk officer, 2017). If the pendulum under Ashton had been near the Council, it was moved noticeably towards the Commission under Mogherini.

EEAS and European Council and Council of the EU

Relations between the EEAS and the European Council cabinet were not as strained as relations with the Commission in the prior phase of consolidation. With a leadership change at the head of the European Council at the same time as the nomination of the High Representative, a new set of political actors might have resulted in changes in interactions. The new President of the European Council Donald Tusk, the former Polish prime minister, exhibited more interest in foreign policy matters than his predecessor (Pomorska and Vanhoonacker 2015; see also Interview 32, EUCO cabinet, 2017), which potentially could lead to a more competitive relationship. Due largely to the nature of the role of the EUCO President, at the service of the heads of state or government of EU member states, and without a large administrative structure, relations have remained less formalised then with other significant EU actors. The cabinet worked closely with both the EEAS and the Council Secretariat, the balance influenced largely by geographic region and the policy environment (Interview 32, EUCO cabinet, 2017). The Council Secretariat also acted as check on the EEAS, 'double, and at times triple-checking with member states' on their positions on a matter (Interview 32, EUCO cabinet, 2017). And while a 'strategic approach to information' by the EEAS was noted (Interview 32, EUCO cabinet,

2017, see also Bicchi 2014), it did not matter much for the work of the cabinet as the EEAS only represented one of various sources of information that fed into the preparation of the European Council. A more serious issue for the cabinet appeared to be access to documents and information by the network of delegations, marred by technological inconsistencies across institutions rather than a strategic attempt to foreclose access. Direct contacts to desk level remain possible and common, but the managing directors of the EEAS need to be informed of the direct requests (Interview 32, EUCO cabinet, 2017), indicating that some level of control on the flow of information is still desired by EEAS senior management.

From the view of officials in the EEAS, contacts with the Council of the EU and member states had actually reduced significantly compared to those with the Commission coordination (Interview 34, EEAS desk officer, 2017). While general collaboration was reported in overall positive terms, in line with previous findings on the first phase of consolidation, this did not hold up for the development of the EU Global Strategy. Here, a cabinet member of the President of the EUCO reported 'being treated like a member state', including having had to ask for information, and finding that access was severely limited and there had been no time for comment (Interview 32, EUCO cabinet, 2017). Some of the difficulties of engagement, however, were also linked to outside events such as the membership vote in the UK, which distracted members of the European Council from the global strategy. The EU Global Strategy process with regard to the European Council and Council confirmed that it was a process run autonomously by the High Representative. There is some irony in these perceptions, considering how much process and consultation was to be included in the strategy-making process (Tocci 2016: pp. 463, 465). The decision to work around the established structured of member states' cooperation (Tocci 2016: p. 466) appear to have left a different mark in these institutions.

EEAS and Parliament

While the European Parliament had also voiced its discontent about the structural arrangements across EEAS, Commission and Council Secretariat by demanding that EEAS '[C]arry out a systematic and in-depth audit in order to unify the external policy-related structures put in place by the Commission and the Council Secretariat, with a view to overcoming current duplications and promoting cost efficiency' (EP 2013b: p. 5), the EP was the most steadfast ally of the EEAS in its consolidation. It also maintained a keen eye on the balance of national diplomats vis-à-vis European officials and other structural issues of employment via the budgetary discharge procedure (Committee on Budgetary Control 2017), the EP's most direct element of control (see Chapter 6). Mogherini's EEAS has obliged and followed the calls of the EP in this instance. The European Parliament, like the European Council President and his cabinet, had been supportive of the EEAS in its early period of operation, repeatedly stressing the relevance of parliamentary involvement and oversight in the

176 *Trajectories of consolidation for the EEAS*

external action of the Union. In the second phase of the consolidation, the relationship became more complicated.

The EP's main concern after the creation of the service proper had shifted to access to the service and information it could provide (Raube 2012). The relevance of this topic is recognisable in the hearing of the High Representative-designate Federica Mogherini in front of the Foreign Affairs Committee of the European Parliament. The chair and other members of the Committee raised the issue of accountability and access to information; specifically, the access to classified information for the EP and its members (AFET 2014a). In her responses during the hearing, Mogherini stressed her willingness to collaborate with parliament above and beyond the agreements that had been achieved in Ashton's tenure (AFET 2014a). Brok, as chair of AFET, also stressed in his opening remarks that there had been an agreement that a senior official of the European Parliament would be hired for the senior management of the EEAS and that he expected that agreement to be honoured (AFET 2014a: p. 4). While only a minor comment, it illustrated that staffing had not entirely slipped the EP representatives' minds as an issue of influence vis-à-vis the service. Brok raised the staffing imbalance in the EEAS, stressing it was unacceptable that 'all the Chiefs [are] from the member states and the foot soldiers from the institutions' (AFET 2014a: p. 4). This issue was picked up by EEAS management in the process of human resource review (see above, Interview 38, EEAS official, 2017).

The evaluation letter written by the Committee Chair, Elmar Brok, highlighted the commitments undertaken by Mogherini towards the Committee (AFET 2014b). Brok noted Mogherini's agreement that 'political reporting should be made available to the Parliament' and that she was 'committed to work in a pragmatic and structured way on enabling access to classified information' (AFET 2014b: p. 2). Access to political assessment by the service was quoted as a relevant source of information in the EP administration, both for EP delegations to other countries (Interview 33, EP official, 2017) and from more thematic parts of the EP administration (Interview 37, EP official, 2017). However, staff also noted the reluctance to share written material (Interview 33, EP official, 2017).

Classified information remained an issue for parliamentarians and staff alike, even though access to some material and classified country reports was made available in a briefing room. The positive, but not very concrete, stance of Mogherini meant that access to classified information was still negotiated one and a half years after the hearing (Interview 37, EP official, 2017). The EEAS, while applying previous inter-institutional agreements in a limited fashion, did not always provide access to the type of information the EP wanted. But after these negotiations, weekly and monthly reports from delegations did become available to selected members and selected staff of the EP (Interview 37, EP official, 2017). Despite the long transition, EP staff was 'very satisfied it has started' and that the goodwill of desk officer did not have to be imposed upon for information gathering (Interview 37, EP official, 2017). Here a downside of the status decision on the EEAS continues to have effect; as the EEAS is not an

Trajectories of consolidation for the EEAS 177

institution in a EU legal sense, yet at the same time wasn't covered fully in its operation by the Commission, or the Council, a grey area existed in which the service could ignore requests for information. Especially with regard to the EU Global Strategy process, while the EP remained strongly supportive of the process, individual disapproval of access to the process by MEPs never subsided (Interview 35, EP official, 2017). Nevertheless, this did not prevent an overall positive assessment of the development of information flows during the Mogherini tenure for the EP.

An overview of the development of EEAS relations with the EU institutions has shown some trends that set apart Federica Mogherini's tenure from the tenure of Catherine Ashton. The most notable difference is a much closer association of the HR and the EEAS with the European Commission. This has resulted in a less fractious relationship with the Commission and improved working relations and decision-making processes which have been achieved by, among other factors, adjusting its internal organisation. It has also, as a consequence, allowed decision-making to be more procedural and consultative in nature; something that still sits uneasily with the foreign policy tasks of the EEAS and HR. The link to the Council and member states has weakened at headquarters, even as member states have taken on a dominant role in staffing in the EU delegations' most senior posts. The European Parliament has continued its position of support in exchange for diplomatic support and, most importantly, access to information. Within the EEAS, the organisational structure has still changed and is adapting to external pressure for staff reduction, coordination needs and stronger authority by senior management and political leadership. Will this rebalancing of the EEAS have an impact on potential trajectories for the role of the EEAS in EU external action over the remainder of the Mogherini tenure and beyond? The following section will thresh out a number of potential avenues for the EEAS and its orientation in the 'politics of Eurocratic structure' (Kelemen 2002; Kelemen and Tarrant 2011).

Charting the course ahead: the politics of diplomatic structure and trajectories of the EEAS

The bureaucratic-institutionalist model has a number of core tenets that are helpful in developing trajectories of institutional change: following Moe (1989), it expected the actors involved to continue renegotiating the agreed bargain up to the point of reversal of decisions, even if reversal would be considered much less likely. A new institutional path had been charted at the European Convention with the EEAS as joined-up external action administration, but the 'game of structural politics never ends' (Moe 1989). Whereas Ashton chose to stand more in the line of an autonomous EEAS that kept its distance from the Commission, Mogherini from the start has adopted a stance of close collaboration with the Commission. As one official noted, the 'pendulum' had swung in the other direction (Interview 34, EEAS official, 2017). This trajectory of the Commission's Associate was the most visible aspect of Mogherini's first tenure.

178　*Trajectories of consolidation for the EEAS*

The Commission's Associate approach

The Commission's Associate approach will naturally always find favour with two particular EU institutions: the European Commission and the European Parliament. In that way, this trajectory is a sustainable path as long as no major opposition is encountered from member states. Member states have not recently insisted on the 'equidistance' formula and have at least publicly accepted the move towards the Commission. This institutional strategy has a tradition linking back all the way to the Convention debates: debates on the network of delegations, the large proportion of former Commission staff in the EEAS, and the idea that the EEAS would be fully integrated into the Commission that had been floated again and again by, for example, members of the European Parliament (see Chapters 4 and 5). Ultimately, the strategy finds its justification in the rhetoric used for the creation of the EEAS, because ensuring coherence in the EU's external action will always require strong coordination with the European Commission's other directorates with external functions such as development and humanitarian aid. Mogherini's push towards coordination has clearly been an improvement in this area (see e.g. Politico Europe 2017).

The Commission's Associate trajectory derives its stability from the main objectives of the Convention's discussion on the role of the then 'EU Foreign Minister': that the EU is fully represented by one person with a 'double hat', or even 'triple hat', of High Representative, Commission Vice-President and Chair of the Foreign Affairs Council. No other alternative structure or reorganisation with an independent EEAS brings the Commission closer to EU foreign policy decision-making. On the other hand, it is an inherently unstable arrangement as the current legal arrangement appears to favour an 'equidistant' role of the EEAS. This means that another HR/VP may again opt to rebalance towards the EEAS as a more autonomous body that works closely with Council structures. Due to procedural and budgetary intertwining with the Commission, this would be difficult, but achievable in the framework of the current legal setting. The trajectory would only be set on an even firmer path, should the EEAS be integrated, or 'folded into' the Commission, either by an adaptation of the Council Decision setting up the EEAS, or in the framework of an unlikely, but repeatedly discussed, revision of the treaties. As a full integration of the EEAS into the Commission is, however, highly unlikely in the near future, administrative competition will continue to shape the operation of the EEAS on this trajectory. The recent focus set by Mogherini on security and defence policy and her 'third hat' as director of the European Defence Agency would likely set some limits to this close association, as member states' buy-in would be more difficult to achieve in security and defence.

The President's Wingwoman

In addition to the Commission-centred trajectory, there is a little-discussed alternative model that also links back to the ideas discussed at the European

Convention among the many options for the post of High Representative. There is no natural guarantee that member states will continue to allow a process of association between the HR/VP and the EEAS and the Commission to continue indefinitely. As their original interest in access to senior positions in the service is currently largely met, their acquiescence may not be sustainable. The first signs of a shift in personnel policy have already become apparent in the EEAS and through demands by the European parliament. As foreign policy shifts ever upward, through the involvement of the European Council to deal with crises, as opposed to the Foreign Affairs Council, member states may well demand that the EEAS resume a more distant role vis-à-vis the Commission.

Here, any institutional change will depend on large-scale institutional shifts, like those developed during the Convention on the Future of Europe. An alternative model for the HR/VP proposed by French government representatives had after all been a 'foreign minister'-like post not autonomous or linked to the Commission but attached organisationally to an elected President of the European Council. The head of the European People's Party in the EP, Manfred Weber, only recently tweeted his support for a 'breakthrough for democracy' in Europe, demanding that 'in the long term, all Europeans should vote directly for the President of the European Council' (Weber 2017). The institutional reform programme presented by Commission President Jean-Claude Juncker in his 'State of the European Union' address of 2017 has added an element of credibility to this particular path. Juncker called for the merger of 'presidents', joining the office of the President of the European Commission with the office of the President of the European Council (Juncker 2017). This proposal has its origins in the Convention debates on the leadership of the EU outlined earlier in this book. While it did not find favour with most delegates and with member states in the resulting intergovernmental conferences, some members of the Convention insisted that a loophole for this solution existed as the draft treaty did not preclude the holding of both offices by one person. In line with the 'presidentialisation' of the Commission solidified by Juncker in his first term, and the strengthening of the Vice-President's role in management, this merger would change the nature of the EU executive fundamentally.

While on the surface this does not concern the EEAS and its political leadership, it links back to the alternative structural models of the EU polity, which do impact on the EEAS. A democratically more legitimate President of the European Council would need to be endowed with a stronger administrative and political resource base, of which the EEAS could more naturally form part than elements of the Commission proper. Due to the chosen institutional path that has solidified in the consolidation phases, this alternative model is less likely than a continued close association with the Commission, but it is an alternative polity idea that may be reactivated. Should the merger of positions in the 'Union President' occur, the distinction of association with European Council President versus Commission President falls away and the role of HR/VP could indeed become a linchpin of this unified EU executive.

180 *Trajectories of consolidation for the EEAS*

Brexit and the EEAS

The external event that will have an impact on the EEAS, even though it is not directly linked to the politics of diplomatic structure, is the fact that the United Kingdom is set to leave the European Union and its institutional structure in the coming years. The decision has briefly shaken up EU decision-makers, but as negotiations began a united position among the 27 member states emerged. Nevertheless, the EEAS was considering the impact of 'Brexit' on the organisation. One main concern is the loss of resources, which could result in a reduction by 10% of the EEAS's operating budget (Interview 38, EEAS official, 2017) if another across the board reduction were to be asked of the EU institutions. In terms of human resources, British diplomats may be difficult to replace within the EEAS. The loss for both sides in terms of, among other things, access to the expertise and reporting of the UK diplomatic network (Dijkstra 2016b) as well as access to the Foreign Affairs Council and to have seconded diplomats in the EEAS for the UK (Bond 2016), is hard to measure, but significant.

The UK government has repeatedly stated its willingness to remain associated to and contribute to European security and defence as well as to cooperate in foreign policy (Bond 2016), but how this cooperation could be achieved structurally is unclear (Whitman 2016). Whitman showed that even prior to the vote to leave the EU, domestic arrangements in foreign and security policy sought to assign the EU a subordinate role in British foreign and security policy (Whitman 2016: p. 2). While Whitman demonstrated that a range of options for British engagement in EU foreign policy structures (Whitman 2016), the minimalist fall-back option will only be as observer and through bilateral arrangements. Focusing on the ongoing negotiations, Lord Kerr, who had been in the Secretariat of the European Convention as well as the head of the UK diplomatic service, argued that its role in foreign policy was the key negotiation chip the UK had to offer to the EU (Kerr 2017). European commentators have mirrored this in spelling out the undesirable risk of the UK being completely cut off from EU coordination meetings (Dijkstra 2016b). The current mood of observers of UK diplomacy with regard to Brexit is probably best captured by Whitman, who described the current efforts as 'punk diplomacy', intent on 'smash[ing] the system' (Whitman 2017).

But not all aspects of Brexit are negative for the EEAS. With the UK on the outside of EU foreign policy making, one obstacle to the role of the EEAS in international organisations and fora will have been removed. It was after all the UK that objected most vigorously about the EEAS making statements on behalf of the EU in a number of international organisations (Interview 13, Commission official, 2012; Foreign and Commonwealth Office 2013). The main thrusts for a 'value-added' construction of the EEAS, the push for a 'budgetary neutral' EEAS, had their origins in the UK government (see Chapter 5). The absence of the UK may not mean, of course, that the remaining EU governments are now willing to spend lavishly on the EEAS as other governments will take up the torch of savings and budget-neutrality (Foreign and Commonwealth Office

Trajectories of consolidation for the EEAS 181

2013). But it is unlikely that the obstacle would be as consistent and as singularly focused on this line, allowing the EEAS to further bend the 'budget neutrality' in its own organisational favour.

These different trajectories are an exercise in informed speculation, and only the next term will tell whether the path taken by Mogherini will indeed be the trajectory of the EEAS in the future. But as institutional shifts appear more likely in the light of Brexit and a unifying push by the Juncker Commission for the remaining 27 member states, the EU is likely to turn inward again, renegotiating its institutional structure in the recurring 'game of structural politics'. The EEAS will find itself at the heart of that game by virtue of its unique position as an 'in-betweener', connecting two very different institutions. Understanding how the bureaucratic institutionalist model explained this development and where the model exhibits limitations will be the main objective of the final chapter.

References

Becker, Stefan; Bauer, Michael; Connolly, Sara; and Kassim, Hussein 2016: The Commission: boxed in and constrained, but still an engine of integration. *West European Politics*, vol. 39, no. 5, pp. 1011–1031.

Bicchi, Federica 2014: EU Foreign Policy and the Politics of Information. In Blom, Tannelie and Vanhoonacker, Sophie (Eds.), *The Politics of Information*. European Administrative Governance series. Palgrave Macmillan: London.

Bond, Ian 2016: Brexit and foreign policy: Divorce? *Center for European Reform (CER) Bulletin*, Issue 109. London, 2016.

Davis Cross, Mai'a 2016: The EU Global Strategy and diplomacy. *Contemporary Security Policy*, vol. 37, no. 3, pp. 402–413.

Dijkstra, Hylke 2016a: Introduction: One-and-a-half cheers for the EU Global Strategy. *Contemporary Security Policy*, vol. 37, no. 3, pp. 369–373.

Dijkstra, Hylke 2016b: UK and EU foreign policy cooperation after Brexit. *RUSI Newsbrief*, vol. 36, no. 5, pp. 1–3.

Kerr of Kinlochard, Lord John 2017: Brexit is about foreign policy. Why is Britain being so silent? *Evening Standard*, 2017.

Moe, Terry 1989: The Politics of Bureaucracy. In Chubb and Peterson (Eds.): *Can the Government Govern?* Brookings: Washington, DC.

Politico Europe 2017: Mogherini's mid-term report card. We grade the EU's foreign policy chief on everything from Iran to migration. Brussels, 18.04. 2017. www.politico.eu/article/federica-mogherini-report-card-midterm-grades-eu-foreign-policy/.

Pomorska, Karolina and Vanhoonacker, Sophie 2015: Europe as a Global Actor: the (Un)Holy Trinity of Economy, Diplomacy, and Security. *Journal of Common Market Studies Annual Review*, vol. 53, pp. 216–229.

Raube, Kolja 2012: The European External Action Service and the European Parliament. *The Hague Journal of Diplomacy*, vol. 7, no. 1, pp. 65–80.

Tocci, Nathalie 2016: The making of the EU Global Strategy. *Contemporary Security Policy*, vol. 37, no. 3, pp. 461–472.

Weber, Manfred (@manfredweber) 2017: European democracy needs a breakthrough. In the long term, all Europeans should vote directly for the President of the European Council'. 18 August 2017, 9.49 AM. Tweet. https://twitter.com/ManfredWeber/status/898451668949319680.

182 *Trajectories of consolidation for the EEAS*

Whitman, Richard 2016: The UK and EU Foreign and Security Policy After Brexit: Integrated, Associated or Detached? *National Institute of Economic Review*, no. 238, pp. 1–8.

Whitman, Richard 2017: The UK's punk diplomacy: never mind the bollocks. The UK in a Changing Europe. Blog. http://ukandeu.ac.uk/the-uks-punk-diplomacy-never-mind-the-bollocks/.

Official documents

European Commission

Juncker, Jean-Claude 2014: Mission letter to Federica Mogherini, High Representative of the Union for Foreign and Security Policy/Vice-President of the European Commission. 1 November 2014, Brussels.

Juncker, Jean-Claude 2017: State of the European Union 2017. Brussels, European Commission. Retrieved 14 September 2017. http://europa.eu/rapid/press-release_SPEECH-17-3165_en.htm.

European Council

European Council 2014: European Council Decision appointing the High Representative of the Union for Foreign Affairs and Security Policy. EUCO 146/14, 30. August 2014, Brussels.

European Court of Auditors

European Court of Auditors 2014: Special Report No. 11: The Establishment of the European External Action Service. ECA, Luxembourg.

European External Action Service

EEAS 2013a: EEAS Review 2013. EEAS: Brussels.

EEAS 2017: 2016 EEAS Human Resources Annual Report. Brussels, 30 May 2017.

European Union Institute for Security Studies

European Union Institute for Security Studies (EUISS) 2016: *The EU and the world: Players and Policies Post-Lisbon. A Handbook*. Paris: EU Institute for Security Studies.

European Parliament

AFET (EP Foreign Affairs Committee) 2014a: Verbatim Record of the Hearing of High Representative-designate Federica Mogherini. Brussels, 06.10.2014.

AFET (EP Foreign Affairs Committee) 2014b: Letter to J. Buzek on High Representative-designate Federica Mogherini. Brussels, 08.10.2014.

Committee on Budgetary Control 2017: Report on discharge in respect of the implementation of the general budget of the European Union for the financial year 2015, Section X – European External Action Service (2016/2160(DEC)), P8_TA(2017)0152, Brussels.

Foreign and Commonwealth Office

Foreign and Commonwealth Office 2013: Response to Freedom of Information request FOI 1256–12. London, 27.03.2013.

High Representative

High Representative (HR) 2015: Implementing the EEAS Review: Progress Report of the High Representative/Vice-President to the Council. HR(2015)170.

8 Conclusion

Towards a European foreign ministry?

The contestation over the EEAS and its impact on the organisation and functioning of the EEAS have been at the heart of this book. It set out to answer a seemingly simple question: why did a new administrative organisation created for a purpose run into opposition in its operation, from exactly those political actors who had originally agreed to create it? In order to answer this question, a number of derivative questions needed addressing. These three questions concerned the evolution of the new organisation: why was the organisation created, how was the organisation created and how does it operate? These questions implicitly identified three distinct phases in the creation of the new organisation: inception, establishment and consolidation. These three phases were conceptualised through subsets of institutionalist theories, which capture the political conflict or contestation surrounding the new administrative actor. With an eclectic analytical framework of institutional approaches that encompasses these three stages of institutional evolution, this book has delivered a specifically bureaucratic-institutionalist answer to the contestation of the European External Action Service. The shortcomings of the EEAS are determined and driven mainly by the contestation of outside actors and only partially explained by internal organisational failings.

After a brief review of the expectations derived from the analytical approaches used, as well as a summary of the findings in each phase of development, this chapter addresses the answers given to the core questions on the EEAS's creation. It combines these insights in an evaluation of the analytical power to explain the evolution of the EEAS. It also highlights where the approach falls short in accounting for the findings in this case. The conclusion continues by considering how the insights into the case of the EEAS speak to the analysis of institutional change more generally. Finally, it concludes by highlighting what these insights mean for the future of the EEAS.

Inception is a phase often described in terms of 'critical junctures' in historical institutionalist research. The institutional constraints on political actors are temporarily loosened, leading to an agreement that is beyond the boundary of a regular, bargain-based lowest common denominator. An agreement by this so-called enacting coalition is found through regular bargaining and shaped by the institutional rules in place and the variety of actors' preferences. The phase is embedded in a particular historical institutional setting and the decisions taken

Conclusion: towards a European foreign ministry? 185

within it subsequently shape the later periods of creation. Next is the actual establishment of the new organisation through legal acts, budget amendments and staffing decisions. These decisions are taken a by a set of different political actors that together make up the executing coalition. The establishment phase returns the decision-making to the familiar institutional setting of EU decision-making, described in theoretical terms as the EU politics of bureaucratic structure. Negotiations of an EU inter-institutional nature are broadened somewhat and are played out in a more typical EU decision-making process than in the first phase. With the decision of this executing coalition, the new organisation comes into existence and from that moment on changes the political scene. This phase is the consolidation phase. The organisation establishes its own organisational structure and purpose and begins to enter into conflict with its bureaucratic environment. The actors who agreed to create the organisation interact with it in a competitive sense rather than a coalition-based approach as in the previous two phases. The main objective is to establish control over the new body in order to gain benefits from its operation. After a brief overview of the findings in these respective phases of inception, establishment, and consolidation of the EEAS, the bureaucratic-institutionalist approach is evaluated in relation to this evidence.

Inception

Looking at the historical evolution of the administrative structures in EU external relations and EU foreign policy demonstrated the vast divergence of views on the organisation of these two policy areas (see also Chapter 2). It showed that even in the 1990s a merger of the two administrative traditions, the Commission's external relations as well as the Council Secretariat's foreign policy organisation, had been floated as a solution to the perceived incoherence of the two policy areas. Nevertheless, in the intergovernmental conferences of the time, no majority could be assembled for this type of change. This changed during the Convention on the Future of Europe in the early 2000s, as explained in Chapter 4. The EEAS was conceived and written into the EU's institutional system at the Convention on the Future of Europe because the Convention's format allowed for integrationist positions to be more strongly represented than during a regular intergovernmental conference. In many ways, it was a case of 'realizing the impossible' – a substantive reform of EU structures (Finke *et al.* 2012). The Convention included members of the European Parliament and members of national parliaments, including from candidate states for the 2004 enlargement. Even with the government representatives of the then member states, the overall composition was considerably pro-European in outlook. The leadership of the Convention as well as core members of the Convention were integrationist representatives from the member states and the European Parliament who were able to additionally exert control over the agenda and outcome. Their agenda was to prepare a full draft treaty to be presented to the member states, in order to prevent the proposal from being picked apart (see Chapter 4), and they anticipated a 'lock-in' for most of the structures agreed in its final draft.

186   *Conclusion: towards a European foreign ministry?*

The relatively limited changes that were subsequently introduced during the intergovernmental conferences that transferred the Convention's proposal into actual EU treaty text illustrate the success of this approach. The EEAS entered the scene first in a working document of a working group of the Convention and remained contested in its form and shape until the last full Convention debates in the summer of 2002. But the final agreement was more or less what the working group on external relations in its report had originally proposed. However, these final debates also illustrate the vague and contentious nature of some of the agreements, leaving open to a degree whether the EEAS would be integrated into the Commission or become what Elmar Brok during these debates called a 'Kingdom of the Middle' between Council and Commission. In order to keep the position of foreign minister with an administrative support structure in its proposal, the Convention did not attempt to set out more precise organisational details of this structure as doing so would have re-ignited disagreements among delegates. The Commission was, until late in the Convention, attempting to safeguard its institutional assets, e.g. by attempting to remove the delegations from the reach of the EEAS. The overall outcome reflected both intra-Convention logrolling as well as a Franco-German institutional compromise, which accepted the creation of a President of the European Council for the creation of a foreign minister with a supporting service. Despite opposition to the concept of the EEAS by some member states, they were not able to prevent it during the Convention or afterwards in the intergovernmental conferences, even if they were able to reduce the standing of the political leadership of the organisation from 'foreign minister' to retain the less statesman-like 'High Representative' title. Details of the administrative set-up were left for the next phase of the EEAS's evolution, the establishment of the service.

Establishment

The translation of the proposals of the Convention via intergovernmental conferences had introduced some surface changes to the institutional structure of external relations and foreign policy, but it did not alter the required next steps. The Lisbon Treaty's amendments mandated the creation of the EEAS, which required a decision of the Council and approval by the Commission. Because of the large-scale nature of these administrative changes, several other pieces of institutional legislation, namely those governing the staff and financial regulations, had to be amended too. These legal acts required collaboration with the European Parliament. The latter used its legislative prerogatives in relation to the staff and financial regulations to participate in the negotiations on the Council decision creating the EEAS, the so-called quadrilogue. In addition to the Council, the Commission and the EP, the new High Representative, who was responsible for the proposal, was an active participant in this process. This 'quadrilogue' involved negotiations between the usual collective actors in EU decision-making, with a leading role in the preparatory stage of the decision for member states representatives in Council. Member states proved very cautious about giving authority to the newly

Conclusion: towards a European foreign ministry? 187

established structure and were weary of Commission influence on foreign policy. The member states were equally strongly concerned about how their own staff would enter the service in adequate numbers and seniority. The EP, in contrast, was keen to guarantee Commission involvement specifically in the budgetary field and held on to the position that the EEAS should be part of the Commission for a long time. The Commission was working to minimise the effect of losing such a large group of staff working on external relations by internal reorganisation and strong negotiations on questions of administrative resources.

The final Council decision reflects these political positions. It created an additional layer of hierarchy to accommodate member states' staff and entered requirements of adequate hiring of member states diplomats into the text. The decision also safeguarded the Commission's role in budgetary management and gave the European Parliament some additional guarantees on political accountability. The Council decision itself, however, could not cover all aspects of future operation of the EEAS and its relations with other actors. These were to be negotiated in the following consolidation phase of the service.

Consolidation

As the EEAS started to take shape as an autonomous administrative organisation, it had to establish its own organisation and procedure in more detail than was written into the Council decision. It also had to develop working relations with other actors in Brussels, and most prominently among those, the European Commission. Because the Commission still retained control over other external relations policies, such as trade, and had a guaranteed role in the external aspects of internal competences, a complex system of interaction was agreed between the two organisations. The overall process of consolidation was characterised by attempts to control the organisation by other actors, i.e. the Council and the member states, the European Commission and the European Parliament. With a lower degree of competitiveness and formality, the EEAS also established working procedures with the President of the European Council.

These interactions with the institutional and administrative environment clearly hampered the ability of the EEAS leadership to shape the organisation. At the level of desk officers, the inter-institutional competition had a concrete impact on their daily work. Increased complexity and longer internal processes are among the challenges faced at the level of officials. Trust in other institutions had been impaired by the experiences of consolidation; this is specifically visible for former Commission staff, who did not consider the Commission a supportive partner organisation.

Nevertheless, these observations feed into a visible trend towards a phase of less active contestation of interactions and control towards the end of the period under observation. In spite of the fact that the EEAS decision required the High Representative to review her own organisation and in that review contained the possibility of amending the original decision, the 2013 review shied away from proposing a review of the decision itself (EEAS 2013a). The response to this

188 *Conclusion: towards a European foreign ministry?*

EEAS review and the continued structural contestation of the EEAS had been postponed until the next High Representative, Mogherini, had taken office, rather than completely abandoned. Since some of the core elements of the review, e.g. a move away from collective leadership to clearer hierarchies, relate to strongly contested design features in the consolidation period of the EEAS, a renewed large-scale restructuring would have given additional insights into who drives organisational change at the EEAS. In this respect, the second part of the consolidation revealed that the reorganisation of the EEAS followed the advice prepared by the first High Representative and a stronger hierarchical organisation was introduced. At the same time, this was pursued alongside a clear turn towards the Commission by High Representative/Vice-President Mogherini. The Commission's dominance over the service has been maintained up to the end of the period of observation in 2017.

How well does a bureaucratic-institutionalist approach capture the evolution of the EEAS?

The evidence presented in the book allows for a number of interesting observations on the 'fit' of the bureaucratic-institutionalist model developed in Chapter 3. The model stressed that the three phases of evolution can be conceptualised by using three related but distinct approaches to bureaucratic change in EU foreign policy.

In the inception phase, the analytical framework was centred on a rational choice historical institutionalist explanation, which perceived this phase as the building of a general enacting coalition to create the new organisation. This enacting coalition in the case of the EEAS was a broad one. As the EEAS entered the EU's institutional stage for the first time in the proposed Constitutional Treaty of the Convention on the Future of Europe, it is here where its enacting coalition can be found. It is more specific, however, than the entire Convention's membership. As has been described above, not all members of the Convention wanted to create the EEAS. But the fact that an influential grouping of MEPs, some members of the Convention leadership, and some government representatives did want to create it sufficed. The process by which the Convention outcome was developed was bargaining. In the case of the EEAS, it took the form specifically of logrolling between different visions for the EU's institutional structure – agreeing to a President of the European Council in exchange for an agreement on the foreign minister and the EEAS. At the same time, this bargaining occurred in an institutional structure that was considerably more relaxed than an intergovernmental conference, something captured very well by the concept of 'critical juncture' in the historical institutionalist literature.

Because the Convention was more inclusive than an intergovernmental conference and because the leadership of the Convention decided to push for a complete treaty proposal, the EEAS could be entered into a set of institutional innovations. But the Convention itself was subject to institutional rules, which favoured the members of the praesidium and the leadership of the working

Conclusion: towards a European foreign ministry? 189

groups. The 'critical juncture' was thus, as expected, not an institutional void (Riker 1998), but a set of more relaxed rules combined with a more inclusive group of actors, which shifted the middle ground towards a particular kind of integration. Member states that had opposed this innovation found no way to substantially unravel the bargain over two intergovernmental conferences, and merely stripped the political figurehead of the new service of its ministerial title without major changes to its mandate or undetermined administrative substructure. Nevertheless, the grand bargain approach also shows the limits of this agreement. Not all elements could be worked out because of political disagreements and contestation, leaving the organisational structure of the EEAS undetermined. The details were left for a second round of processes, detached from the Convention. This next phase brings the setting up of the EEAS to a more concrete level.

The establishment phase is equally foreseen in a rational choice historical institutionalist framework, which conceptualises the processes as the working out of an 'executing coalition' (Lindner and Rittberger 2003). The forming of the executing coalition, however, had a very specific EU nature. The legal basis for the EEAS needed to be agreed by Council (i.e. the member states' representatives) with approval of the Commission. When a preliminary agreement was reached that the EEAS would become an 'assimilated' institution, giving it certain autonomous powers without making it a formal institution, it required legislative changes that locked in the negotiation format. The European Parliament's approval was now required to pass amendments to the financial and staff regulations. The ensuing process is captured well by the 'politics of Eurocratic structure' approach (Kelemen 2002), in which the Council tried to limit supranational influence on core policy areas, and the European Parliament in turn attempted to extend them. The Commission mainly defended its own turf by limiting the autonomy of the new organisation and asserting its procedural dominance.

Both of these processes could be observed during the establishment of the EEAS. The main interconnected points of contention were the status and scope of the organisation, staffing, budgetary management and political accountability. The Council members were specifically focused on the relevance of member states' own staff in the newly created organisation, in the expectation that member states would have direct access and links to the EEAS leadership. The EP managed to extract specific concessions on accountability to the European Parliament from the new High Representative and also maintained the Commission's (and thus its own) control over budgetary management. The Commission would be expected to support transfers of authority to itself. However, as in the previous phase, the Commission appeared to be fighting a rearguard action against the EEAS, being more concerned with stifling its autonomy. Here, the politics of Eurocratic structure approach reaches its limit, as the Commission appeared to prefer no transfer of authority from the member states over transfer to the EEAS. In parallel, it worked more predictably towards bringing the EEAS under Commission influence. Its orthodox position on budgetary management

190   *Conclusion: towards a European foreign ministry?*

and the role of the Commission in running delegations remained in line with the position Commission representatives had already defended during the Convention, yet it had not been entered into the treaty text.

With the creation of the EEAS as an administrative organisation through the Council decision, a new phase was ushered in. This consolidation phase was expected to differ from the first two phases by including the EEAS as an autonomous actor in a political environment replete with other actors. The focus of the analysis shifted in this conceptualisation from compromises and coalition building to negotiated or enforced cooperation (or maybe 'coopetition'), i.e. cooperation may be required by treaty rules and secondary legislation. The evidence speaks for viewing the EEAS as a self-interested organisation in competition with other actors that tried to bring it under their control. There is some evidence of the leadership of the EEAS attempting to increase the budget of the organisation, at least at the beginning, as well as to shape its activities. This supports core expectations of two central approaches of bureaucracy theory: budget maximisation and bureau shaping. As an organisation built during a financial crisis, it is however important to note that increases in the EEAS budget have decreased over time. This has been accounted for by another approach to bureaucracy theory, which argues that budget increases are politically costly to the leaders of administrative organisations (Dunleavy 1991).

Externally, the bureaucratic characteristics of the third phase are shown by bureaucratic politics and conflict surrounding the operation of the service: All actors involved in creating the EEAS used their control mechanisms built into the decision, albeit to varying degrees. The EEAS lives up to the abbreviation's possible meaning in the engineering world: it's an 'externally excited adaptive system' (Horwitz *et al.* 1974). The Council maintained its vigilance on staffing matters. The European Parliament, however, shied away from direct confrontation with the service. As bureaucratic politics predicted, the main lines of conflict centred on the other bureaucratic actor in EU external relations, the European Commission. Conflicts over resources, responsibilities and autonomy were fought out over the period of consolidation. Even in the short period until the review of the EEAS in 2013, a trend of decreasing salience set in and continued throughout the second High Representative/Vice-President's tenure. The political contestation that saw the 'institution as policy' was to a degree superseded by foreign policy 'substance' like crisis response and the EU Global Strategy. After conflicts over the rules on procedural cooperation had been settled – largely in favour of the European Commission – routine processes set in and appear to have reduced conflict. The analytical framework does not account for this decrease, but it would be a relevant factor in future analyses. Another reason why the conflict subsided over this period was that the second HR/VP turned her role considerably towards the European Commission, making conflict between the EEAS and the Commission self-defeating. After the limited organisational revisions undertaken as a response to the EEAS review, the question in the future will remain how long member states are willing to entertain the institutional 'equidistance' formula being resolved in favour of the Commission.

Conclusion: towards a European foreign ministry? 191

Looking at the various trajectories for the EEAS in the previous chapter, this could mean further integration into the Commission as much as subordination to the President of the European Council. It is therefore a conflict postponed, rather than abated.

Combining these institutional approaches gives a clear answer to the key question: why did the EEAS have such a difficult start after having been lauded as the panacea for the EU's difficulty in becoming an influential actor in the world? From the very start of the conception of the service, political and administrative actors have hotly contested it. Throughout the phases of its creation, the central or strategic objective of the EEAS has come second to varying political considerations. First, it was introduced during the contests between integrationists and defenders of the status quo at the Convention on the Future of Europe, only to be party to an inter-institutional tug of war over structure, staffing and autonomy during its establishment. Even its early operation and review were strongly influenced by outside actors at the EU level whose interests were often focused on elements of control over the new service rather than on its efficient functioning. The EEAS is after all a political bureaucracy, with limited interest group interaction; it needs to serve many masters who only agree to a certain extent what the organisation is meant to do.

Any fair evaluation must naturally also refer back to the long trajectory of cooperation, and see the EEAS operation in the context of EU member states' foreign policy cooperation. David Allen's insight that any serious engagement with the world by EU member states will require more than a simple secretariat set-up was already true before the creation of the EEAS (Allen 1982), but the EEAS has created the bureaucratic foundation from which to conduct foreign policy. While it is unclear that a genuinely common foreign policy could be achieved given the vastly diverging interests of member states, the EEAS fulfils many of the functions regularly reserved to diplomatic services and is certainly able to report, provide statements and maintain regular relations around the globe. The service in itself is an institutional expression of the increase in value that these links have for the EU member states.

While the respective shift in focus of the analytical framework for each of the three evolutionary phases of the new organisation appears to hold reliably, there is evidence not accounted for and not captured appropriately by the framework. One of these difficulties concerns the linkages between the phases. In many ways, the purpose of the three phases is to distinguish different dynamics, something the approach is well able to do. It sees the phases as distinct, even if previous phases define some of the parameters for the following phase. Nevertheless, this subtle link between phases may actually be too soft to match the evidence. The phases are connected much more strongly than the original analytical framework expects. This connection is built through a variety of mechanisms: the first one is the actors involved. The continuity of actors shaping EU institutional politics is not accounted for. In several instances, the same person is interacting in all three phases with a similar agenda, adapting it only slightly to the changing institutional environment. The best example of this in the case of

192 *Conclusion: towards a European foreign ministry?*

the EEAS is perhaps the role of Elmar Brok, the conservative German MEP. He appears in a central role in all three phases: first as an active member of the European Convention (Chapter 4), then as a negotiator for the European Parliament (Chapter 5), and finally as chair of the AFET Committee in the European Parliament during the EEAS's early years of consolidation (Chapter 6). But several other individuals appear with differing roles across the three phases. David O'Sullivan first represented the Commission on several occasions during the Convention and proposed the removal of delegations from the EEAS structure (see Chapter 4). He then returned in the consolidation phase as Chief Operating Officer of the new-born EEAS. In late 2014, he went on to take up the most prized of EU head of delegation posts in Washington, DC (EEAS 2014b; see also Chapter 2).

Another factor that is under-valued in the framework is the consistency with which precedent determines later activity in the EU's political and administrative system. In the EU's treaty (i.e. rule)-based system, once a decision has been agreed upon, it is difficult to change and will become the baseline of subsequent decisions even if the time horizon is stretched over several years, as in the case of the EEAS. This is why the EU institutions reverted to a preliminary agreement from 2005 when discussing the set-up of the EEAS in 2008/2009 (see Chapter 5). Equally, EU member states largely stuck to the substance of the Constitutional Treaty text when discussing it at an intergovernmental conference. The stability of views did not just exist for compromises. Linking the views on EU foreign policy and external relations structures from the 1990s, it is clear that fault lines across the views of the member states were stable. The orientation of individual countries may have shifted, but the conflicts over integration in these policy areas remained relatively stable. Irrespective of the first-order views on deeper integration, the second-order views on influence over the organisation, for example via staffing, were equally salient across all member states. In a similar vein, views of the European Parliament exhibited a comparable stickiness, reiterating its views on a European diplomatic service and referring to established parliamentary positions with each contribution. Beyond the ironclad commitment to making the EEAS a supranational organisation, in second-order discussions on the establishment of the service the EP also defended the communitarised budget management already in place and thus in many ways fought the corner of the European Commission. This commitment may have played a large role in setting up the conflicts that were to occur between EEAS and Commission in the first consolidation years. This consistent positioning also has implications for the understanding of institutional change in the EU political system.

The EEAS and institutional change in the EU

The EEAS is a strong case to observe the creation of a new administrative actor at the EU level. It exists in a policy space that is contested by both the member states (foreign policy) and the European Commission (external relations, trade). As such it sits at the fault line of the large-scale political conflict about the nature

Conclusion: towards a European foreign ministry? 193

of the EU itself. The disagreement between integrationist views demanding a stronger federalisation and supranationalisation as well as those seeking to safeguard member states' core competences is what both drives and hinders the institutional creation of the EEAS.

The evolution of the EEAS also relates to the debate between rational design of institutions and historical institutionalists. Where Pierson has outlined the 'limits of design' (Pierson 2000b), the evolution of the EEAS tells another variant of the story reminiscent of Miller's argument that 'Rational actors, in the aggregate, can choose dysfunctional institutions even when, as individuals, they perfectly understand what they are doing' (Miller 2000: p. 540). The particular twist in the case of the EEAS is that even if the actors involved in setting up the organisation had acted instrumentally, the outcome would not have been completely functional to one objective. This is because a political institution requires large-scale coalitions and compromises, often in several iterated instances of negotiations, in this case crossing the pro-integrationist and eurosceptical divide. The EEAS is a prime example of these coalitions of various collective actors. An institutional perspective on the EEAS shows these core elements of the EEAS's evolution. First, it highlights that EU institutions and administrative organisations are objects of political contestation or conflict. The EEAS was created through a process that is perhaps best described as political design of institutions, i.e. it is built on compromise decisions between various collective actors in several evolutionary phases.

The institutionalist insight, that one 'should not expect consistency from a group' (Riker 1998) plays out even more strongly as the EU's political processes require not only intra-group or rather intra-institutional negotiations and compromises, but also compromises with other institutions. Any coherent, original purpose, if it ever existed, must thus be diluted with competing interests. The EEAS is not as such a functional tool for a specific problem. Expectations that the Council as collective organ have for the EEAS are different from those that individual member states may have. Expectations that the European Parliament might have are bound to differ even more greatly, as do those of the European Commission. The EEAS was created as an institutional 'fudge' with unclear mandate(s) and expectations attached and has been renegotiated in each political cycle. It will remain an organisation operating under these various pressure fields of EU institutions and member states' reach.

Second, The EEAS evolved and will continue to operate in an environment that is as complex in political expectations as it is in procedural rules. The contestation of the organisation will continue; as Moe has put it, 'the game of structural politics never ends' (Moe 1989: p. 284). The EEAS shows that even where contestation is solved, it is merely solved temporarily, or passed on. The Council decision necessitates negotiations between the EEAS and the Commission, i.e. it shifts conflicts into another format or arena. It is this triggering or connectedness of different stages of conflicts that shows how relevant the historical institutional argument is, both because each decision triggers another one and also because each decision tends to narrow the scope of the next decision. In other words, it

194 *Conclusion: towards a European foreign ministry?*

creates path dependency. This is especially the case in an EU institutional environment, as the evidence has shown. On several occasions during the creation of the EEAS, a discussion was moved forward by referencing an earlier decision taken at a higher hierarchical level: the concept of 'acquis', of a joint position that has been achieved, works not only on a legislative level, but on a political one as well. This can only be breached by institutional change on a higher level, such as the proposed merger of Commission and European Council Presidents.

Another challenge the EEAS brings to the debate is the view that time horizons of political actors are limited, or 'short-lived' (Pierson 2000b: p. 479). In the case of the EEAS, the surprising element is rather how long-lived political and administrative actors alike are. Several individuals re-appear throughout the evolution of the EEAS. This includes politicians like Elmar Brok, but also senior administrators like David O'Sullivan who during the inception represented the Commission in the Convention only to later become the Chief Operating Officer, or senior manager, of the EEAS. Even the elite interviews undertaken for this study speak of this muted continuity; a large number of the interviewees were involved in different functions across the evolution of the EEAS: once as national diplomats, then as EU officials; once as a leader of member state's government, then as a Member of the European Parliament. This continuity is an interesting avenue for further research.

Time horizons are also relevant in the evolution of the EU's administrative structures in foreign policy and external relations. Combining the historical information in Chapter 2 with the evidence from the Convention in Chapter 4 provides an illustration of the long view of institutional change in the EU. Even in the 1990s there had been proponents of a merged administration in the Commission and Secretariat General. These ideas were on a smaller scale than the eventual EEAS, but they nevertheless anticipated the most basic features of it. However, the more limited unanimity and veto-based development of treaty reforms via intergovernmental conferences did not allow these ideas to reach fruition. The underlying conflict between integrationist positions and more sceptical positions appears extraordinarily stable, despite the changes in government and majority parties. These findings lead back to considerations by March and Olsen in 'Rediscovering Institutions' (1989: p. 94):

> Although it is difficult to guess when an opportunity to attach a favorite solution to some problem will arise, a solution that is persistently available is likely to find an occasion. The implication is not that governing is impossible. Rather, it is that governance becomes less a matter of engineering than of gardening (Szanton 1981: p. 24); less a matter of hunting than of gathering.

It is the long time horizon of some of the actors, both individual and collective, that eventually ensures that an institutional solution that has been floated on several occasions is finally attached to a problem.

Future research agenda

The findings of this book underscore the overall strength of a bureaucratic-institutionalist approach to the emergence of administrative organisations, yet they highlight specific gaps in understanding the disruptions as well as continuities of the various phases a new bureaucracy goes through. Both from the strength of the approach and from the blind spots identified, several avenues for future research emerge. Below these avenues are identified, both on an empirical as well as theoretical level, and some thoughts are offered on their direction.

Following the approach developed in this book, various relevant empirical cases could be used to explore the power of the model further. A comparable case of a bureaucratic structure that has developed through similar political processes, but has experienced more changes to its structure and status, is the European Defence Agency. Its design options were extensively debated in the security and defence working group of the European Convention. Unlike the EEAS, its establishment was not delayed by treaty ratification and it was agreed upon as an intergovernmental agency as far back as 2004. These outcomes differ considerably from those of the EEAS, and in-depth process tracing of the creation of the agency may reveal relevant insights about the role of member states in the process of the Convention and the role of external actors such as industry on the decision-making during and after the Convention, as well as on the peculiarities of this particular policy area. With security and defence policy regaining renewed interest from policy-makers and the High Representative, organisational changes will be worth a closer look.

There are several gaps of the bureaucratic-institutionalist framework that are worth exploring. The main element emerging from the evolution of the EEAS is the persistence of actors within the changing institutional structures of decision-making. In studies of institutional continuity and change, the role of actors, and specifically individual actors, still merits additional attention. Further studies could look into in how far individuals may be agents of continuity with fixed preferences and policy ideas that they seek to attach to specific policy problems until they succeed, or whether they act as agents of change producing amalgamated policy solutions through negotiating over time. Drawing on the literature of policy entrepreneurs both traditional (Frohlich *et al.* 1971) and more recent (Narbutaite *et al.* 2015) may provide insights into what role they may play in institutional emergence and evolution. The role of these entrepreneurs will also shed additional light on the processes determining the direction of change during a critical juncture, as discussed above.

Finally, and most specifically regarding the EEAS, further research needs to address the recent significant drop in the salience of Commission–EEAS conflict. It will be relevant to learn whether this is a temporary phenomenon, prompted by the alignment of the new High Representative Mogherini within the Juncker Commission. It will also be of interest to students of the EEAS whether this realignment will come at a significant cost in terms of collaboration with other relevant stakeholders of the EEAS, namely the member states.

196   *Conclusion: towards a European foreign ministry?*

Contested diplomacy – the future of the EEAS

One of the core insights of the institutional analysis of the EEAS is that the organisation had to go through various periods of contestation from inception to consolidation. And despite the increase in routine decision-making and decreasing conflicts with other actors, in particular with respect to the central competitor the European Commission, the 'game of structural politics' is likely to return to the EEAS. The policy debate around the EEAS had identified organisational as well as political shortcomings (Hemra *et al.* 2011; Helwig *et al.* 2013; Vanhoonacker and Pomorska 2013; Pomorska and Vanhoonacker 2015). The official review of the EEAS in 2013 followed suit and concluded that in various matters, such as the senior management structure and relations with the Commission, the EEAS's organisation and functioning needed to be improved. The minor changes proposed by the new High Representative/VP Mogherini left the door to a full revision of the decision ajar, but there are no signs of it being opened in the current tenure. After Brexit and with a new Commission, this may change.

The diverging opinions of member states about what the EEAS should do will resurface at every turn. Despite these difficulties, it is important to note that the history of the EEAS not only shows the continuity of structural politics, it also highlights how determined actors can use their political and institutional influence to shape the organisation in the direction of their preferences. A High Representative with political capital, clear preferences and persistence may take this opportunity to shape the EEAS from a Brussels bureau into a more modern diplomatic actor. The EEAS may still become, as per its 'founders'' original intent, a European Foreign Ministry, led by a European Foreign Minister under the tutelage of a joint President of the European Commission and European Council. Another part of the institutional road always lies ahead.

References

Allen, David 1982: Postcriptum. In Allen, Rummel, Wessels (Eds.), *European Political Cooperation.* Butterworth: London.

Dunleavy, Patrick 1991: *Democracy, Bureaucracy and Public Choice. Economic Explanations in Political Science*. Harvester: New York.

Finke, Daniel; König, Thomas; Proksch, Sven-Oliver; and Tsebelis, George 2012: *Reforming the European Union: Realizing the Impossible*. Princeton University Press: Princeton.

Frohlich, Norman; Oppenheimer, Joe; and Young, Oran 1971: *Political Leadership and Collective Goods*. Princeton University Press: Princeton.

Helwig, Niklas; Ivan, Paul; and Kostanyan, Hrant 2013: *The New EU Foreign Policy Architecture. Reviewing the first two years of the EEAS*. CEPS: Brussels.

Hemra, Stefan; Raines, Thomas; and Whitman, Richard 2011: *A Diplomatic Entrepreneur: Making the Most of the European External Action Service*. Chatham House Report. The Royal Institute of International Affairs: London.

Horwitz, I.; Smay, J.; and Shapiro, A. 1974: A synthesis theory for the externally excited adaptive system (EEAS). *IEEE Transaction on Automatic Control*, vol. 19, no. 2, pp. 101–107.

Kelemen, R. Daniel 2002: The Politics of 'Eurocratic' Structure and the new European agencies. *West European Politics*, vol. 25, no. 4, pp. 93–118.

Lindner, Johannes and Rittberger, Berthold 2003: The Creation, Interpretation and Contestation of Institutions – revisiting Historical Institutionalism. *Journal of Common Market Studies*, vol. 41, pp. 445–473.

March, James G. and Olsen, Johan P. 1989: *Rediscovering Institutions. The organizational basis of politics.* Free Press: New York.

Miller, Gary 2000: Rational Choice and Dysfunctional Institutions. *Governance*, vol. 13, no. 4, pp. 535–547.

Moe, Terry 1989: The Politics of Bureaucracy. In Chubb and Peterson (Eds.): *Can the Government Govern?* Brookings: Washington, DC.

Narbutaite Aflaki, Inga; Petridou, Evangelia; and Miles, Lee (Eds.) 2015: *Entrepreneurship in the Polis. Understanding Political Entrepreneurship.* Ashgate: Farnham, Surrey.

Pierson, Paul 2000b: The Limits of Design: Explaining Institutional Origin and Change. *Governance*, vol. 13, no. 4, pp. 475–499.

Pomorska, Karolina and Vanhoonacker, Sophie 2015: Europe as a Global Actor: the (Un) Holy Trinity of Economy, Diplomacy and Security. *Journal of Common Market Studies*, vol. 53, pp. 216–229.

Riker, William 1998: The Experience of Creating Institutions. The Framing of the United States Constitution. In Knight and Sened (Eds.), *Explaining Social Institutions*, pp. 121–144. University of Michigan Press, Ann Arbor, MI.

Vanhoonacker, Sophie and Pomorska, Karolina 2013: The European External Action Service and agenda-setting in European foreign policy. *Journal of European Public Policy*, vol. 20, no. 9, pp. 1316–1331.

Official documents

European External Action Service

EEAS 2013a: EEAS Review 2013. EEAS: Brussels.

EEAS 2014b: Catherine Ashton appoints new Head of EU Delegation to the United States. Press release, 05.05.2014.

Appendix 1

Overview of Plenary Discussion in Convention on the Future of Europe on External Service (own compilation)

Date	Proponent(s)	Document number	HR	Service	Other
	Secretariat	CONV/161/02	Discussion paper	–	–
11.07.2002	Brok (EP)	Verbatim	Merger HR and Commissioner	Single administration	No 'Super-President' at Council level
	Van der Linden	Verbatim	Merger HR and Commissioner into COM		More co-decision
	Puwak (Romania)	Verbatim	Fusion of HR and Commissioner		
	McDonagh	Verbatim	Stronger cooperation	More resources for Council SG	
	Attalidis (Cyprus)	Verbatim	Better coordination, HR/Commissioner. tandem	European institute of foreign relations and European diplomatic academy	
	Bonde (MEP)	Verbatim	Cooperation between sovereign nations		Adopt only recommendations
	Michel (Belgium)	Verbatim	Strengthen HR, closer collaboration with COM		Right of initiative and chair of GAERC/FAC
	Hain (UK)	Verbatim	HR chair FAC, right of initiative, attend COM meetings on external policy		Joint proposals HR and Commissioner

				President would create more confusion
	Lennmakers (Swedish Parliament)	Verbatim	'When it comes to the decision-making procedures, it is time we no longer had three units: the Commission, the Council and the foreign office of the presidency. It is time to merge them into one. We cannot have three foreign ministries or state departments.'	Single diplomatic representation
11.07.2002	Fayot (Luxembourg Parliament)	Verbatim	COM VP that coordinates strongly	
	Katiforis (Greece)	Verbatim	Merger HR and COM within a given time	
	Hamzik (Slovak Parliament)	Verbatim	Merger in the long term	
	Glotz (Germany)	Verbatim	'Doppelhut' (double-hat)	Effective diplomatic service forged from 3 elements, DG RELEX, Foreign Policy Unit from Secretariat and under responsibility of Council, external representation by Union delegations (from COM del) under double-hatted HR
	Maij-Weggen (EP)			'Patten is building diplomatic service'; time for a coordinating status for this service

continued

Date	Proponent(s)	Document number	HR	Service	Other
11.07.2002	Muñoz Alonso (Spanish Parliament)			European foreign service on horizon to serve MS	Centre of gravity European Council
	Nahtigal (Slovenia)		Enhanced cooperation between the Council and the Commission on external policies through HR		
	Fini (Italy)		Merge HR and Commissioner		Single external representation
	Avgerinos (Greek Parliament)		Gradual merger of HR into Commissioner for RELEX and CFSP		
	Dini (Italian Parliament)		Merger HR and Commissioner with separate mandates		
	Barnier (Commission)		Gradual merger, start with right of initiative		
	Tiilikainen (Finland)		COM must be made key actor		
	Meyer (German Parliament)		Double-hat as 'personal union'	European diplomatic corps, more regular exchange of personnel between MS and COM/CSG	
	Maij-Weggen (EP)		Merger HR and Commissioner		

	Kiljunen (Finnish Parliament)	Merge the Office of High Representative in a new way with the function of the Commission Vice-President, creating a new office of Foreign Affairs Representative		
11.07.2002	Vassiliou (Cypriot Parliament)	Merger into COM		
	Wittbrodt (Polish Parliament)	Merger into COM		
	Migas (Slovakia)	Gradual merger of posts		
	Farnleitner (Austria)	Foreign Minister with special status at COM		
	Hjelm Wallen (Sweden)	If merger becomes necessary, should be located at Council		
	Boesch (Austrian Parliament)	Security Council	Any staff at Secretary General of the Security Council	
	Oleksy (Polish Parliament)	Gradual bringing together of posts through joint actions/ projects		
	Carnero Gonzalez (EP)	COM in charge, HR approved by EP		Community method
	Muscovici (France)	Double-hat needs to be studied carefully	Diplomatic system needs to be located at Council	President of European Council
	Einem (Austrian Parliament)	Supports Brok *et al.*		

continued

Date	Proponent(s)	Document number	HR	Service	Other
	Szent-Ivanyi (Hungarian Parliament)		Merger of posts		
12.07.2002	Giannakou-Koutsikou (Greek Parliament)		Merger of posts HR and Commissioner		
2nd day focus: defense	Huebner (Poland)		HR with more resources, more powers		Chair GAERC
	Frendo (Maltese Parliament)		Merger HR and Commissioner		
	Stuart (UK Parliament)		More responsibilities HR		President of European Council
	Kohout (Czech Republic)		Merger of HR and RELEX Commissioner with Development Commissioner		
28.10.2002	Praesidium	Preliminary Draft CT	Role of HR to be determined	To be determined	To be determined
06.12.2002	Dehaene/ Presentation WG Report	Verbatim	Double-hat, separate procedures	Joint administration DG RELEX, CSG External, MS	Chair of FAC, single diplomatic service with diplomatic academy, Union embassies
20.12.2002	Working Group Final Report	CONV 459/02	European External Representative (merger) and VP Commission	One joint service (EEAS) from DG RELEX, CSG, MS national diplomats	External Action Council, Chaired by EER, EU delegations/embassies

Date	Name		Statement		Remarks
	Dehaene		Presents report		
	Van der Linden	Verbatim	Majority in group for merger into COM, but accepts double-hatted compromise	Diplomatic service and academy	Linked to discussion of President, which the majority group rejects
	Hain (UK)	Verbatim	Expressed worries on double-hat	Cooperate more pragmatically	
	Michel (Belgium)	Verbatim	Double-hat (refers to Belgian memorandum)		
	Avgerinos (Greek Parliament)	Verbatim	Merger of the two posts	Diplomatic service with EU embassies	
	Tiilikainen (Finland)	"	Long-term merger into COM as goal		
20.12.2002	Duff (EP)	"	Supports option 2 of WG (full merger into COM)		Several remarks on admin position of HR vis-à-vis COM President
	Dini (Italian Parliament)	"	Double-hat, Foreign Minister of Europe or European External Representative		
	Hjelm Wallen (Sweden)		Against merger, would not solve problems and would create new ones		
	Fogler (Polish Parliament)		Merger of HR and Commissioner		
	Kelam (Estonian Parliament)		Option one (practical measures to improve HR-COM coordination)		
	Christophersen (Denmark)		Double-hat HR, remove SecGen functions		Against President's external function

continued

Date	Proponent(s)	Document number	HR	Service	Other
	Spini (Italian Parliament)		Double-hat		
	Cushnahan (EP)		Prefers full merger, but accepts double-hat	Single service	
	Attalidis (Cyprus)		Supports compromise double-hat		
	Lequiller (French Parliament)		Support double-hat, but call it Foreign Minister		Chair FAC
	Roche (Ireland)		Supports double-hat		
	Brok (EP)		Double-hat and focus on single administration	Single administration at the Commission	
20.12.2002	De Vries (Netherlands)		Double-hat	Single administration	
	Haensch (EP)		Compromise double-hat, Foreign Minister		
	Carnero Gonzalez (EP)		Double-hat HR		
	Skaarup (Danish Parliament)		No support		Against diplomatic academy
	Lopes (Portugal)		Double-hat		
	Borrel Fontelles (Spanish Parliament)		Double-hat as consensus		
	Fini (Italy)		Double-hatted EU External Representative		Reference to institutional debate

	Hololei (Estonia)	HR separate, but doesn't exclude double-hat	Delegations under HR	
	Hain (UK)	No agreement on double-hatting without agreement on President		
	Kauppi (EP)	Double-hat not best solution, but realistic		
	Dastis (Spain)	Separate roles, study double-hat		Strong Council President
	Kristensen (Danish Parliament)			Connection President-HR decision
20.12.2002	De Villepin (France)	Minister of Foreign Affairs under President of European Council		
	Maij-Weggen (EP)	Double-hat, but clarity on lines of authority		Diplomatic service, supported by Bruges
	Azevedo (Portuguese Parliament)	Merger of functions needs more study, more caution		
	Peterle (Slovenian Parliament)	Double-hatting sufficient compromise		
	Figel (Slovak Parliament)	Support European External Affairs Representative if appropriate inter-institutional arrangement can be found		
	Yakis (Turkey)	Supports merger of HR and Commissioner		

continued

Date	Proponent(s)	Document number	HR	Service	Other
	MacCormick (EP)		Competing logics in merged function		
	Wittbrodt (Polish Parliament)		Merger into Commission		
	Santer (Luxembourg)		Double-hatted European External Representative/VP		
	Meyer (German Parliament)		All factions of Bundestag support double-hat, Foreign Minister	Appropriate support	Transfer delegations to EU embassies
	Szent-Ivanyi (Hungarian Parliament)		Enhanced role of HR		
20.12.2002	Abitpol (EP)		Doubts double-hat		
	Stuart (UK Parliament)				Permanent chair of Council as external voice
	Muñoz Alonso (Spanish Parliament)		Supports HR role from the WG		
	Akcam (Turkish Parliament)		Double-hat HR/VP of COM		
	Fahrnleitner (Austria)		Support double-hat		

	Kohout (Czech Republic)		Option 3, double-hat	
	Lennmarker (Swedish Parliament)		Supports double-hat compromise	
	Fischer (Germany)		Double-hat for HR and Commissioner RELEX to replace Troika, Foreign Minister	Necessary resources	Personal union, not mixture of offices
	Barnier (Commission)		Had supported HR in COM above single administration of CSG, COM, MS	
04.07.2003	Peterle (Slovenia)	Verbatim		Clarify relation of diplomatic service with 'famille RELEX'/ EPP amendment
	Brok (EP)			Wrong to create new service in footnote, service should be inside COM, as is disturbs institutional balance
	Maij-Weggen (EP)		Institutional balance if new service at Council, link to external policy areas	
	Fischer (Germany)		Double-hat	Service will be under Commission staff regulation and control of Parliament, but services like trade will not be subsumed

continued

Date	Proponent(s)	Document number	HR	Service	Other
	Tiilikainen (Finland)		Foreign Minister should not undermine COM role	EEAS under authority of the COM	
	Van der Linden (Dutch Parliament)			Diplomatic service under COM	
	Brok (EP)	Verbatim		Unclear text, not what Fischer pronounced, against creation of third service 'Kingdom of the Middle'	
	Einem (Austrian Parliament)			Service in COM and not in between Council and COM	
	Maij-Weggen (EP)			Fischer and Brok amendment awaited	
	Kiljunen (Finnish Parliament)			Service should work in COM	
	Dini (Italian Parliament)			Clarification relationship service and COM, do not create a body that is entirely unique, autonomous and independent of the COM	

Peterson (Sweden)		Strong support within current system for FM	
Barnier (Commission)		Use existing resources in CSG, COM and MS, not create new administration	Maintain efficiency of delegation system, which also works for Community
McDonagh (Ireland)		Service needs links to both COM and Council, supports Barnier	
Tusek (Austria)	Foreign Minister and QMV	COM needs unfettered access to diplomatic service	
MacLennan of Rogart (UK Parliament)		No bifurcation of bureaucracy, EA WG called for single unified diplomatic service	
Adreani (France)		Support Fischer on service	

Appendix 2

Overview of proposed institutional changes in the Convention Working Group on External Action (own compilation)

Date	Proponent(s)	Document number	HR	Service	Other
23–4.09.2002	Elmar Brok (MEP)	WD 2	VP/Commissioner for Foreign Relations (merging HR and RELEX Commissioner)	COM	
24.09.2002	Louis Michel	WD 4	Strengthening and integrating HR into COM with link to Council	COM, reinforced Policy Unit as 'centre commun' au service des deux institutions	Lose functions of Sec Gen of Council SG; Preside over GAERC
15.10.2002	Javier Solana (HR, non-delegate)	WD 8	HR permanent chair of FAC	Pragmatic pooling of resources to develop European Foreign Ministry at pace MS are comfortable with	Financing
	Poul Nielsen (COM on delegate)	WD 9	HR part or wholly in COM	'Centre of gravity in control of policy initiative'	
28.10.2002	Adrian Severin	WD 11	Merger HR and RELEX Commissioner/VP of COM	CSG staff transferred to COM, EU diplomatic corps within COM	Communitarisation of CFSP, Diplomatic academy, EU institutions coordinating MS, common representation, delegations=embassies

05.11.2002	Bobby McDonagh (Irish alternate)	WD 16	HR attends COM meetings, separate from SecGen duties, creation of Deputy High Representatives (DHRs)	Reinforced CSG with MS diplomats, common services CSG and COM DGs	HR Right of initiative, common system of representation of COM and CSG staff
	Guenter Pleuger (German alternate)	WD 17	'Double-hat' merger of HR and RELEX Commissioner., chair of GAERC, 2 deputies for Community/CFSP with right of vote	Separate 'apparatuses'; 'consolidated Policy Unit (European Foreign Policy Unit)', joint cabinet	EU delegations merged from COM and CSG
07.11.2002	Danuta Huebner (delegate)	WD 18	Merger 'EU Representative', chair GAERC		Connects to Pres of EuCo, EU political delegation network
08.11.2002	(Ms) Teija Tiilikainen (delegate)	WD 19	Merger of both functions into COM	'Single structure' in COM	Problems of double-hatting
	Louis Michel	WD 20	HR into COM with special status to Council and to COM, participate in COM meetings, long term full integration	Strengthened policy unit detached from Council, service to both institutions	Merged network of Union delegations
	Preliminary draft final report (Options and summary discussion)	WD 21	a) practical measures, b) full merger into COM, c) 'double-hat', 'EU Minister of Foreign Affairs or EU Foreign Secretary'	'Enhanced co-operation between (their) services, including possible merger of services in certain areas', national seconded diplomats, reinforced Policy Unit	EU diplomatic service and academy, Commission delegations to be EU embassies under HR, also servicing MS

continued

Appendix 2 Continued

Date	Proponent(s)	Document number	HR	Service	Other
	Goeran Lennmaker	WD 23	HR/Commissioner chairing external action council	'One single coherent centre of external action, a "Foreign Office" that is part of or closely related to the Commission'	
11.11.2002	Elmar Brok	WD 26	'One person, one administration' = Commissioner for Foreign Relations legitimised by Council		EU diplomatic representations, diplomatic corps, college of European diplomacy, 'bridging system' between Community and MS
15.11.2002	H. M. Bury (Germany)	WD 28	'Double-hat', two deputies for CFSP and one for Community, Chairman of PSC	Separate offices, strengthened Policy Unit, joint cabinet	Decision making separate, merged EU delegations
18.11.2002	Severin, Brok, Lamassoure, v. d. Linden	WD 30	'Foreign Minister of the European Union FMEU' VP of COM, chair	–	Opposition to President of EuCo
19.11.2002	Jan Kohout (Czech Republic)	WD 33		Based on experiences of Policy Unit, combining resources from MS and EU	'Europeanisation of MS foreign services'

	Ernani R. Lopes (Portugal)	WD 34		'[Find] premature the setting up of a EU diplomatic service. And I also have reservations on the idea that the Delegations of the Commission could become EU Embassies.'	
	Gerhard Tusek (AT alternate)	WD 36	'Double-hat' gradually introduced, HR in COM meetings, long-term integration into COM	Potential merger of some substructures (COM and CSG), objective 'Foreign Service'	HR Right of initiative, Chair of GAERC, opposition to President of EuCo
	Michel Barnier (COM delegate, Praesidium)	WD 37	'Secretary of the Union'		QMV, majority rejected President of EuCo, EU delegations/embassies managed by COM
	Louis Michel (Belgium)	WD 38	'Double casquette' supported		
19–20.11.2002	Lamberto Dini (Italian Parliament)	WD 39	'Minister of Foreign Affairs' under two mandates, VP of COM		Also Development responsibility
	Peter Hain (UK)	WD 40	Deletes reference to Minister of FA, questions feasibility of merger into COM	Existing resources and avoiding duplication, delete delegations servicing of MS	
	John Cushnahan (MEP)	WD 41	'European Union Foreign Secretary' merged from HR and Commissioner		

continued

Date	Proponent(s)	Document number	HR	Service	Other
	Lena Hjelm-Wallen (Sweden)	WD 42	Separate functions, supports option (1)		Delete HR chairing GAERC, shared right of initiative
	Jose Borrelles (Spanish Parliament)	WD 43	HR		Combine national diplomatic offices into a single European
	Klaus Haensch (EP)	WD 45	Double-hatted 'EU Representative for Foreign Affairs', coupled resources Council-Commission, also Member of COM, several deputies	DG RELEX and DG Foreign Relations in Council SG	Chair GAERC, merged EU embassies
	Brok, v.d. Linden (Dutch Parliament), Cushnahan (MEP), Lamassoure	WD 46	VP-Commissioner for Foreign Relations, full merger into COM,	Diplomatic service within COM and diplomatic academy, with bridging system to MS; if double-hat a single administration needed (2×)	FAC Chair, critical of President of EuCo
	Gijs de Vries (Netherlands)	WD 47	VP-Commissioner, deletes Minister of FA text; double-hat with several deputies	Council Secretariat officials have access to European diplomatic service/academy	

21.11.2002	Pierre Lequiller (French Parliament)	WD 49	Merged 'ministre des Affaires étrangères de l'Union européenne'	Separate structures und Minister	
	Danuta Huebner (Poland)	WD 51	'Double-hatted Foreign Policy Chief', member of College	Opportunity to do away with two services RELEX and SG and to create 'Foreign Policy Commission'; single diplomatic service drawing heavily on seconded officials from MS and services of Commission	
22.11.2002	Dominique de Villepin (France)	WD 52	'Ministre des affaires étrangères de l'Union, placé auprès du Président du Conseil européen'	Operational means	Under President of EuCo, Chair of FAC
	Revised draft final report	WD 21 (1)	a) Separate functions with practical measures, b) full merger into COM, c) double-hatted merger, several titles with c1) several deputies or c2) 2 deputies for CFSP and Community policies, and d) EU Minister of Foreign Affairs under the President of EuCo	Under c) double-hat: a) joint service of DG RELEX officials, the Council Secretariat, and seconded staff from national diplomatic services or b) distinct administrations with separate merged service for CFSP with a joint Private Office	Majority opposed President of EuCo, duplication of services should be avoided, staff should be Commission, Council SG and seconded officials, EU delegations under HR, some opposition

continued

Date	Proponent(s)	Document number	HR	Service	Other
25.11.2002	H.M. Bury (Germany)	WD 53	Detailed explanation of 'double-hat' arrangement	Separate structures under double-hat; DG RELEX and 'European Foreign Policy Unit' from CSG parts on foreign policy, seconded national officials and seconded COM officials	Chair of GAERC
29.11.2002	Revised draft final report including Recommendations	WD 21 (2)	(Recommendations) Double-hatted 'European External Representative' as 3rd option before	(Recommendations) 'Creation of one joint service (European External Action Service) composed of DG RELEX officials, Council Secretariat officials and staff seconded from national diplomatic services' – creation of EU diplomatic service and EU diplomatic academy	One focal point in COM, Specific FAC chaired by Representative, EU delegations including officials from Council SG and MS, trend in favour of option 3

15.11.2002, circulated 03.12.2002	Inigo Mendez de Vigo (delegate)	WD 55	'Common European diplomacy' based on Galeote report	Increase permeability of foreign services, personnel from the MS diplomatic services, Commission and Council officials for external relations	Delegations of the European Union
09.12.2002	Revised draft final report	WD 21 (3)	(Recommendations) European External Representative, double-hatted	Creation of EEAS, in case of EER under his/her authority; creation of EU diplomatic service and diplomatic academy	Specific FAC chaired by HR, VP coordinating in COM, merged EU delegations
12.12.2002	Teija Tiilikainen (Finland)	WD 61	EER but inserts long-term goal of merger of functions into COM with timetable		
	H. M. Bury (Germany)	WD 63		Reiterates need for staff from MS, COM and CSG supporting HR	
	Bobby McDonagh (Ireland)	WD 64			Insert opposition to HR chairing FAC/GAERC
12.12.2002	Peter Hain (UK)	WD 66	Insert opposition to double-hat	Deletion of EU diplomatic service	Deletion of embassies
	Lena Hjelm-Wallen	WD 68 REV	Doubts about double-hatting, stresses intergovernmental nature of CFSP, keeping function separate		MS chair FAC

continued

Date	Proponent(s)	Document number	HR	Service	Other
	Elmar Brok (MEP), John Cushnahan (MEP)	WD 70	'European External Representative'	'Establishment of one joint service (European External Action Service) based on DG Relex, supported by Council secretariat officials and staff seconded from national diplomatic services.'	
	Pervenche Beres (MEP)	WD 71	'Representant europeen pour les affaires exterieures'		
13.12.2002	Pascale Adreani (France)	WD 72	Doubts about double-hat, coherence from MS FPs coming closer		
16.12.2002	Final report	CONV 459/02	'European External Representative, double-hatted, COM VP	'Establishment of one joint service (European External Action Service) composed of DG RELEX officials, CSG officials and staff seconded from national diplomatic services. In the hypothesis of the creation of a new post of European External Representative, this service would work under his/her authority.'	'Creation of EU diplomatic academy and EU diplomatic service, alongside those of Member States. The Commission's delegations would become EU embassies', staffed by COM, CSG, seconded MS officials under authority of HR/EER

Appendix 3

Overview Plenary Treaty Drafts in Convention on Future of Europe on HR and EEAS (own compilation)

Date	Proponent(s)	Document number	HR	Service	Other
28.10.2002	Praesidium	CONV 369/02	Future role of HR in art. 41 no substance.		
23.04.2003	Praesidium	CONV 685/03	Minister of Foreign Affairs, VP of COM, double-hatted, Title V, art. 5 External Action, Title IV, art. 19 Institutions.		Union delegations under authority of EFM.
09.05.2003	Delegates	CONV 709/03	Art. 17a Institutions: Preference for title of 'Secretary of Union' (Duff +5 (am.11)); 'European External Representative' (Hain (am.16)); 'Foreign Representative' (Huebner (am.21)); 'Foreign Minister' ("Aussenminister") (Kaufmann (am.22)); 'Minister for Foreign Affairs' (Kelam +3 (am.19)); 'External Representative of the European Union' (Liepina +3 (am.28)); 'European Representative for External Relations' (Queiro (am.34)); 'Union Minister for Foreign Affairs' (Roche +2 (am34)). Prefer no title ('Member of the Commission') (Helle (am.18)).	Art. 17a Institutions: Additional paragraph detailing administration, which will support the Minister (Barnier +3 (am.4), Brok +33 (am.8), Fischer (am.15), Huebner (am.21), Meyer (am.30)).	Art 17 a Institutions: Remove reference to FAC being chaired by Foreign Minister Barnier + Vitorino (am.4), Bonde (am.7), Einem (am.15), Helle (am.25), Palacio (am.40).

continued

Date	Proponent(s)	Document number	HR	Service	Other
			Addition of new paragraph creating: two deputy posts (Huebner (am.21), Liepina +3 (am.28)): up to five Deputy posts (Roche +2 (am.35)).		State that Minister is appointed on basis of proposal from the President of European Council; procedures are same for terminating the appointment (de Villepin (am.10)).
			Specify that Minister's office in the Commission (Andriukaitis +2 (am.2)).		
			Specify that Minister is a member and Vice-President of Commission (Attalides (am.3)).		
26.05.2003	CONV 724/03	Praesidium	Title IV Union Institutions, Art I-27 The Foreign Minister/VP COM.		
10.06.2003	CONV 797/03	Praesidium	Title IV Union Institutions, Art I-27 The Foreign Minister/VP COM.		
12.06.2003	CONV 802/03	Praesidium			Chapter IV, Article III-225 (ex Article 36) 1. Union delegations in third countries and to international organisations shall represent the Union.

			2. Union delegations shall operate under the authority of the Union's Minister for Foreign Affairs and in close cooperation with Member States' missions.
12.06.2003	CONV 811/03	Article I-27: The Foreign Minister (footnote 1) Footnote 1: The establishment of a Joint European External Action Service, to assist the Minister, will be addressed in a Declaration/Part III.	
27.06.2003	CONV 821/03	Art. III-192 (ex-5) Proposal for the addition of a paragraph on a joint European service for external action/ European diplomatic service which would assist the Minister for Foreign Affairs to carry out his mandate (am. 2/Fischer, am. 4/Michel+4). Mr Fischer proposes the text of a declaration to be annexed to the Constitution, on the establishment of such a service. Insert a new initial paragraph before the present paragraph 1 under which the Union would have at its disposal a diplomatic service of its own composed of officials of the Commission and the Council Secretariat, as well as of staff seconded from the Member States (am. 1/ Farnleitner).	Art. III-203 (ex-16) Proposal to add that the Political and Security Committee shall be chaired by a representative appointed by the Union's Minister (am.2/Fischer). State that delegations/ representations will operate under the joint authority of the Union's Minister for Foreign Affairs and the Commission (am. 1/Farnleitner, am. 5/Tiilikainen).

continued

Appendix 3 Continued

Date	Proponent(s)	Document number	HR	Service	Other
22.07.2003/ received 08.07.2003	CONV 829/03	Amendments Brok, Amato, Duff		2 options: EEAS as joint service inside COM with CSG MS officials and EEAS as joint service of COM CSG MS and work as mandated by Council.	
27.06.2003/ adopted 4.06.2003	CONV 836/03	Draft Constitution Vol. II		Art III-192 inserts paragraph 3: EEAS, inserts footnote one declaration, inserts declaration on EEAS.	Union delegation staff part of EEAS.
30.06.2003	CONV 839/03	Commission delegates Barnier and Vitorino		'Joint European External Action Service', at HQ services of COM and CSG in COM ('not divorced institutionally', all services of the 'famille RELEX').	Union delegations also in the JEEAS.
08.07.2003	CONV 847/03	Amended draft Constitution parts III and IV		III-192 EEAS as service to FM; footnote to Declaration on EEAS; inserts Declaration on EEAS.	

09.07.2003	CONV 848/03	Draft Constitution vol. II, parts III and IV	Title V, Chapter II, III-192 (ex-5) 'the Union Minister for Foreign Affairs shall be assisted by a European External Action Service. This service shall work in cooperation with the diplomatic services of the Member States' 2. Annex III – 'EEAS composed of officials from relevant departments of the General Secretariat of the Council of Ministers and of the Commission and staff seconded from national Diplomatic Services within 1st year of entry into force.'

Appendix 4

EEAS in Treaty versions

EEAS across Treaty documents	Draft Constitutional Treaty	IGC	Lisbon Treaty
Location	Part III: The Policies and Functioning of the Union Title V: The Union's External Action Chapter II: CFSP Art III – 197 (3) Part IV General and Final Provisions Declaration on the creation of a European External Action Service	Part III: The Policies and Functioning of the Union Title V The EU's External Action Chapter II CFSP Art III – 296 (3)	AMENDMENTS TO THE TREATY ON EUROPEAN UNION AND TO THE TREATY ESTABLISHING THE EUROPEAN COMMUNITY Article 1 General Provision on Union's External Action The Common Foreign and Security Policy Nr. 30) The following new Article 13a shall be inserted: Article 13a (3)
Full text	Text Art III – 197 In fulfilling his or her mandate, the Union Minister for Foreign Affairs shall be assisted by a European External Action Service. This service shall work in cooperation with the diplomatic services of the Member States 1.	Text Art III – 296 (…) 3. In fulfilling his or her mandate, the Union Minister for Foreign Affairs shall be assisted by a European External Action Service. This service shall work in cooperation with the diplomatic services of the Member States and shall comprise officials from relevant departments of the General Secretariat of the Council and of the Commission as well as staff seconded from national diplomatic services of the Member States. The organisation and functioning of the European External Action Service shall be established by a European decision of the Council. The Council shall act on a proposal	Art. 13a (…) 3. In fulfilling his mandate, the High Representative shall be assisted by a European External Action Service. This service shall work in cooperation with the diplomatic services of the Member States and shall comprise officials from relevant departments of the General Secretariat of the Council and of the Commission as well as staff seconded from national diplomatic services of the Member States. The organisation and functioning of the European External Action Service shall be established by a decision of the Council. The Council shall act on a proposal from the High Representative after consulting the European Parliament and after obtaining the consent of the Commission.

		from the Union Minister for Foreign Affairs after consulting the European Parliament and after obtaining the consent of the Commission.	
Declaration Full text	'To assist the future Union Minister for Foreign Affairs, introduced in Article I-27 of the Constitution, to perform his or her duties, the Convention agrees on the need for the Council of Ministers and the Commission to agree, without prejudice to the rights of the European Parliament, to establish under the Minister's authority one joint service (European External Action Service) composed of officials from relevant departments of the General Secretariat of the Council of Ministers and of the Commission and staff seconded from national diplomatic services. The staff of the Union's delegations, as defined in Article III-230, shall be provided from this joint service. The Convention is of the view that the necessary arrangements for the establishment of the joint service should be made within the first year after entry into force of the Treaty establishing a Constitution for Europe.'	A. Declaration Concerning Provisions of the Constitution Declaration 24. Declaration on Article III-296 The Conference declares that, as soon as the Treaty establishing a Constitution for Europe is signed, the Secretary-General of the Council, High Representative for the common foreign and security policy, the Commission and the Member States should begin preparatory work on the European External Action Service.	A. DECLARATIONS CONCERNING PROVISIONS OF THE TREATIES 15. Declaration on Article 13a of the Treaty on European Union The Conference declares that, as soon as the Treaty of Lisbon is signed, the Secretary-General of the Council, High Representative for the common foreign and security policy, the Commission and the Member States should begin preparatory work on the European External Action Service.

Appendix 5

List of interviewees 2011–17

Interview No.	Date	Institutional affiliation	Seniority	Phase I	Phase II	Phase III	Phase IIIb
1	28.01.2011	Council Secretariat General (CSG)	Desk officer	X	X		
2	02.02.2011	CSG	Director		X		
3	08.02.2011	Member State (MS)	Director	X	X	(X)	
4	06.04.2011	MS/EEAS	Cabinet		X	X	
5	21.02.2011	MS	Former Head of Government	X	X		
6	11.02.2011	European Commission (COM)	Director	X			
7	14.02.2011	COM	Director	X			
8	13.05.2011	MS	Ambassador		X		
9	19.04.2011	CSG	Director-General	X	(X)		
10	10.05.2011	EEAS	Head of Unit		X	X	
11	11.05.2011	COM/EEAS	Desk officer		X	X	
12	11.05.2011	COM	Desk officer		X		
13	30.01.2012	COM	Senior desk officer		X		
14	22.03.2012	COM/EEAS	Director	X	X	X	
15	26.03.2012	COM	Head of Unit	X			
16	02.04.2012	CSG	Head of Unit	X	X		
17	23.05.2012	EEAS	Head of Unit	X	X	X	
18	08.06.2012	CSG	Desk officer		X	X	
19	31.05.2012	EEAS	Head of Unit		X	X	

No.	Date	Institution	Function				
20	30.05.2012	EEAS	Director		X	X	
21	01.06.2012	COM	Head of Unit		X	X	
22	31.05.2012	European Council (EUCO)	Cabinet of President			X	
23	20.06.2012	COM	Desk officer		X	X	
24	12.06.2012	European Parliament (EP)	Political assistant		X	X	
25	18.06.2012	EP	Member European Parliament	X	X		
26	08.02.2012	MS	Desk officer		X	X	
27	08.02.2012	MS	Desk officer	X	X		
28	27.02.2013	COM	Head of Unit		X	X	
29	27.02.2013	EEAS	Desk officer		X	X	
30	28.02.2013	COM	Desk officer		X	X	
31	01.03.2013	COM	Desk officer		X	X	
32	28.02.2017	EUCO	Cabinet			X	X
33	28.02.2017	EP	Desk officer				X
34	28.02.2017	EEAS	Desk officer				X
35	01.03.2017	COM	Deputy Head of Unit			X	X
36	01.03.2017	COM	Desk officer			X	X
37	01.03.2017	EP	Desk officer			X	X
38	02.03.2017	EEAS	Head of Division				X

Index

Page numbers in **bold** denote tables, those in *italics* denote figures.

administration of EEAS: bureaucratic politics in 140; civil 152; collaboration and competition in 145; by Council Secretariat 152–158; decision-system system for 55; EU foreign policy and 152; game of structural politics in 177; political level of 141; Presidency 163

American Foreign Economic Policy 48

Amsterdam Treaty 29

Arrow, Kenneth 56

Ashton, Catherine 2–3, 13, 114, 127–128, 130, 139, 158, 170, 172, 174, 177

Balkans War 34

Barroso–Solana report (2005) 109, 116, 118

Basic Treaty of the European Union 80

Berlin Wall, fall of 26, 34

Bertelsmann Foundation 28

Brexit, impact of 180–181

Brok, Elmar 86–87, 92, 97–99, 101, 122–126, 176, 186, 192, 194

Brok–Verhofstadt (2010) working paper 124–126

Brusselisation 26

budget maximization thesis 59, 135, 137–138

budget neutrality 111, 157, 161, 180–181

budgetary control 98, 124, 131, 163

budgetary process, for the EEAS: budgetary discharge procedure 175; Council Secretariat role in 157–158; European Commission role in 150–152; European Parliament role in 160; management of 189

bureau shaping 59, 135, 137, 138–140, 161, 190

bureau territoriality 60

bureaucracy 71–72; changes in EU foreign policy *see* bureaucratic change, in EU foreign policy; characteristics of 58; consolidation of 67; defined 136; hypotheses about internal functioning of 58–59; public 57, 58, 59, 136; theory of 136, 190

bureaucratic behaviour: drivers of 59; principles of 136–137

bureaucratic change, in EU foreign policy: analysis of 48–50; budget maximisation and bureau shaping 58–59; bureaucratic institutions, emergence and change of 46–48; bureaucratic politics and 57–63; centralization and coherence of 48; competition and control 59–60; critical junctures of 50–52; institutional approach to 45; institutional change and analysis of 48–50; inter-organisational relationships and 59–60; mechanism of reproduction 52; new institutionalism, notion of 47; politics of *see* bureaucratic politics; positive feedback loop on 52; public administration 57; 'public choice' approach to 57, 58, 136; rational choice and 54–55

bureaucratic emergence, stages of 72–73

bureaucratic politics 59, 60–61, 71–72, 144, 169; 'fire alarm' monitoring 63; and foreign policy decision-making 61; governmental politics and 61; indicators for 141–142; internal effects of external contestation 140–144; inter-organisational competition and control 61–63; Krasner's views on 61; and models of decision-making process

Index   229

60–61; observable 61–63; operationalisation of 62; paradigm of 61; 'police patrol' mechanism 63; on political interactions between organisations and officials 68; Principal Agent (PA) analysis 62–63; structural choice 55–57; turf wars 60

bureaucratic-institutionalist framework 1–2, 13, 195

bureaucratic-institutionalist model 177

career development 156

Carnegie Endowment for International Peace 3

Center for European Policy Studies (CEPS), Brussels 3

civilian crisis management 31

Civilian Planning and Conduct Capability (CPCC) 31

collective leadership, idea of 139, 188

College of Commissioners 122, 149

College of European Diplomacy 36

Commissioner for External Relations 28, 85–86, 88, 93–94

Commissioner for Foreign Relations 87

Committee of Permanent Representatives (COREPER II) 108

common defence policy 31

Common Foreign and Security Policy (CFSP) 18, 118; Council Secretariat's role in 34; decision-making, nature of 27; elements of 27; Franco-German proposal for 27; functioning of 29; High Representative for 29–34; member states' positions on integration of **30**; member states' views on organisational structures in **32–33**; other modes of 52–53; Treaty on the European Union (TEU) on 27

competence creep, process of 155

Constitutional Treaty 80, 107, 117; Common Foreign and Security Policy of 99; Convention on the Future of Europe 9, 100, 122, 179, 188, 191, **198–209**; fate of the draft 99–100; rejection of 83

Consultative Committee on Appointments (CCA) 148, 162

contested diplomacy, notion of 196

Convention on the Future of Europe 9, 100, 122, 179, 188, 191, **198–209**

Convention paradox 81

Copenhagen Report (1973) 25

Council of the EU 4, 10, 22, 73, 109, 153, 175

Council Secretariat (CSG) 27, 29, 31, 34, 79, 92, 108, 110, 142, 146; administrative procedures of 153–155; budgetary process for the EEAS 157–158; civil administration of the EEAS 152–158; foreign policy 39, 156; inter-bureaucratic rivalry with EEAS 157; oversight of 152–153; role in CFSP 34; Secretariat General 154; staffing and organisation 155–156

crisis management: in European External Action Service (EEAS) 116; in European Union 139; and planning directorate 31

critical junctures, concept of 50–52, 53, 64, 188–189

Cuban missile crisis 45

Davignon Report (1970) 25

decision-making system 55, 64, 106, 195; Allison and Zelikow's models of 60–61; 'bureaucratic politics' model of 61; collective decisions 56; in EU institutions 54, 70–71; in European Commission 114, 146; foreign policy 61, 85; inter-institutional 51; models of governmental 60; 'organisational behaviour' model of 60; president's involvement in 61; rational actor model of 60; rational choice perspectives on 54; treaty change *versus* inter-institutional 68

declaration on accountability (DPA) 127, 158–159

Development Cooperation 171

diplomatic service, creation of 91

Directorates-General Trade, Development and Enlargement 118

Downs, Anthony 46, 57, 58–60, 62, 136

Draft Constitutional Treaty 95, 99–100

Economic Commission for Latin American (CEPAL/ECLA) 20

EEAS negotiation: Barroso–Solana report (2005) 109; Issues Paper 109, 120; Joint Progress Report on 113, 117; on lines of command and operational expenditure 120–121; by Member States 107–116; other topics of 115–116; scope of 111–113; on staffing of EEAS 113–115; status of 108–111; Swedish Presidency Report of 2009 on 129; towards the 2010 decision 127–130

EU diplomatic academy 91

230 *Index*

EU foreign policy 1, 6, 24, 174; associated with Council Secretariat 31; bureaucratic change in *see* bureaucratic change, in EU foreign policy; consensus on organisation of 26; and external relations 192; institutional change in 48–50; intergovernmentalist and supranationalist views on 34; Member states and reorganisation of 28–29; organisational structure of 28; reform of 26; revision of 28

EU Military Staff (EUMS) 31

Eurocracy, politics of 70

Eurocratic structure, politics of 67, 70–71, 130, 177, 189

European Coal and Steel Community (ECSC) 20

European Commission (EC) 1, 5, 10, 18, 40, 70, 131, 190; administrative procedures of 146–148; appointments in 148; Commission's Associate 178; attempt to include the EEAS in 97–99; autonomy of 118; on budgetary process for the EEAS 150–152; conditions of employment 98; conflict with EEAS 195; decision-making 114; Directorate-General for External Relations (DG RELEX) 20, 22, 111, 118, 147, 149, 154, 171; dominance over EEAS 188; as an emerging bureau 136–144; external representation (1954–1993) 19–24; general budget proposals of 137; history of 20, 21; independence in field of external affairs 118; influence over staffing of EEAS 119–120, 163; institutional relaunch of 27; organisation of 148–150; planning staff 28; President of 9; presidentialisation of 179; President's Wingwoman 178–179; protecting prerogatives of 116–121; relation with European Union diplomatic service 98; relation with EEAS 3, 195; role in foreign policy 22; on scope of EEAS 117–119; staff structure of 122, 148–150; on status of EEAS 116–117; Unified External Service 23; Vice-Presidents of 172

European Commissioner for External Relations 28, 86, 93

European Communities 19–20, 24, 80, 167

European Convention 9, 73, 79, 145, 177, 195; actors of 81–84; background of 80–87; categories of reform considered during **90**; fault lines of 85–86;

fundamental disagreements in 84; on future of Europe on external service 80, **198–209**; on future of Europe on HR and EEAS **219–223**; Laeken declaration (2001) 80; linchpin in external action 86–87; mandate of 81; membership of *82*; objective of 80–87; organisation of 80–87; reform process 69; Secretariat of 87; structure of *82*; Working Group on External Action **210–218**

European Council 28, 196; Group of Wise Men 80; High Permanent Representative for CFSP 29; leadership change at 174; President of 10, 91, 143, 157–158; Regulation 401/2004 126; relation with EEAS 174–175

European Court of Auditors (ECA) 4, 144, 170

European Defence Agency 178, 195

European Defence Community 24

European Development Fund 19, 21

European diplomacy 7, 13, 18, 36, 38

European diplomatic service *see* European External Action Service (EEAS)

European diplomatic space 7

European External Action Service (EEAS) 63, 93; administrative agreements 147; administrative procedures for 148; administrative structures of 8; attempt to include in the Commission 97–99; autonomy of 150; Brexit and 180–181; budget for 2011–2016 **137**; budget maximisation for 59, 135, 137–138; budgetary neutral 180–181; bureaucratic change and the long road to 8–10; bureaucratic politics of 10; bureaucratic-institutionalist approach on evolution of 188–192; categorisation of 8; from coalition to competition 67–68; conflict with European Commission 195; consolidation of 10, 13, 67–68, 187–192; control mechanisms for **162**; creation of 1, 9, 18, 19, 36, 80, 83, 127; crisis management in 116; decision to set-up 122; development phase of **11**; developments inside 169–171; diplomatic structure and trajectories of 177–181; enacting coalition of 64–65; establishment of 9–10, 65–67, 99, 137, 145, 186–187, 189; European Commission role in budgetary process for 150–152; and European Council 174–175; evolution of 2, 45, 193–194; executing coalition of 65–67; framework of bureaucratic creation **8**; future of 196; future research agenda on 195; High Representative on 117; inception of 9, 64–65, 185–186; and institutional change in the EU 192–196; institutionalisation of 108; inter-bureaucratic rivalry with Council Secretariat 157; inter-institutional agreement on 135; as interstitial organisation 7; and its institutional environment 145–146; and Juncker Commission 171–174; literature on 5–8; member states' control of 155; negotiation on *see* EEAS negotiation; new bureaucracy 67–68; nomination procedures of heads of delegation 148; objectives of 191; as organisation 5; organisation and functioning of 10; organisational hierarchy of 159, 189; origin of 100; Principal Agent (PA) relationships of 72; perception of support by other EU bodies **143**; performance assessment of 2–5; phases of emergence of 63–68; policy on human resources allocations 171; position of European Commission on status of 116–117; principal aims of 112; process tracing of 12; relation with European Commission 3; relation with European Parliament 175–177; role in strategic allocation of assistance funds 112; role of EP in organisation of 36, **37**; 'self'-review (2013) 169; service-level agreements 147; shortcomings of 184; as social body 7; staffing of 113–115; time horizon in evolution of 194; training for officials in 36; Treaty Drafts in Convention on Future of Europe on **219–223**; in treaty versions **224–225**; as 'tripartite' organisation 100; value to Global Europe 2–5; 'value-added' construction of 180

European External Representative 91–94, 96

European foreign ministry 4, 19, 88, 196

European Foreign Policy Unit 88, 92

European Neighbourhood Policy 112, 160

European Parliament (EP) 7, 10, 22, 29, 40, 70–71, 73, 83, 107, 110, 131, 137, 143, 171, 186, 189, 192; activism over two decades 34–38; administration of the EEAS 158–160; budgetary control of 98, 160; Committee on Foreign Affairs 36; common Community diplomacy 36; on decision to set-up the EEAS 122; Declaration on Political

Accountability 158–159; on expansion of political cooperation 36; Galeote I Report (2000) 36; Galeote II Report (2001) 36; on institutional aspects of setting up EEAS 123; legislative power of 36; Members of 84; on organisation of EU external affairs 36, **37**; oversight of 158–159; on political accountability of EEAS 126–127; political control of 98; political influence on nominations 164; relation with EEAS 175–176; resolution of 22 October 2009 122–123; resolution on the institutional aspects of EEAS 122; role in staffing and organisation of EEAS 159–160; Rotating Presidency 130; views on setting up of the EEAS 121–127

European People's Party (EPP) 86, 179

European Planning Staff 28

European Political Cooperation (EPC) 18, 22, 28, 34; and European Commission 26; institutionalisation of 26, **35**; organisation of 24–28; Presidency of 26; Troika Secretariat 26, 27

European Representative for External Relations 96

European Security and Defence Policy (ESDP) 18, 31, 39

European Treaty reform 80

European Union (EU) 6, 19; Basic Treaty of 80; common foreign and security policy 24; contribution in external relations 1; crisis management structures 139, 190; decision-making process 70–71; diplomatic service 1; EEAS and institutional change in 192–196; Eurocratic structure, politics of 70–71; external action dilemma 85–86; first and second pillar elements of 118; foreign policy *see* EU foreign policy; Global Strategy 174–175, 177, 190; member states 26; political and administrative system 192; rules on operation and financial processes 111; stages of institutional development in 68–72

European University Institute 80

executing coalition, forming of 65–67, 189

External Representative of the European Union 96

Famille RELEX 23, 39

financial management, of EEAS 150–151, 153, 159, 161, 163; *see also* budgetary process, for the EEAS

232 Index

Fischer, Joschka 96–99
Foreign Affairs Council 86, 92, 97, 100, 178–180
foreign minister, position of 96, 122, 186
Foreign Policy Chief 89
Foreign Policy Instruments Service (FPI) 121, 151
Foreign Representative 96

Galeote I Report (2000) 36
Galeote II Report (2001) 36
game of structural politics 2, 56, 169, 177, 181, 193, 196
Genscher-Colombo initiative 26
gradual institutional change, theory of 53
Group of Correspondants 25
Group of Wise Men 80

Hain, Peter 86, 89, 92–95
High Representative (HR) 9–10, 29–34, 83, 85, 91, 93, 101, 117, 139, 186, 188; for Common Foreign and Security Policy 39, 87; declaration on accountability (DPA) 127; nomination of 174; in relation to information flow to the EP 131; relation with European Commissioner for External Relations 86; Treaty Drafts in Convention on Future of Europe **219–223**; of Union for Foreign Affairs and Security Policy 127
historical institutionalism 47, 48, 52; criticisms of 53; distribution of power 54; model for dealing with change in 50
Huebner, Danuta 89
human resources allocations, EEAS policy on 171

Inside Bureaucracy (1967) 46
institutional change, in foreign policy 48–50
institutional creation 193; phases of 55, 63, 71–72, 115, 135; process of 1, 13, 67–68; stages of 66, 79
institutional development, stages of 68–72; consolidation stage 71–72; establishment stage 70–71; inception stage 68–70
institutional loyalties, concept of 142
intergovernmental agreements 69; plenary struggles and 95–99
Intergovernmental Conference (IGCs) 9, 28, 80–81, 84, 99, 188, 192; decision-making processes 29; determinants of

government positions in 69; Progress Report from the Chairman of the Reflection Group on 28; on veto-based development of treaty reforms 194
inter-institutional competition 187
inter-organisational: competition and control 61–63; decision-making 68; relationships 59–60, 62

Joint European External Action Service 97
Juncker Commission 169, 181, 195; EEAS and 171–174; Political Guidelines 172; services of 172–174
Juncker, Jean-Claude 171–172, 179

Kerr, Lord 180
Kosovo War 29

Laeken declaration (2001) 38, 80, 81
Laeken European Council 80
Le Roy, Alain 170
Leinen, Jo 122
Lisbon Treaty 1, 40, 71, 100, 102, 107, 122, 157, 160; on creation of the EEAS 186; implementation of 109–110
London Report (1981) 26

Maastricht, Treaty of 28
Matutes Report (1995) 23
Member States 29; control of EEAS activities 155; economic integration of 27; EEAS negotiation by 107–116; foreign policy cooperation 191; national intelligence services 31; Parliamentary activism 34–38; positions on CFSP integration **30**; and reorganisation of EU foreign policy 28–29; views on organisation structures in CFSP **32–33**
Minister for Foreign Affairs 95–96
Miozzo, Agostino 139
Mission Letters 172
Moe, Terry 2, 62, 127, 177, 193
Mogherini, Federica 13, 73, 169, 171–178, 176, 181, 188, 195–196
multiple complementary hypotheses 13

negotiation contexts, diversity of 69
new institutionalism, notion of 45, 47–48, 60–61, 66, 157, 177
Nice Treaty 31, 38, 80
nomination procedures, of heads of delegation 148
Non-paper on the European External Action Service 152

Non-paper on the Strengthening of the European External Action Service 153
North Atlantic Treaty Organization (NATO) 31

organisational: learning and innovation 7; self-interest, notion of 59, 137; settlement 5
organisation's search, Downs' concept of 59
O'Sullivan, David 96, 192, 194

Pan-Europa Union's 'Draft Constitution for a United States of Europe' (1942) 19
path dependence 49, 66, 69, 131; path-dependent processes 49, 52
police patrol 63
Policy Planning and Early Warning Unit (PPEWU) 31, 89; Situation Centre 31
Policy Unit see Policy Planning and Early Warning Unit (PPEWU)
Political Co-operation machinery 25
political institutions 145, 193; development of 48; duality of 47; efforts to reform 48; government bureaucracies 49; historical analyses of 50
political union 26, 34
Politics of Bureaucracy (1965) 58
polity ideas 84
power balance, between Secretariat-General and Commission President 150
President of the European Council (PEC) 10, 91, 143, 157, 164, 179, 191, 196; Franco-German institutional compromise on creation of 186; relationship of the EEAS with 158; working procedures with EEAS 187
Principal Agent (PA) 6, 62–63, 72, 164
public choice bureaucracy theory 57, 58, 59, 72, 136
punctuated equilibrium, idea of 50
punk diplomacy 180

rational choice institutionalism 47; and change in EU foreign policy 54–55
rational design, of international institutions 54
Riker, William 56
rolling secretariat 25

St Malo British-French declaration (1998) 31
scope of EEAS: European Commission views on 117–119; European Parliament

position on 124–125; Member States views on 111–113
Secretariat General, of the Commission 117, 150, 163, 172–173; of the Council 29, 89, 145, 153–154, 194
Secretary of Union 96
Single European Act (1987) 26, 34, 38–39
Situation Centre 31, 118, 129
sociological institutionalism 47, 54
Solana, Javier 29, 34, 86, 88, 91, 118
Solemn declaration (1983) 26
Soviet Union 23
Spinelli, Altiero 19
staffing of EEAS 113–115; Council Secretariat administration of 155–156; European Commission views on 119–120; European Parliament role in 125–126, 159–160; Member States views on 113–115
stakeholders of EEAS 144
status of EEAS: defined 145; European Commission views on 116–117; European Parliament views on 122–124; Member States views on 108–111
structural choice, politics of 55–57, 67, 70
structural politics 2, 56, 116, 145, 169, 170, 177, 181, 193, 196

Tindemans Report (1975) 25
Trade Commissioner 128
transfer of powers 130
treaty making, phase of 68
Treaty on European Union (TEU) 18; Common Foreign and Security Policy 27
Tullock, Gordon 57–58
Tusk, Donald 174

UK diplomatic network 180
Unified External Service 23–24, 38–39
Union for Foreign Affairs and Security Policy 127
Union Minister of Foreign Affairs 99
United States: foreign policy 45; government system of 56

van den Broek, Hans 28
veto-based development, of treaty reforms 194
von Rompuy, Herman 157

Warsaw Pact 23
Weber, Manfred 179
Weber, Max 57
Westendorp, Carl 28

234　Index

Western European Union 28
Williamson Report (1996) 22
Wilson, Woodrow 57
Wirtschaft und Gesellschaft (1922) 57
Working Group on External Action 87–95;
proposed institutional changes in
210–218; tableau of options 90–94;
from working group to plenary 94–95
Working Group on the Network of
Delegations 170